D0473147

NutriSearch
Comparative Guide to
Nutritional
Supplements™

5th Professional Edition
for Canada and the USA

CALGARY PUBLIC LIBRARY

OCT   2014

NutriSearch Comparative Guide to Nutritional Supplements™

5th Professional Edition
for Canada and the USA

by Lyle MacWilliam, MSc, FP

for NutriSearch Corporation

NutriSearch.ca

NutriSearch Comparative Guide to Nutritional Supplements™
5th Professional Edition

All Rights Reserved

Copyright © 2014 NutriSearch Corporation.

Published by Northern Dimensions Publishing / 2014

Printed and bound in the United States of America.

No part of this book may be reproduced or transmitted in any form or by any means, electronic or mechanical, including photocopying, recording or any information storage and retrieval system, without express written permission from NutriSearch Corporation.

This guide is produced for educational and comparative purposes only. No person should use the information herein for self-diagnosis, treatment, or justification in accepting or declining any medical treatment for any health-related problems. Some medical therapies, including the use of medicines, may be affected by the use of certain nutritional supplements. Therefore, any individual with a specific health problem should seek advice by a qualified medical practitioner before starting a supplementation program. The decision whether to consume any nutritional supplement rests with the individual, in consultation with his or her medical advisor. Furthermore, nothing in this manual should be misinterpreted as medical advice.

This guide is intended to assist in sorting through the maze of nutritional supplements available in the marketplace today. It is not a product endorsement and does not make any health claim. It simply documents recent findings in the scientific literature.

This guide was not commissioned by any public sector or private sector interest, or by any company whose products may be represented herein. The research, development, and findings are the sole creative effort of the author and NutriSearch Corporation, neither of whom is associated with any manufacturer or product represented in this guide.

NutriSearch, the NutriSearch logo, the NutriSearch.ca logo, Northern Dimensions Publishing, the Northern Dimensions Publishing logo, NutriSearch Comparative Guide to Nutritional Supplements, the NutriSearch Comparative Guide to Nutritional Supplements logo, NutriSearch Medal of Achievement, and the various medals associated with the NutriSearch Medal of Achievement program, including the Editor's Choice medal, are trademarks of NutriSearch Corporation. None of the trademarks may be used without express written permission of NutriSearch Corporation.

Other product names, logos, brands, and other trademarks featured or referred to within NutriSearch's products and services and within the *NutriSearch Comparative Guide to Nutritional Supplements* are the property of their respective trademark holders. These trademark holders are not affiliated with NutriSearch Corporation in any way.

Library and Archives Canada Cataloguing in Publication

MacWilliam, Lyle Dean
    NutriSearch comparative guide to nutritional supplements : a compendium of products available in the United States and Canada / by Lyle MacWilliam. -- 5th ed.

Previous ed. had title: NutriSearch comparative guide to nutritional supplements.
Includes bibliographical references and index.
ISBN 978-0-9812840-4-0

    1. Dietary supplements. I. Title.

To my wife

Arlene

the wind beneath my wings

Table of Contents

Figures and Tables

ON A PERSONAL NOTE

Since its inaugural publication in 1999, the *Comparative Guide to Nutritional Supplements* has evolved into a recognized standard for the rating of nutritional supplements in the global marketplace. Now in its second decade and published in Canada, the United States, Australia, New Zealand and Mexico, the guide serves as an indispensable tool in helping health-conscious consumers make informed choices. With translations into French, Spanish, Chinese and Korean, our work at NutriSearch has taken on a global dimension. Soon we will be releasing a guide with product ratings specific to Colombia, the first market in South America to be added to our roster.

The concept for the guide germinated from my work as a consultant for Health Canada during the late 1990s. At that time, I was appointed by the Hon. Allan Rock, Canada's former Minister of Health, as a member of a team of experts charged with developing an innovative regulatory framework for the manufacture and sale of nutritional supplements in the Canadian marketplace. Our report, with all of its 51 recommendations accepted by the Canadian Government, called for sweeping changes in the licensing of products and manufacturers that would ensure Canadian consumers access to nutritional products that were safe, effective and of high quality. During the deliberations of the advisory team and through the writing and development of its final report, it became clear to me that Canadian consumers—and consumers elsewhere—were largely in the dark about how to assess the quality and efficacy of nutritional products. Thus, as a personal mission, I began to explore a means of helping the consumer separate the 'wheat from the chaff' on the question of nutritional quality. The *Comparative Guide to Nutritional Supplements* is the culmination of this effort.

Now in its 5th edition, the *Comparative Guide to Nutritional Supplements* is an independent publication under license to NutriSearch, a Canadian company

> I have been witness to innumerable testimonies regarding the astounding curative powers attributed to optimal nutrition. It is not magic. It is Mother Nature at her best.

specializing in the evaluation of nutritional products in the global marketplace. The production of the guide is not funded or commissioned by any public sector entity, nor by any nutritional manufacturer whose products may be represented in the guide. The research, development and findings are the sole creative efforts of NutriSearch Corporation and the author.

From its beginnings, the *Comparative Guide to Nutritional Supplements* employed an analysis model that was developed from the published recommendations of several recognized nutritional authorities. Rather than rely on the recommendations of any single individual or authority, we chose to stand on the shoulders of those whose contributions to nutritional science have collectively advanced the concept of optimal nutrition. With each edition of the guide, we have added new recommendations from authorities who have more recently come to the forefront, incorporating new research that has added to our knowledge base and pooling this information to provide an increasingly robust model of optimal nutritional supplementation.

In this 5th edition of the guide, we incorporate very recent findings on two nutrients whose pivotal roles in cellular nutrition have long been misunderstood and neglected. The emergent science on vitamin D and iodine in disease prevention is simply breathtaking, heralding a new understanding of their biological functions as true medical breakthroughs. Both of these nutrients are ancient, their evolutionary assimilation into biological systems far predating all but the earliest of life forms. As such, their biochemical roles in cellular growth and metabolism are deeply imbedded in the genetic blueprint of every cell in our body.

Keeping with our desire to offer this guide both as an educational and consumer-based tool, we review the biology of vitamin D and iodine, and we present to you some startling new scientific revelations about how absolutely critical it is to supplement with these two nutrients, neither of which is particularly prevalent in our modern diet.

This guide is the work of several dedicated people without whom this production would not have been possible. My thanks go to my wife, Arlene, whose research and editing skills—and dogged determination to dig out every last product we could find—are unmatched. To Gregg Gies for his tireless efforts in conducting our online data search, and for his invaluable computer skills in the development, testing and modification of our analytical model, and for the final layout of the guide. Also, my thanks go to Bryden Derber, who was able to put "boots on the ground" and dig out hard-to-locate retail products, and to Kathleen Tite and Tammy Simpson, for their valued help in data verification. Lastly, my thanks go to you, the reader, whose financial contribution through the purchase of our guides makes our continued efforts possible.

In summary, the last 15 years I have spent in creating, developing and writing all five editions of this guide have truly been a labour of love. As an educator and biochemist whose early research focused on the protective effects of the antioxidant vitamin E, enlightening myself and others on the paradigm of preventive health—and the importance of supplementation and lifestyle change as components of that paradigm—has been a journey nothing short of a life's mission.

Through much of the last two decades, I have been blessed with countless opportunities to speak to audiences around the world regarding the virtues of good diet, proper supplementation and positive lifestyle change in disease prevention. In turn, I have been witness to innumerable testimonies regarding the astounding curative powers attributed to optimal nutrition. It is not magic. It is Mother Nature at her best—testimony to the fact that, when provided with the proper nutritional tools to do so, the human body has an amazing capacity to heal. It is what Nobel Laureate Linus Pauling called 'orthomolecular medicine'—healing at the *cellular* level.

I hope that the information provided through these guides will enlighten you in your quest for better health. I hold the belief that the most important legacy one can create is to have made a positive contribution to the lives of others. Through these guides, and through my global speaking engagements on the pursuit of optimal health, it is my hope that I have met this challenge.

To your health,

Lyle MacWilliam

February 17, 2014

You can observe a lot just by watching.

~ Yogi Berra
New York Yankees from 1946–1965

INTRODUCTION:

WHAT'S NEW IN THE GUIDE

The 5th edition of the *NutriSearch Comparative Guide to Nutritional Supplements* introduces several changes since the 4th edition was published in 2007. These changes are prompted by a wealth of emergent scientific evidence regarding the astonishingly wide-ranging preventive powers of two nutrients that have recently come to the forefront: iodine and vitamin D.

While the US Institute of Medicine has yet to increase the recommended daily intakes for the element iodine, both the US Food and Nutrition Board and Health Canada have made recent changes to the recommended intakes for vitamin D. Accordingly, NutriSearch has developed an important new Health Support criterion and modified several criteria used in our analytical model.

Extensive Review of the Marketplace

Information on the nutritional products evaluated for this guide was compiled through extensive fieldwork and internet researches on American and Canadian products conducted from 2011 to 2014. This research involved visiting several retail locations in geographically diverse regions throughout both the United States and Canada; this was followed by exhaustive internet–based research to locate products and companies listed in previous generations of our guides. Searches were also conducted to identify companies and products new to the marketplace.

While NutriSearch attempts to identify and catalogue every available nutritional product that meets our qualification criteria, it is acknowledged that our capture rate is never 100%. Despite our best efforts, it is nearly impossible to cast the net far or wide enough to capture every qualifying product out there. Consequently, if you identify a product that is not included in our data, we would like to know about it. NutriSearch would be pleased to review the product and, provided it meets our qualifying criteria, include the information in future updates to this guide. Please contact us at *cs@nutrisearch.ca* to provide us with details of the new products. In turn, we will do our utmost to identify and review them on your behalf.

Despite our best efforts to include all products and manufacturers previously registered in the 4th edition of the guide, this was not possible due to changes in the marketing of some products, including name changes and product removal, and due to companies that have discontinued operations since our last market review. As well, we have eliminated the product category for *Combination (Pack) Products* that was included in previous editions of this guide in order to avoid the confusion caused by having differing product categories. In the future, an analysis of *Combination Products* may be published separately. While there are consequently slightly fewer products in the 5th edition than in the 4th, several new products and new companies are included in this edition.

Levels of Iodine and Vitamin D Increased

The *Blended Standard* is an evolving and comprehensive set of recommendations based initially on the published recommendations of selected independent nutritional authorities. Readers of previous editions of this guide will be familiar with the NutriSearch *Blended Standard* and how the recommended nutrients and respective dosages have been used to develop our analytical model. Where emergent scientific evidence has eclipsed these original recommendations, NutriSearch has modified the specific criteria or nutrient intakes accordingly. In the past, this has included the addition of gamma tocopherol and mixed tocopherols to the criteria for vitamin E, and the addition of polyphenols as an important nutrient category. In light of emergent scientific evidence, NutriSearch has substantially modified the recommended daily intakes for two selected nutrients, iodine and vitamin D. Further to this, we have expanded and strengthened the role played by these two important nutrients in our 18 Health Support criteria.

Increased Iodine levels

NutriSearch has increased the *Blended Standard* Recommended Daily Dose of iodine from the previous 100 µg/day *(4th Edition, 2007)* to 1,000 µg/day. The scientific rationale for this increase is discussed later in this guide.

Increased Vitamin D levels

NutriSearch has increased the *Blended Standard* Recommended Daily Dose of vitamin D from the previous 400 IU/day *(4th Edition, 2007)* to 1,000 IU/day. The scientific rationale for this increase is discussed later this guide.

A New Criterion on Immune Support

Much of the recent evidence on vitamin D centers on its innate ability to regulate our immune response at the cellular level. Having a healthy immune response is critical, not only in fighting off infection and wound healing, but in preventing the aberrant growth of cells that can lead to cancer and other disease processes. The recent discovery that vitamin D can influence over 2,000 genes in our cells, almost 6% of the total human genome, illuminates the hormone's profound influence in immune support and general health maintenance. NutriSearch has consequently developed an important new Health Support criterion on *Immune Support*. For

details on this new criterion, please refer to Chapter Six of this guide.

Two Criteria Become One

In order to accommodate the new criterion on Immune Support without increasing our eighteen Health Support criteria, NutriSearch has combined two criteria into one. We have taken the criterion on vitamin E forms and the criterion on gamma and mixed tocopherols (both employed in the *4th Edition* of this guide) and condensed them into a *single* criterion that considers synthetic versus natural forms of vitamin E as well as the various vitamin E isomers, including gamma and delta tocopherols, and tocotrienols.

Three Criteria Modified for Vitamin D

Three Health Support criteria have been modified to incorporate new scientific evidence of the importance of vitamin D in general health maintenance. The criteria on *Heart Health, Metabolic Support* and *Inflammation Control* now take into consideration new scientific evidence of the important role played by vitamin D in each of these functions. For details on the changes to these criteria, please refer to Chapter Six of this guide.

Six Criteria Modified for Iodine

Six Health Support criteria have been modified to incorporate new scientific evidence of the importance of iodine in general health maintenance. The criteria on *Immune Support, Heart Health, Metabolic Support, Inflammation Control, Liver Health* and *Antioxidant Support* now take into consideration new scientific evidence of the important role played by iodine in each of these functions. For details on the changes to these criteria, please refer to Chapter Six of this guide.

Calculation of Daily Dose Modified

In all previous editions of this guide, our policy was to present the products of a manufacturer in the best possible light—to put their 'best foot forward,' so to speak. Consequently, when we reviewed products that provided a recommended range in their daily dose, we evaluated the product based on the *highest* value in that range. Doing so gave that product the highest possible score based on the nutrients on the product label. For example, if a product label specified to *take two to four capsules daily*, we evaluated the product based on the *maximum* daily intake of four capsules.

However, it has been brought to our attention that, while recommending a dosage range (i.e., take *one to four* capsules per day), some manufacturers would package and price their product based on the *lowest* dosage (where one capsule per day was the equivalent of one month's supply). With respect to our analysis, this did two things:

✓ it provided the product with the highest possible rating; and

✓ in relation to those products with a specific daily dosage (i.e., take *four* capsules per day) on the label (also generally packaged for a month's supply), it gave the dosage-range product a distinct price advantage over its specified-dose competitor.

NutriSearch has responded to these concerns by modifying the calculated Daily Dose in our analysis to evaluate dosage-range products by their *median* dosage as calculated from their dosage range stated on the label. Using this approach in the example above, a product label stating *take two to four capsules daily* would be evaluated at a *median* daily dose of three capsules. It is our intention that, by doing this, we have helped level the playing field for all manufacturers.

Products Graphed by Market Share

New to this edition of the guide, NutriSearch provides a graphical analysis of the top-rated multivitamin products from the 30 leading brand names in North America according to 2013 market data by *Euromonitor International*, a global market-research database. These graphs provide the reader with a detailed comparison of the performance of these top-rated products according to our 18 Health Support criteria and in relation to other leading brand names.

Product Ratings Displayed in Product Tables

The ratings for all products are shown in the *Product Tables* found in Chapter Nine of the guide. Each product is shown with its appropriate star rating, based on half-star increments, to the maximum rating of five stars. These ratings are prominently displayed in a full-colour format.

Summary

Emergent research on the importance of iodine and vitamin D in the maintenance of daily health have prompted NutriSearch to amend its analytical model for rating of all nutritional products evaluated in this guide. These changes provide NutriSearch with an opportunity to enhance the power of our analysis and improve our ability to sort the 'wheat from the chaff' within the maturing nutritional marketplace.

Nations endure only as long as their topsoil.

~Henry Cantwell Wallace
U.S. Secretary of Agriculture from1921-1924

CHAPTER ONE:

NUTRIENT DEPLETION OF FOODS

We are made of the stuff of the earth.

Our daily bread comes from the plants that form the 'roots' of the human food chain. They provide us with important macronutrients, the carbohydrates and sugars, proteins, fats and oils that are manufactured through photosynthesis and are needed to fuel our bodies. Plants also provide us with important micronutrients, the vitamins manufactured by the plant and the minerals absorbed from the soils, which are obligatory for healthy cellular function.

Vitamins and minerals serve as essential components in enzymes and coenzymes (helper enzymes), the biological catalysts that speed up chemical reactions necessary for cellular function. They work in concert to either join molecules together or break them apart in the myriad chemical reactions that take place every second within the living cell. Simply put, without enzymes and their essential vitamins and minerals life could not exist.

Reflecting on this, the calculus becomes simple: plants can't make minerals; they must absorb them from the soil—and without minerals, vitamins don't work. Accordingly, if important minerals are depleted from our soils, they are *also* depleted from our bodies.

Chronic mineral deficiency leads to disease. Consequently, it is not surprising that any degradation in the mineral and nutrient content of our soils leads to a commensurate increase in nutritionally related diseases in both animal and human populations.

The bottom line is this: our physical health ultimately depends upon the health of our topsoil.

The alarming fact is that foods—fruits, vegetables and grains—now being raised on millions of acres of land that no longer contain enough of certain needed nutrients, are starving us—no matter how much we eat of them.

~ US Senate Document 264

The remarkable thing about the above declaration, found in US Senate document 264, is that it was issued nearly eight decades ago—in 1936. Since that time, the United States and other industrialized nations have been losing arable land at an unprecedented rate. In the United States topsoil is eroding at a rate today that is ten times greater than the rate of replenishment. In countries such as Africa, India and China soil erosion exceeds the replenishment rate by 30 to 40 times. Current estimates place the chronological reserves of our global topsoil at less than 50 years. As the topsoil goes, so go the vital nutrients—and so goes our health.[1]

Findings released at the 1992 RIO Earth Summit confirmed that mineral depletion of our global topsoil reserve was rampant throughout the 20th century. During that time, US and Canadian agricultural soils lost 85% of their mineral content; Asian and South American soils dropped 76%; and throughout Africa, Europe, and Australia soil mineral content was depleted by 74%.[1] Little has been done since to forestall the inevitable exhaustion of these precious mineral stores.

In March, 2006, the United Nations recognized a new kind of malnutrition—*multiple micronutrient depletion.* According to Catherine Bertini, Chair of the UN Standing Committee on Nutrition, the overweight are *just* as malnourished as the starving. In essence, it is not the *quantity* of food that is at issue; it is the *quality.*[2]

Modern Agriculture Impoverishes our Soils

The earth's topsoils are a wafer-thin envelope of mineral-containing, carbon-based materials. Soils act to buffer and filter water and airborne pollutants, store critical moisture and important minerals and micronutrients, and are essential reservoirs for carbon dioxide and methane. Global warming aside, soil degradation is one of the most ominous threats to the long-term environmental sustainability of our planet.

Soil depletion was well understood in primitive societies, which would migrate every few years to new lands or would replenish the soils with organic wastes. In more recent history, the western migration of Europeans to the New World witnessed families moving every few years as their dry-land farming practices repeatedly played out the soil. The first sign of nutrient exhaustion did not come from crop failure; rather, it appeared as increased illness and disease amongst both the animals and humans who relied upon the land.[3] Those who did not leave their farms or practise soil replenishment observed inevitable declines in crop production, followed by outright collapse of the land, as was witnessed in the great dust bowl formations of the 1930s.

Today, we have nowhere else to go. We can no longer simply pick up and leave for greener pastures because there are none left. We must make do with what we have; soil erosion, contamination with industrial pollutants and depletion of our limited mineral resources has now gone global.[4-11] Nevertheless, modern agricultural practices continue to consume water, fuel and topsoil at alarmingly unsustainable rates, seemingly oblivious to nature's inviolate dictate to give back to the earth what we have taken. Instead of renewing and replenishing our soils, commercial agriculture has corrupted nature's natural cycles—and for this there will be a steep price to pay.

> The US Department of Agriculture standards for fruits and vegetables are limited to size, shape, and colour—they do not even consider nutritional value.

Impoverished Soils, Impoverished Crops

Soil depletion through unsustainable agricultural practices results in an inevitable loss of nutrient content in our crops. Historical data shows that the average mineral content of vegetables grown in US soils has declined precipitously over the last century.[1] Research published in the *Journal of the American College of Nutrition* in 2004 found significant declines in the mineral and vitamin content of 43 garden crops grown in US markets.[12] As well, an investigative report published by Life Extension Foundation in 2001 demonstrated that the vitamin and mineral content of several foods dropped dramatically between 1963 and 2000. Collard greens showed a 62% loss of vitamin C, a 41% loss of vitamin A and a 29% loss of calcium. Potassium and magnesium were down 52% and 84% respectively. Cauliflower had lost almost half of its vitamin C, thiamine and riboflavin, and most of the calcium in commercial pineapples had all but disappeared. When asked to explain the precipitous drop in the calcium content observed in commercial corn, the US Department of Agriculture responded that the 78% loss was not significant because "no one eats corn for calcium," unbelievably adding that the nutritional content of produce is not as important as appearance and yield.[13]

The US data corroborate findings for vegetable crops grown between 1940 and 2002 in Great Britain, which show mineral losses ranging from 15% to 62% for common minerals and trace elements.[2] In an earlier study, detrimental changes were found in the natural ratio of minerals, such as calcium and magnesium, in the foods tested.[14] Similarly, a Canadian study found dramatic declines in the nutrient content of produce grown over a 50 year interval to 1999. During that time, the average Canadian spud lost 57% of its vitamin C and iron, 28% of its calcium, 50% of its riboflavin, and 18% of its niacin. The story was the same for all 25 fruits and vegetables analyzed. The Canadian data revealed that nearly 80% of the foods tested showed large drops in their calcium and iron content, three-quarters showed significant decreases in vitamin A, one-half lost vitamin C and riboflavin, and one-third lost thiamine.[15]

Selective breeding of new crop varieties that places a premium on yield, appearance and other commercially desirable characteristics has also been attributed to depletion of the nutritional value of our foods.[16] Dr Phil Warman of Nova Scotia's Agricultural College argues that the emphasis on appearance, storability and yield—with little or no emphasis on nutritional content—has added considerably to the overall nutrient depletion of our food supply. The US Department of Agriculture standards for fruits and vegetables are limited to size, shape and colour—they do not even consider nutritional value.[1] With standards like these, it is not surprising that you have to eat eight oranges, today, to get the same amount of vitamin A that your grandparents got from a single orange.[15]

How Nutrients are Removed from Soils

Erosion of topsoil by wind and water is accelerated by over-cultivating, over-grazing and destruction of natural ground cover. The loss of organic matter results in a concurrent loss of nitrogen, minerals and trace elements, and it reduces the ability of soil to hold moisture and support the growth of healthy plants. The nutrient demands from high-yield crops place a further burden on the limited nutritional capacity of our depleted soils. For example, in 1930 an acre of land would yield about 50 bushels of corn. By 1960, yields had reached 200 bushels per acre—far beyond the capacity of the soil to sustain itself.[17]

Erosion, in combination with high-yield nutrient extraction, also depletes the soil of its alkalizing minerals (calcium, potassium and magnesium). This loss of natural buffering capacity results in the release of acids from natural clay deposits, and the soil becomes increasingly acidic. Conversely, over-irrigation with hard (alkaline) water causes some soils to leach important minerals while accumulating others (such as calcium). As a result, the soil becomes too alkaline to sustain crop growth.

It is true that nitrate, phosphate and potassium (NPK) fertilizers, first introduced in the early 1900s, significantly increase crop yield; but, they do so at great expense. Over-use of these chemical fertilizers has been found to *accelerate* the depletion of other vital micronutrients and trace elements and reduce their bioavailability to plants.[18] NPK fertilizers will gradually reduce soil pH, rendering the soils too acidic to support beneficial bacteria and fungi. These symbiotic organisms assist the plant in absorbing nutrients from the soil. Once gone, uptake of micronutrients by plants is significantly impaired.[19] Moreover, in acidic soils NPK application has been found to bind soil-based selenium, making it unavailable for root absorption.[20]

The use of NPK fertilizers to replenish the principal growth-promoting nutrients fails to address the concurrent losses of valuable micronutrients and trace elements (such as copper, zinc and molybdenum) which occur in intensively cultivated soils. According to Dr William Albrecht of the University of Missouri, the use of NPK fertilizers ultimately leads to malnutrition; attack by insects, bacteria and fungi;

Figure 1: Crop Duster
Airplanes have long been used to spread pesticides and fertilizers on crops.

weed encroachment; and crop loss in dry weather.[21] Albrecht contends that the use of chemical fertilizers to chase yield actually weakens the crop, making it *more* susceptible to pests and disease. Consequently, the commercial farmer has no choice but to rely on an armoury of dangerous and harmful chemical pesticides to protect his crop and his investment.

Nutrient Depletion forces Pesticide Abuse

The weakening of our soils and crops through the indiscriminate practices of commercial agriculture creates a destructive cycle of dependence on pesticides and herbicides. These extremely toxic organochlorine (OC) and organophosphorus (OP) derivatives kill our soils by slaughtering the symbiotic bacteria and fungi that promote nutrient uptake in plants; they inactivate critical enzyme systems within the plant roots that are involved in mineral absorption;[19] they destroy the soil micro-organisms needed to create the organic-mineral complexes that naturally replenish the soil.[18]

To make matters worse, these environmental poisons end up on our dinner table.

Dr Jerome Weisner, Science Advisor for President John F Kennedy, said in 1963: "The use of pesticides is far more dangerous than radioactive fallout." Unfortunately, he may have underestimated their potential. Most atmospheric radioactive fallout soon decays to harmless background levels. Pesticides, on the other hand, are *persistent* environmental toxins that accumulate and concentrate along the food chain, their residues sequestered in the fatty tissues of the body. All of us carry a lifetime body burden of these environmental poisons, and many of us unknowingly suffer their cumulative effects.

The evidence is unassailable: human exposure to pesticides is ubiquitous and occurs most commonly through the food we eat.[22-46] What *is* in dispute is whether low levels of exposures to these persistent environmental toxins and their residues can cause harm. Some studies refute the claim that exposure is harmful;[47-49] other studies provide startling evidence that pesticide exposure can elicit harmful biological effects—sometimes at exquisitely low levels—as a result of chronic environmental exposure.[24-26,37,43,50,51]

Furthermore, harmful synergistic effects from combinations of pesticides and chemical agents have been found to occur at *normal* levels of environmental exposure.[37,52] In some cases, pesticide 'cocktails' have been found to elicit toxic effects at levels significantly *below* those expressed by the individual chemicals.[53-56] In one study, a cocktail of aldicarb, atrazine and nitrate at levels approximate to that found in groundwater across the United States induced endocrine, immune and behavioral changes at doses that, for the individual compounds at the same concentrations, could not be observed.[55]

While the industry claims that pesticides and herbicides are safe and effective, a recent study suggests that women with breast cancer are five to nine times more likely to have significant levels of pesticide residues in their blood.[57] As well, pesticides and herbicides have been linked to a wide range of human health effects, including immune suppression, hormone disruption, diminished intelligence, reproductive abnormalities, neurological and behavioral disorders, and cancer.[50,51] They are also potent endocrine hormone disruptors and can be passed easily through the placenta to the unborn infant, who is extremely vulnerable to toxins that disrupt the developmental process.[58-61] Children are particularly susceptible to these agents because of a higher level of food intake for their body weight and a still-maturing immune system.

No matter how conscientious we may be, we are constantly exposed—through the foods we eat, the water we drink and the air we breathe—to environmental levels of these toxins that may manifest in subtle or profound ways. That is why it is exceedingly important

> No matter how conscientious we may be, we are constantly exposed—through the foods we eat, the water we drink and the air we breathe—to environmental levels of these toxins that may manifest in subtle or profound ways.

to protect yourself and your children, as much as you can, by choosing sensible dietary alternatives to commercially gown and processed foods—the principal sources of pesticide and herbicide exposure.

Organic Agriculture Improves Nutrient Content

For most of human history, agriculture has used organic growing practices. Only during the last 100 years has the use of synthetic chemicals and their widely destructive consequences been introduced to the food supply. Fortunately, an increasing number of progressive growers are, today, shunning commercial growing techniques; they are, instead, returning to their organic roots and the traditional ways of caring for the soil.

The natural mulching and cultivation techniques employed through organic gardening feed the soil rather than the plant by returning many of the nutrients lost through plant growth and by encouraging the growth of beneficial fungi, nitrogen-fixing bacteria, and other beneficial micro-organisms. Healthy *living* soil, in turn, promotes the symbiosis of plants with these soil microbes, thereby enhancing the transfer of essential nutrients into the plants. In contrast to conventional agriculture, organic agriculture *embraces* the natural replenishing cycles of nature.

In a 2003 exposure study in Seattle, Washington, children two-to-four years of age who consumed organically grown fruits and vegetables had urine levels of pesticides six times lower than children who consumed conventionally grown foods. According to the authors of the study, the consumption of organic fruits, vegetables and juices can reduce children's exposure levels from *above* to *below* the US Environmental Protection Agency's current guidelines,

> Despite our best intentions to eat a balanced diet—the dictates of modern lifestyles and prevalence of ready-made meals that now pervade our culture make it inordinately difficult to do so.

thereby shifting exposures from a range of *uncertain* risk to a range of *negligible* risk.[62]

There is a growing body of evidence confirming the health promoting effects of organically grown foods. Studies confirm that organic crops are higher in vitamin C, iron, natural sugars, magnesium, phosphorus and other minerals, and lower in harmful nitrates than conventional crops.[63,64] An independent review, published in the *Journal of Complementary Medicine*, found that organically grown crops had markedly higher levels of nutrients for all 21 nutrients evaluated than did conventionally grown produce. Organically grown spinach, lettuce, cabbage and potatoes expressed particularly high levels of minerals.[64]

Research conducted by the University of California (Davis) showed that organically grown tomatoes and peppers had higher levels of flavonoids* and vitamin C than conventionally grown tomatoes.[65] The health promoting effects of these secondary plant metabolites, manufactured by the plant to protect it from the oxidative damage caused by strong sunlight, are well established. High intensity conventional agricultural practices appear to disrupt the production of these natural plant metabolites, leading to a loss of flavonoid content in conventional crops. Conversely, organic growing practices are known to stimulate the plant's defence mechanisms, leading to enhanced production of these important botanical nutrients.[66] It is precisely because organic crops are not protected by pesticides that their fruits contain higher levels of flavonoids than conventional fruits—including up to 50% more antioxidants.[66-68] A good example is the polyphenol content of red wine. This heart-healthy nutrient is found in much higher concentrations in wine made from organically grown grapes, which manufacture the nutrient to protect against a naturally occurring fungus that attacks the skin of the grape.

---

* *Flavonoids are a group of plant pigments that are responsible for the bright colours of many fruits and flowers. Designed by nature to protect the plant against the damage caused by sun exposure and disease, they elicit powerful antioxidant, cell signalling, and anti-inflammatory properties.*

Conclusions

The conveniences of modern living involve many trade-offs when it comes to eating a healthy diet. Most of us are completely unaware of the consequences of chronic exposure to persistent environmental toxins through the chemically laced foods we place daily on our dinner table. Nor do we appreciate the degree to which the nutritional value of our food supply has been bludgeoned by our over-reliance on commercial, chemically based agriculture. The fact is, unless we complement our diet with a high quality nutritional supplement, most of us will not even come close to meeting our daily nutritional requirements. Less than one-third of North Americans eat the minimum recommended five servings of fruits and vegetables every day. Now we find that even if a person accidentally *does* eat a vegetable, it doesn't have nearly the nutrition that nature intended.

What's a mother to do?

To start with, we can begin to identify those foods most highly exposed to chemical fertilizers, and we can choose to enhance our diets with organically grown alternatives. We can learn to grow our own produce on family-owned or community garden plots, and we can use organic growing techniques, such as composting and feeding the soil, to replenish the vital nutrients. If we can't grow our own gardens, we can choose to support local farmers and agriculturalists, encouraging the growth of a local organic farming culture, and we can support organic growers the world over with the purchase power of our consumer dollar. Within the home, we can learn to adapt culinary and cooking techniques that *optimize*, rather than *compromise*, the nutritional value of the foods we purchase. We can also learn to stop treating vegetables as a *side* dish, and we can prepare our meals with the understanding that optimal nutritional intake of fresh fruits and vegetables is our *best* defense against illness and disease.

Finally, we must accept the fact that, despite our best intentions to eat a balanced diet, the dictates of modern lifestyles and prevalence of ready-made meals that now pervade our culture make it extraordinarily difficult to do so. That is why daily supplementation with a high quality, broad-spectrum nutritional supplement—one with a full range of the necessary vitamins, minerals and plant-based antioxidants—is a prudent preventive measure that will reduce the risk of chronic disease and promote long-term health.

And that is *precisely* what the venerated American Medical Association now recommends.

Vitamins, if properly understood and applied, will help us to reduce human suffering to an extent which the most fantastic human mind would fail to imagine.

~Albert Szent-Györgyi, (1893–1986)
Nobel Laureate, Physiology and Medicine

CHAPTER TWO:

WHY WE NEED TO SUPPLEMENT

The word is out—it pays to take your vitamins.

In 2002, the American Medical Association (AMA) reversed its long-held anti-vitamin stance and began to encourage all adults to supplement daily with a multiple vitamin. A landmark review of 38 years of scientific evidence by Harvard researchers Drs Robert Fletcher and Kathleen Fairfield convinced the conservative *Journal of the American Medical Association (JAMA)* to rewrite its policy guidelines regarding the use of vitamin supplements. In two reports, published in the June 19, 2002 edition of *JAMA,* the authors concluded that the current North American diet, while sufficient to prevent acute vitamin-deficiency diseases, such as scurvy and pellagra, is inadequate to support long-term health.[1,2]

Insufficient vitamin intake is apparently a cause of chronic diseases. Recent evidence has shown that suboptimal levels of vitamins (below standard), even well above those causing deficiency syndromes, are risk factors for chronic diseases such as cardiovascular disease, cancer and osteoporosis. A large portion of the general population is apparently at increased risk for this reason.

~ Drs Robert Fletcher and Kathleen Fairfield

In the study, the authors examined several nutrients, including vitamins A, B_6, B_{12}, C, D, E, K, folic acid, and several of the carotenoids (including alpha and beta carotene, cryptoxanthin, zeaxanthin, lycopene and lutein). Among their conclusions, they noted:

✓ folic acid, vitamin B_6 and vitamin B_{12} are required for proper homocysteine metabolism, and low levels of these vitamins are associated with increased risk of heart disease (homocysteine is a sulphur-containing amino acid that, at high blood levels, can damage the cardiovascular system);

✓ inadequate folic acid status increases the risk of neural tube defects and some cancers (a neural tube defect is an incomplete closing of the spinal cord that occurs early in foetal development);

✓ vitamin E and lycopene (the red pigment found in ripe tomatoes) appear to decrease the risk of prostate cancer;

✓ vitamin D is associated with a decreased risk of osteoporosis and fracture when taken with calcium (osteoporosis is a hollowing out of the bones caused by the loss of calcium);

✓ inadequate vitamin B_{12} is associated with anaemia and neurological disorders (anaemia is a decrease in number of red blood cells or a lack of hemoglobin in the blood);

✓ low dietary levels of carotenoids, the brightly coloured pigments in peppers, carrots and fruits, appear to increase the risk of breast, prostate and lung cancers (carotenoids belong to the family of nutrients called bioflavonoids);

✓ inadequate vitamin C is associated with increased cancer risk; and

✓ low levels of vitamin A are associated with vision disorders and impaired immune function.

In a striking departure from *JAMA's* long-held anti-vitamin stance, the authors concluded that, given our modern diet, supplementation each day with a multiple vitamin is a prudent preventive measure against chronic disease. The researchers based their guidance on the fact that more than 80% of the American population does not consume anywhere near the five servings of fruits and vegetables required each day for optimal health.

JAMA's previous comprehensive review of vitamins, conducted in the 1980s, concluded that people of normal health do not need to take a multivitamin and can meet all their nutritional needs through diet alone. Since that time, nutritional science has compiled an impressive wealth of studies affirming the health benefits of supplementation as an adjunct to a healthy diet. The American Medical Association's about-face in light of the Fairfield-Fletcher studies, and its public declaration that supplementation is now deemed important to your health, underscores the strength of the scientific evidence that now prevails.

The Case for Supplementation

We now have convincing evidence that the lifetime risk of cancer; heart disease; stroke; diabetes; neurological disorders, such as multiple sclerosis and amyotrophic lateral sclerosis (Lou Gehrig's disease); macular degeneration; osteoporosis; Alzheimer's disease and other forms of dementia can be reduced by providing the cells of the body with sufficient amounts of the right nutrients.

One of the first human studies to substantiate the benefits of vitamin supplements was announced in 1992 and showed that men who took 800 mg/day of vitamin C lived six years longer than those who consumed the US Food and Nutrition Board's recommended daily allowance of 60 mg/day.[3] Published in the journal *Epidemiology*, this ten year follow-up study showed that high vitamin C intake extended average life span and reduced mortality from both cardiovascular disease and cancer.[4]

A compelling report that high-potency supplements extend human life span was published in August, 1996, in the *American Journal of Clinical Nutrition*. The study involved 11,178 elderly people who participated in a trial to establish the effects of vitamin supplements

on mortality. Supplementation with vitamin E, alone, reduced the risk of overall mortality by 34% and reduced the risk of coronary disease mortality by 47%. However, when vitamin C and E were used in combination, overall mortality was reduced by 42% and coronary mortality dropped by 53%, demonstrating the synergistic effects of multiple vitamin therapy. What made these findings of even greater significance was that the study compared people who took low potency one-a-day multiple vitamins to those who took higher potency vitamin C and E supplements. Only those participants taking high-dose vitamin C and E supplements benefitted.[5]

A 1997 study published in the *British Medical Journal* evaluated 1,605 healthy men with no evidence of pre-existing heart disease. Those men deficient in vitamin C were found to have a 350% increased incidence of sudden heart attacks compared to those who were not deficient in vitamin C. The authors concluded that vitamin C deficiency, as measured by low blood levels of ascorbate, is a significant risk factor for coronary heart disease.[6]

A massive cohort study, published in 1998, investigated the risk for colon cancer in 88,756 nurses who took folic acid (a B-complex vitamin) as part of a daily multivitamin supplement.[7]

The study found that intakes of 400 mg/day or more of folate, compared to intakes of 200 mg/day or less, were strongly related to lowered risk. While no significant protective effects were noted over shorter periods, an inverse relationship between folate intake and cancer risk became apparent after five years of use. After 15 years, a remarkable 75% reduction in the risk of colon cancer was noted among those women taking the supplements containing the B-complex vitamin. The authors concluded that long-term use of multivitamins might substantially reduce the risk for colon cancer, an effect likely related to the folic acid contained in these products.

In this same study, nurses who took multivitamins containing vitamin B_6 also reduced their risk of heart attack by 30%. The evidence revealed that the more vitamin B_6 they took, the lower was the risk of suffering a sudden cardiac event. These findings support those of another cohort study conducted in Norway that demonstrated a combination of folic acid and vitamin

B[6] can reduce homocysteine levels by up to 32% in healthy individuals. Homocysteine, a harmful amino acid at high blood levels, can markedly increase the level of inflammation and oxidative stress in blood vessels, which can precipitate both heart attack and stroke.[8]

In 2005, an international coalition led by Canadian researchers at McMaster University, Ontario, provided evidence that a comprehensive 'cocktail' of nutritional supplements can significantly improve lifespan in animal models. The nutrient mixture, containing 31 nutrients common to many better quality broad-spectrum supplements available in the market, targeted key factors in the aging process, including the proliferation of reactive oxygen species (free radicals), inflammatory processes, insulin resistance and mitochondrial* dysfunction. In the study, the treatment group of mice exhibited an 11% increase in lifespan compared to normal mice who did not receive the supplement cocktail. Previously, the same researchers established that that the supplement cocktail completely abolished severe cognitive decline expressed by aging untreated mice. The results from these animal-model experiments demonstrate that broad-spectrum dietary supplements may be effective in ameliorating the effects of aging and age-related pathologies where simpler formulations have generally failed.[9,10]

The benefits of supplementation with n-3 polyunsaturated fatty acids (omega-3 fats) after a heart attack are well documented. Omega-3 fatty acids, commonly found in cold-water fish, nuts and grains, dramatically reduce the risk of premature death in high-risk individuals. A 2008 study on post-myocardial infarction (heart attack) patients revealed a significantly lower likelihood of dangerous cardiac arrhythmia and an 85% reduction in the risk of premature death by

> All of us grew up believing that if we ate a reasonable diet, that would take care of our vitamin needs. But, the new evidence, much of it in the last couple of years, is that vitamins also prevent the usual diseases we deal with every day—heart disease, cancer, osteoporosis, and birth defects.
> ~ Dr Robert Fletcher, 2002

simply maintaining an optimal level of omega-3 fats in the diet.[11] Moreover, these protective effects are also seen in healthy populations.[11-15] In healthy people with no evidence of heart disease, men and women appear to achieve the same level of protection against premature death by supplementing with omega-3 oils from fish and nuts. In a 2010 Norwegian study, elderly men with no evidence of overt heart disease who supplemented with fish oil experienced a 47% reduction in the risk of premature death compared to those who did not supplement.[16] Similarly, a large Australian study found that women with the highest levels of omega-3 consumption from nuts and fish had a 44% reduction in the risk of premature death from inflammatory disease. The protective effect was dose-related to the level of omega-3 intake.[12] The ability of omega-3 fats to reduce the level of systemic inflammation through the production of anti-inflammatory prostaglandins (primitive cell signalling hormones) appears to be the source of their protective talents.

A 19-year study of colorectal cancer rates found the relative risk in men with poor vitamin D status was almost triple that of men with sufficient vitamin D.[17] In a meta-analysis (a study of studies) conducted on research worldwide from 1966 to 2004, researchers from the University of California concluded that 1,000 IU/day of vitamin D lowers an individual's risk of developing colorectal cancer by as much as 50%.[18] A 2006 review of vitamin D status and cancer risk in the northeastern United States concluded that efforts to improve vitamin D status through vitamin D supplementation could markedly reduce cancer incidence and mortality at low cost and with few or no adverse effects.[19] A 2008 review of current research findings on the cancer-protective effects of vitamin D concluded that intakes of between 1000 and 4000 IU

---

*   *Mitochondria are tiny organelles that are the power centres of the cell. It is in the mitochondria that many of the energy-producing reactions of cellular respiration take place. In the terminal process of respiration, reactive oxygen species are created that can damage the delicate membranes of these organelles if left unprotected through lack of antioxidants. Oxidative damage to the delicate mitochondrial membrane is believed to be a principal cause of cellular aging.*

per day protect against cancers of the breast, colon, prostate, ovary, lungs and pancreas.[20] Lastly, a 2009 review on ultraviolet radiation, vitamin D and cancer concluded that circulating levels of vitamin D play an important role in determining the outcomes of several cancers.[21] According to the authors of this review, support for the sunlight/ vitamin D/cancer link is scientifically strong enough to warrant the use of vitamin D in cancer prevention and treatment protocols.

These studies and their findings are but a few of the thousands of independent scientific reports confirming the efficacy of supplementation with high quality nutritional supplements as a prudent, preventive measure for optimal health and disease prevention.

> Firstly, the consumer must understand that out of 100 clinical studies that investigate a particular effect, probability dictates that five of these studies—no matter how well designed— will show results that are *not* real. There will always be a statistical fluke in the bunch.

The Other Side of the Coin

To be certain, the premise of life extension and disease prevention through supplementation does not have universal support amongst the scientific community. As is inevitably the case, in an evidence-based discipline there will arise conflicting studies that cast doubt on the evidence. Many researchers argue that supplements provide a convenient and effective means for supplying the optimal intakes of essential nutrients required to support long-term health; others counter that there is no conclusive proof that supplements provide any real health benefits at all.

Unfortunately, much of the debate is framed by a media more interested in selling newspapers than in ferreting out the truth. Sloppy reporting, distorted editorial sensationalism, and conflicts of interest by researchers and publishers have unnecessarily alarmed the public and have threatened to destroy its trust in complementary health care. Health-conscious consumers and medical practitioners alike have become frustrated at the mixed messages promulgated through the headlines: one day we are told something is good for us and the next day we are told it is not. Why do so many recently published studies appear to refute the prevailing scientific evidence about the benefits of natural approaches to wellness? How can vitamin E be good for us one day and bad for us the next? For once, why can't the experts just get it straight?

If there is any consolation, it is helpful to understand that science never progresses smoothly—there will always be new findings that appear to refute long-established theories. Controversy is the crucible for change and paves the road that science must travel to arrive at a final truth. Unfortunately, media bias and conflicts of interest place unnecessary detours along the way.

Firstly, the consumer must understand that out of 100 clinical studies that investigate a particular effect, probability dictates that five of these studies—no matter how well designed—will show results that are *not* real. There will always be a statistical fluke in the bunch.

Secondly, about one-fifth of clinical trials investigating a particular effect will not have the needed number of subjects to show a statistically significant result. This occurs because in most clinical trials the probability of finding a real result, known as the power of a test, is set at a minimum of 80%. Consequently, there is up to a 20% chance of missing your mark and failing to find a difference when one actually exists. This is merely the gremlin of probability at work.

Thirdly, some investigations are just bad science, improperly conducted, poorly reported and inadequately reviewed. Unfortunately, as has been the case in several recent studies, their findings attract an inordinate amount of attention from a media hungry for headlines.

Poor Science, Poor Journalism—or Both?

A good example of one of these studies, which set the medical and scientific communities astir, is the 2005 Johns Hopkins University announcement that high-dose vitamin E can increase the risk of death among elderly patients.[22] Here was a finding at complete odds with a surfeit of evidence supporting the vitamin's long established protective benefits.

The study was a meta-analysis, a statistically based methodology that combines the data from several published clinical trials. Properly done, a meta-analysis is a powerful investigative tool; mishandled, the results can be powerfully misleading. In selecting their studies for inclusion in the analysis, the authors disqualified several smaller investigations and those where there were fewer than ten deaths reported in the trial. This served to introduce a sampling bias, which skewed the data to *support* the argument of harm. Moreover, some of the studies included in the analysis involved elderly subjects—many of whom were already seriously ill—rather than healthy adults. In one such trial, 31% (60) of the subjects *died* during the study period. Nutritional intervention with gravely ill individuals can be a legitimate objective for a clinical study within a therapeutic context; however, applying the findings to the general population within the context of prevention is *not* legitimate.

On a final point, the studies included in the Johns Hopkins research used the synthetic *(d/l)* form of vitamin E. While there is no evidence of adverse effects from the consumption of the natural *(d)* form of vitamin E, the US National Academies of Science has long warned of adverse effects from taking high doses of synthetic vitamin E, including hemorrhagic toxicity—a serious and potentially fatal complication with elderly subjects who are already likely to be on blood thinners.

While publicly suggesting that high-level intake of vitamin E may be dangerous, the authors commented in their published report that: "Overall, vitamin E supplementation did not affect all-cause mortality." The authors also reported that at the highest dosages the risk of death was actually *lower*, a finding that the media completely missed—or *chose* to ignore.

So, where does the Johns Hopkins study leave us? The findings fail to make the case that high-dose vitamin E intake will increase the risk of death. More importantly, the study involved elderly people, many of whom were gravely ill; consequently, whatever the findings, they simply *cannot* extend to the general healthy population.

> While there is no evidence of adverse effects from the consumption of the natural *(d)* form of vitamin E, the US National Academies of Science has long warned of adverse effects from taking high doses of synthetic vitamin E.

Unfortunately, when announcing their findings to the Press, the authors disregarded their own written guidance not to generalize the results, thus raising the spectre of harm to the public. The fallout was predictable: giving no consideration to the wealth of scientific evidence to the contrary, the media took the bit at a full run, declaring that high-dose vitamin E may be deadly. Reacting with fear, consumers dumped vitamin E down the toilet by the truckload.

To review more examples of these questionable studies, please refer to an investigative article written by this author for *Life Extension Magazine* in 2006, entitled, *Media Bias, Conflicts of Interest Distort Study Findings on Supplements.* This review article is available at the following URL: *http://www.lef.org/magazine/mag2006/jun2006_cover_media_01.htm.*

Through the Looking Glass

Much of the controversy regarding the efficacy of nutritional supplements stems from peering through the lens of the prevailing drug-based model of treatment/cure—the looking glass through which we evaluate the effectiveness of standard medical therapies. While this approach is certainly appropriate for drug products, it is entirely inappropriate for natural health products. Such products are, by nature, *preventive,* rather than *curative.*

Within the drug-based model, the objective of most clinical trials is to evaluate a single drug for its therapeutic effect on a particular symptom or disease. Once a positive therapeutic effect is established, the drug is licensed for a specified treatment protocol. This *Magic Bullet* approach of high-tech, disease-centered medicine promises powerful, fast-acting drugs that quickly produce therapeutic results. Unfortunately, it has absolutely *nothing* to do with prevention.

The drug-based approach is a disease-centric approach and the clinical trials employed by its adherents focus on treating already-ill subjects. This is called *secondary* prevention—averting further progression of an existing condition. It is fundamentally different from that of *primary* prevention—thwarting the development of chronic disorders in a healthy population. Primary prevention is a lifelong undertaking to avoid disease, not a quick fix to rectify collateral damage from a poor lifestyle. Such an approach requires a far *different* investigative lens.

Tragically, the majority of clinical studies on the health benefits of natural health products continue to test individual supplements as though they are prescription drugs, able to work in isolation, targeting a single biochemical lesion, and expected to provide dramatic health benefits over the short term in acutely ill people. This is *not* how vitamins work and, viewed within the paradigm of treatment/cure, it is no wonder they come up short.

For example, epidemiological and observational research supports the position that vitamin E, administered over the long term, helps prevent atherosclerosis (primary prevention). However, in a clinical setting, vitamin E is ineffective in preventing the onset of a heart attack or stroke brought on by the rupture of an *existing* atherosclerotic plaque (secondary prevention). The findings of several clinical studies support this view. As such, vitamin E passes muster as an effective long-term measure for the *prevention* of heart disease; however, it fails the test when standard clinical trials evaluate its effectiveness as a *treatment* in patients with established disease.[23]

Does this mean that vitamin E is useless? Of course not. It simply demonstrates that the value of vitamin E as an agent in prevention is fundamentally different from its value as an agent of intervention.

As instruments of wellness, natural health products, such as vitamins, minerals and botanicals, lie outside the standard acute-care paradigm. For this reason, it is folly to evaluate the efficacy of such products and therapies through the looking glass of treatment/cure. When evaluated within that paradigm they most often fail. These failures are subsequently paraded by the media as evidence that natural health products have no health benefits—cheered on by an international drug cartel whose over-riding interest is to protect its bottom line.

Clearly, it is time for a new paradigm.

Nothing makes sense in biology except in the light of evolution.

~ Theodosius Dobzhanski
Evolutionary biologist and
Orthodox Christian scholar

CHAPTER THREE:

THE VITAMIN D STORY

Vitamin D is ancient, its metabolic functions incorporated into countless cellular activities in both primitive and advanced life forms. So central is the vitamin's role to the maintenance of life, we can trace its origins back to the unicellular zooplankton and phytoplankton that flourished in the ancient seas over 750 million years ago—a time well before vertebrate life forms had evolved.[1]

A Short History

Through countless millennia of evolutionary change, vitamin D's core biochemical functions have remained inviolate. The vitamin's development early in the evolutionary timeline and its innate capacity to modulate calcium metabolism allowed evolving life forms to develop the necessary calcified skeletal structures that would later carry their successors onto land. *Emiliana huxleyi,* an ancient phytoplankton with a global distribution from the tropics to the subarctic, is uniquely adorned with ornate calcite disks, a good example of an early life form that retains its capacity to manufacture vitamin D. While the role of vitamin D in lower non-vertebrate life forms is not well understood, it is vital that most vertebrates obtain an adequate source of vitamin D, also called calciferol, in order to develop and maintain a healthy mineralized skeleton.[2]

A steroid hormone, vitamin D is manufactured in skin cells in direct action to sunlight. Evolutionarily speaking, the hormone forms an integral component in the metabolic machinery of virtually all vertebrate life forms. As with the iguana, humans were built to obtain vitamin D through exposure to solar radiation. With the exception of some marine species, the vitamin is not found in any significant degree in foods. It is truly the 'sunshine vitamin.'[3] Constant exposure to the penetrating ultraviolet beta (UVB) rays of ancient sunlight, and the consequent synthesis of calciferol, allowed advancing life forms to manufacture skeletons strong enough to support their weight on land. In essence, the emergence of terrestrial vertebrate life on earth was *predicated* upon the evolution of the metabolic pathway for the photosynthesis of vitamin D, a hormone central to the process of bone mineralization.

Of Man and Beasts

In his seminal work *The Vitamin D Solution,*[4] renowned vitamin D researcher Dr Michael Holick

Figure 2: Vitamin D and Early Life Forms
Sea Whip (*Leptogorgia virgulata*) is a soft-bodied colonial coral with an internal skeleton found in the western Atlantic Ocean. This ancient organism is also known to manufacture vitamin D as well as the iodine-containing hormone thyroxine.

suggests that the extinction of the dinosaurs, the dominant vertebrate life form for over 160 million years, may have been a consequence of acute vitamin D deficiency brought on by a catastrophic global reduction in light intensity.[5] Holick purports that a weakening of the bones as a result of insufficient vitamin D would have rendered the skeletons of these reptilian monsters incapable of supporting their enormous weight. Their extinction, 65 million years ago, coincides with an enormous asteroid impact off the Yucatan Peninsula that spread a massive global dust cloud, likely obscuring sunlight for an extended period of time.[6]

From the beginnings of human evolution, some 600,000 years ago, our hunter-gatherer forbearers were constantly exposed to strong sunlight. The dark-skin pigmentation of today's African tribes and other equatorial populations is evidence of an early protective adaptation to the intense tropical sun, blocking excessive exposure while allowing penetration of sufficient UVB rays to permit vitamin D production. One hundred and fifty thousand years ago, spreading waves of humanity flowed outward from the equatorial plains of Africa, their northward migration creating selective pressure to lighten the skin—a necessary adaptive response to the lower intensity sunlight of the northern latitudes.

This persistent decrease in light intensity, in fact, appears to have played a critical role in the differences in bone structure recorded in early fossilized human remains.[7] The extinction 30,000 to 50,000 years ago of the Neanderthals, the first human lineage to colonize northern Europe, may have been a consequence of their particular inability to adapt to these lower light conditions. Paleontological records of their stooped posture and bowed legs suggest severe bone deformation and calcium imbalance, a likely consequence of poor vitamin D status.[6]

Eventually, early man's northward journey ran out of the sun; the inability to manufacture sufficient vitamin D likely limited further northward migration until the discovery of a novel source of dietary vitamin D—marine mammals and oily fish. Today's Inuit of Northern Canada, Greenland and Siberia survive the harsh low-light conditions of the high arctic only because of this rich marine source of calciferol found in the surrounding arctic waters.

Today, the further north you go, the lighter is the pigmentation of the skin. Peoples of the northern latitudes, the Swedes, Norwegians and Scots, for example, are much fairer in complexion than their southern European counterparts and demonstrate successful adaptations to lower intensity sunlight. Modern-day migrations are, however, distorting these established polygenetic patterns. Today, it is common to see people of darker complexion living in temperate climates where the seasonal light intensity is highly variable. Such individuals are at high risk for vitamin D deficiency because their darker skin blocks the penetration of the meager sunlight available for vitamin D synthesis, particularly during the winter months.

Studies confirm that increased skin pigment can *greatly* reduce the photosynthesis of vitamin D.[8] Consequently, people with darker complexions must spend much longer in the sun to manufacture as much vitamin D as a person of northern European descent. This is likely why African-Americans and other dark-skinned populations living in temperate climates suffer from significantly higher rates of heart disease, hypertension, cancer, diabetes and other diseases related to poor vitamin D status. They are just not manufacturing enough of the sunshine vitamin.[9]

Here Comes the Sun

Over the millennia, several cultures have embraced heliotherapy, which is the practice of using sunlight to affect healing. The ancients of Egypt, Greece and Rome worshipped the sun as a wellspring of health. Indian medical literature dating to 1500 BC, Buddhist literature from 200 AD, and 10th-century Chinese literature also document solar therapies in many healing practices. From the Aztecs of Mexico, the Incas of Peru, and from the Aborigines of Australia to the indigenous cultures of North America, past civilizations have instinctively known that the sun was their source of both spiritual *and* physical healing. [10,11]

It was during the Industrial Revolution in the 18th and 19th centuries that modern man first witnessed the importance of sunlight in daily health. The migration of citizens from the fresh air and open sunlight of the countryside to cloistered cities with smoggy air and little direct sunlight triggered health challenges not previously experienced. Physicians began to observe a new affliction in young children that caused bowed legs, weakened bones and other skeletal deformities. Then, in 1889, the British Medical Association reported that rickets, a disease rarely seen in rural districts, was increasingly prevalent in large industrial centers. First discovered in 1651 by English physician Francis Glisson,[12] rickets is a disease of acute vitamin D deficiency, which continues to afflict modern society. By the turn of the 20th century, around the time researchers discovered that sunlight was essential for the production of vitamin D, 80% of the children living in northern Europe and the northeastern United States were afflicted with this debilitating bone-deforming disease.[13]

> Studies confirm that increased skin pigment can *greatly* reduce the photosynthesis of vitamin D.[8] Consequently, people with darker complexions must spend much longer in the sun to manufacture as much vitamin D as a person of northern European descent.

Also around this time, Danish physician and Nobel Laureate, Niels Finsen, developed the first therapeutic artificial light source and successfully used it to treat *lupus vulgaris,* a painful tuberculosis skin lesion that appears on the face and neck. Modern medicine had stumbled upon what the ancients had known for millennia—that exposure to sunlight cured *many* diseases. Physicians soon began treating patients by exposing them to sunlight on rooftop solaria. Throughout Europe and North America, heliotherapy quickly became the 'de rigueur' treatment for diseases such as rickets, tuberculosis and psoriasis. It worked—we just didn't know *why*.

A Misguided Fear

Tragically, the use of sunlight as a modern source of healing was short-lived, pushed aside in favour of antibiotics, vaccinations and other "wonder drugs" discovered in the early 20th century and promoted heavily by a growing pharmaceutical industry. During the 1960s, after it was discovered that over-exposure to sunlight could also contribute to skin cancer and premature wrinkling, a massive shift in public perception was engineered by the global drug and cosmetic industries, which realized immense profits from pedalling the notion that the sun was *bad* and must be avoided at all costs. Over the next 50 years, "cover up and slap on the sunscreen" became the marketing slogan for a global

campaign that would prove largely responsible for a worldwide epidemic of vitamin D deficiency that was *entirely* avoidable.

While *over-exposure* to strong sunlight *can* damage the skin, the fear about skin cancer has been pure hyperbole. Researchers have known since 1937 that UV radiation, while increasing the risk of benign and easily treatable skin carcinomas, can actually *protect* against the development of a much wider range of more deadly cancers. In reality, the risk of death from serious internal cancers caused by the *avoidance* of sunlight is far greater than the risk of death from skin cancer. Non-melanoma skin cancer has a very low death rate (0.5%) compared to colon and breast cancer, which have kill rates between 20% to 65%.[5] According to vitamin D authority Dr Michael Holick, there is no credible evidence that moderate sun exposure causes melanoma.[5] In fact, increased sun exposure can actually *increase* survival rates for this more lethal form of skin cancer.[14]

Ironically, early sunscreens effectively blocked the sun's burning UVB rays while allowing unintentional over-exposure to the damaging UVA rays, known to be a primary cause of skin melanoma. Consequently, since the 1960s, application of these sunscreens actually contributed to the rapid rise in death rates from this type of cancer. While modern sunscreens now protect against both types of radiation, these sunscreens filter out virtually all of the capacity of the skin to manufacture vitamin D. Application of SPF 8 eliminates 90% of the skin's ability to manufacture vitamin D, while SPF 30 stops vitamin D formation dead in its tracks.

Even today, the misguided fear and the avoidance of the sun, and blind allegiance to the mantra of "cover up and slap it on," dangerously hinder our ability to obtain sufficient vitamin D.

The bottom line is this: sunlight IS healthy. Moderate whole-body exposure to strong sunlight is *essential* for good health. Fifteen to thirty minutes a day, depending on the season, is all the vitamin D you need; then, you can cover up to protect against over-exposure. During the fall and winter months, when it may not be possible to get sufficient sun exposure, everyone should supplement with 1,000 to 2,000 IU of vitamin D.

How Vitamin D is Manufactured

In the presence of skin-penetrating UVB rays, dehydrocholesterol, a precursor of cholesterol, is transformed into pre-vitamin D_3, which is quickly converted to vitamin D_3. Once formed, vitamin D_3 is metabolized in the liver to 25-hydroxyvitamin D_3 (calcidiol), the major circulating form of vitamin D in the blood. Circulating calcidiol then reports to the kidneys, where a small amount is converted to 1,25-dihydroxyvitamin D_3 (calitriol). This *active* circulating form of vitamin D is responsible for the regulation of calcium metabolism and bone health; without sufficient calcitriol, you absorb less than 15% of the calcium available through your diet. Circulating calcidiol is also shunted to body tissues, such as the prostate gland, breast, brain, colon, parathyroid glands and immune cells; it is this stored form of vitamin D that has so recently caught the attention of the scientific community.

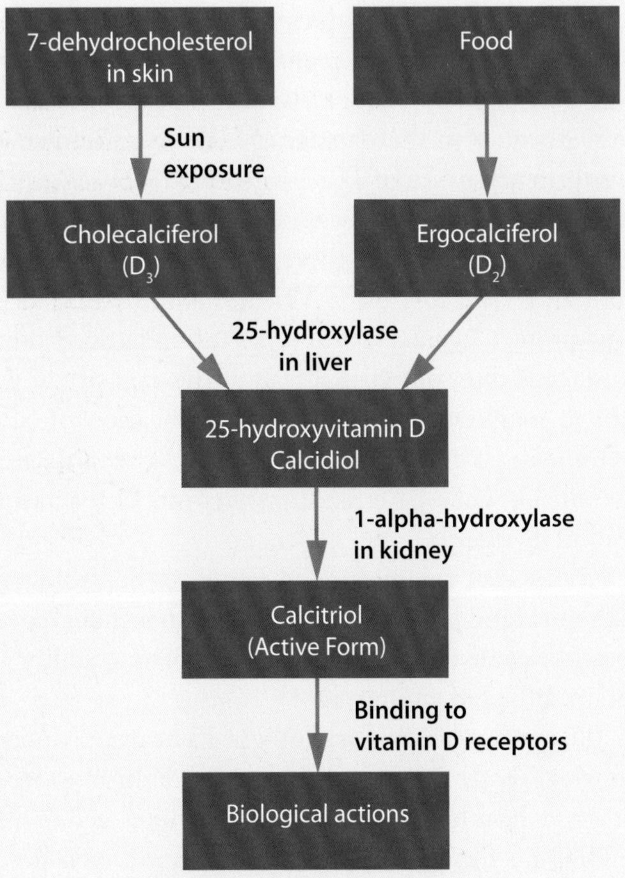

The skin's ability to manufacture vitamin D is prodigious, provided you spend some time in strong sunlight. Fifteen to thirty minutes exposure when the sun is high in the sky—enough to cause a slight pinkening of the skin within 24 hours—is the equivalent of taking 15,000-20,000 IU of vitamin D in supplement form.

Incidentally, if you are taking a cholesterol-lowering statin drug, such as Lipitor®, you may be shorting yourself on the very substance that is essential for the formation of vitamin D. Artificially lowering circulating cholesterol with powerful pharmaceutical drugs unintentionally inhibits the metabolic pathway responsible for the formation of vitamin D, the glucocorticoids, sex hormones and other important steroid hormones necessary for good health. This renders such individuals susceptible to a host of disorders that can be avoided with more natural methods of cholesterol reduction. Anyone taking statins should make certain they supplement with plenty of pre-formed vitamin D to avoid this problem.

More than Just Calcium

Once formed, activated vitamin D circulates in the blood to interact with the cells of the small intestine and bone. Specialized proteins, called nuclear receptors (located within the nuclei of these cells), respond by absorbing calcium from the gut and depositing it in the bone to maintain calcium balance. This is something we have known for years.

But, that's not all there is to vitamin D.

Very recently, an immense volume of new research has revealed vitamin D's prodigious powers to regulate cell metabolism throughout the body, creating a quantum shift in our understanding of the importance of this essential hormone. Researchers have now discovered vitamin D receptors in *all* our body tissues. The hormone interacts with these receptors to create a *multitude* of important physiological effects. That is why, when you think about it, your health and well-being depend upon developing an intimate relationship with the sun.

Figure 3: Vitamin D Synthesis

Research has recently uncovered that virtually every tissue in the body, such as found in the colon, breast, heart, brain, muscle, lung, prostate and thymus gland, has the enzymatic machinery to produce activated vitamin D (calcitriol)—*on the spot*—from the vitamin D stored within. Once activated, the hormone then 'rolls up its sleeves,' interacting with nuclear receptors located on the cell membranes of these tissues, to regulate cell growth and proliferation. Calcitriol's actions target over *2,000* genes in our cells—about 6% of the total human genome, providing the hormone with an unprecedented degree of control over cellular function and growth. This finding has lifted the veil on vitamin D's actions, revealing a new understanding that the vitamin D story is *so much more* than just calcium balance. It also explains why the hormone appeared so early in the evolution of all advanced life-forms: its influence lies at the very core of our biochemical make-up.

The ability of vitamin D to regulate genetic expression and cellular homeostasis at so many levels is unparalleled. Working throughout the body and at the cellular level, vitamin D can: improve fertility; safeguard pregnancy; reduce chronic inflammation; help control weight; protect against infectious agents; prevent strokes; prevent neurological disorders, including dementia; bolster our immune response; boost mental cognition; modulate heart function; and support muscle strength.[4]

All-in-all, that's not a bad day's work!

> Researchers have now discovered vitamin D receptors in *all* our body tissues. The hormone interacts with these receptors to create a *multitude* of important physiological effects.

New Findings on Vitamin D

For most practitioners in mainstream medicine, it is simply incomprehensible that an ordinary vitamin can: reduce the risks of heart attacks by as much as 50%; decrease the risks of cancers of the breast, colon and prostate by a similar amount; reduce infectious diseases, including influenza, by as much as 90%; combat both type-1 and type-2 diabetes; diminish the risk of dementia and associated neurological dysfunctions; and dramatically impede the incidence of multiple sclerosis and other autoimmune diseases.[15]

But, this is no ordinary vitamin.

In the following discussion, we will investigate three disease processes, cancer, heart disease and immune dysfunction, and we will learn about some of the most recent exciting discoveries regarding the extraordinary preventive powers of this unique nutritional powerhouse.

Vitamin D and Cancer

More than 2500 published studies confirm vitamin D's role in the prevention of cancer. Together, the findings suggest that vitamin D from strong sunlight or provided in supplement form is responsible for preventing a host of internal cancers.

Three of the most prevalent and feared cancers, breast, colorectal and prostate cancer, are highly influenced by the amount of sun exposure and vitamin D status. Supplementation with 1,000 IU per day of vitamin D will substantially reduce your risk of developing these cancers. There is abundant evidence that vitamin D prevents human breast cancer cell proliferation and enhances the differentiation of cells into normal healthy tissue.[16-21] The risk of metastasis (spread) of breast cancer is 94% greater among women who have a deficiency in vitamin D at the time of diagnosis. These women also have a 75% greater risk of dying from this disease. Moreover, the risk of prostate cancer in men with low vitamin

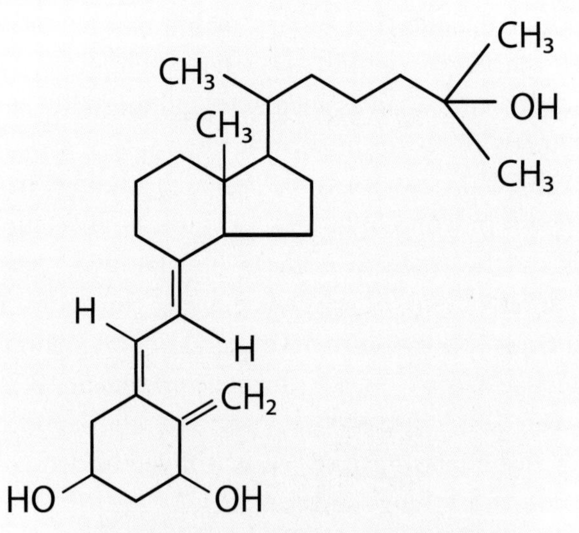

Figure 4: Molecular Structure of Calcitriol

D status is three times that for men with sufficient vitamin D;[22-25] high blood levels of vitamin D have been shown to increase survival rates for colon cancer in both women and men by almost 50%.[26]

Twenty-five years of research confirms that high vitamin D intake may be especially important in averting colon cancer. A 19-year study of colorectal cancer rates found the relative risk in men with poor vitamin D status was almost triple that of men with sufficient vitamin D.[27] In a meta-analysis (a study of studies) conducted on research worldwide from 1966 to 2004, researchers from the University of California concluded that 1,000 IU/day of vitamin D lowers an individual's risk of developing colorectal cancer by as much as 50%.[28]

Epidemiological, ecological and observational studies all confirm that the further away you live from the equator, the *poorer* is your vitamin D status and the *higher* is your lifetime risk of contracting cancer. While such studies, by design, cannot establish causality, findings dating back to 1941 confirm that cancer rates, including cancers of the breast,[29-31] prostate,[29,30] colon,[30] ovaries,[29,32] kidney,[33] brain,[34] pancreas,[35,36] lung and childhood cancers,[37,38] are strongly related to latitude, solar intensity and the lack of vitamin D.

A 2006 review of vitamin D status and cancer risk in the northeastern United States has also found evidence of a strong protective relationship.[29] The authors conclude that efforts to improve vitamin D status through vitamin D supplementation could markedly reduce cancer incidence and mortality at low cost and with few or no adverse effects.

A 2008 review of current research findings in cell biology, epidemiology, and preclinical and clinical trials on the protective effects of vitamin D against the development of several cancers concludes that calcitriol, the active form of vitamin D, offers significant protective effects. The authors posit that intakes of between 1000 and 4000 IU per day offer significant protective effects against cancers of the breast, colon, prostate, ovary, lungs and pancreas.[39]

A 2009 review on UVB radiation, vitamin D and cancer has also concluded that circulating levels of

vitamin D play an important role in determining the outcomes of several cancers.[40] According to the authors of this review, support for the sunlight/vitamin D/cancer link is scientifically strong enough to warrant the use of vitamin D in cancer prevention and treatment protocols. This view is widely supported by other researchers, some of whom have called for obligatory preventive national programs of vitamin D supplementation in countries where widespread insufficiency exists.[41]

Lastly, a recent four-year, population-based, double-blind, randomized, placebo-controlled clinical trial—the gold standard for medical proof—has reported an astounding finding. Post-menopausal women who supplemented with 1,100 IU of vitamin D and 1,500 mg of calcium per day reduced their risk of dying from ALL cancers by more than 66%.[42] This remarkable finding suggests that vitamin D could be the *single* most effective means of preventing cancer, even outpacing the benefits of a healthy lifestyle.

According to Michael Holick, whose ground-breaking research led to the discovery of the activated form of vitamin D, when you are exposed to strong sunlight or supplement with vitamin D, excess vitamin D is stored in cellular tissues in its inactive form as *calcidiol* (25-hydroxyvitamin D). This stockpiled vitamin D can then be activated at any time to *calcitriol* (1,25-dihydroxyvitamin D), which can regulate aberrant cell growth that leads to cancer. Acting at the cellular level, calcitriol halts the chaotic reproduction and growth of these aberrant cells by inducing apoptosis, or cellular suicide, and it inhibits the formation of new blood vessels needed to nourish cancerous growth, effectively snuffing out cancer *before* it takes hold.

This revelation provides us with *enormous* capacity for prevention. It is the singular reason why scientists at the University of California, San Diego, now contend that low vitamin D status may be *the* root cause of all cancers.

Vitamin D and Heart Disease

The further north or south you live from the tropics, the higher is your risk of heart attack (myocardial

> This revelation provides us with *enormous* capacity for prevention. It is the singular reason why scientists at the University of California, San Diego, now contend that low vitamin D status may be *the* root cause of all cancers.

infarction).* Low light levels during the winter months reduce vitamin D synthesis and encourage excess cholesterol synthesis, thereby concurrently elevating the risks of atherosclerosis (plaque formation) and myocardial infarction (MI).[43] A 1990 New Zealand study provided the first hint that a deficiency in vitamin D might be related to heart disease when researchers discovered that MIs were strongly correlated with low vitamin D status. The results were observed over all seasons but were most pronounced during the spring and winter months.[44] This finding was later corroborated in an analysis of almost 300,000 heart attacks registered in the US National Registry of Myocardial Infarction. The latter study revealed that heart attacks surged by 53% during the winter months when sunlight and vitamin D production were low,[45] unlike MI incidents in tropical climates, where the sun shines year-round and seasonal variation is not seen.[46]

People who are deficient in the sunshine vitamin are also much more likely to have hypertension (high blood pressure), type-2 diabetes and elevated triglycerides (a major risk factor for heart disease).[47-49] Vitamin D reduces blood pressure by relaxing the smooth muscles lining the artery walls and by regulating the release of renin, a hormone manufactured by the kidneys that increases vasoconstriction (constriction of the arteries). As well, vitamin D is a potent anti-inflammatory agent; the hormone expresses a powerful effect in reducing levels of C-reactive protein (CRP), a principal biological marker of inflammation and heart disease.[50] In fact, the ability of vitamin D to reduce CRP levels appears to be far more pronounced than that of the statin drugs commonly used by the drug industry to reduce the risk of heart attack.[3] Moreover, the vitamin's benefits in stimulating general cardiovascular function are now recognized as being on par with that of aerobic exercise. A deficiency of vitamin D diminishes the contractile function of the heart, contributes to dysfunction in the endothelial lining of the blood vessels, exacerbates atherosclerotic plaque formation and contributes to congestive heart failure.[51-53]

A recent Harvard University study reveals that low vitamin D status can increase the risk of a cardiac event in a *graded* manner by up to 242%, the level of risk increasing proportionately with *decreasing* levels of circulating vitamin D.[54] As well, vitamin D status is inversely related to the risk of deep vein thrombosis, a dangerous clotting of the major veins in the legs, which can, in turn, lead to acute pulmonary embolism (a sudden blockage in the arteries of the lung resulting from dislodged clotted fragments) and death. The findings of this Swedish study also show that the risks of thrombotic complications exhibit a seasonal variation, peaking in winter and dropping in summer. High levels of vitamin D appear to enhance the body's anti-clotting capacity to reduce both inflammation and the risk of clot formation.[55]

Researchers now understand that inflammation of the arteries is a major contributory factor in congestive heart failure. Vitamin D offers protective benefits to the endothelial lining of the arteries and the heart muscle by quelling the production of inflammatory proteins, called cytokines, which contribute to heart failure. The authors of a recent German study conclude that supplemental vitamin D could serve as a new anti-inflammatory agent for the treatment of this disease.[56]

Vitamin D and Immune Support

For years, the evidence has mounted that sun exposure is an effective prevention and treatment for immune disorders. Like cancer and heart disease, the prevalence of these disorders also correlates directly with latitude—the further you deviate from the equatorial zone, where the sunlight is always strong, the higher is the incidence of these diseases. The importance of sunlight to the body's immune response is demonstrated dutifully each year when the waning sunlight of autumn presages the onslaught of the flu season.

> The importance of sunlight to the body's immune response is demonstrated dutifully each year when the waning sunlight of autumn presages the onslaught of the flu season.

---

* *The medical term for a heart attack, derived from Latin, meaning "death of the heart."*

Contrary to conventional wisdom, many researchers now believe that seasonal infections, such as colds and influenza, may actually be the result of *decreased* levels of vitamin D rather than of *increased* wintertime viral activity.[57] Several studies suggest that vitamin D is required for proper activation of specialized immune cells in our blood that are responsible for killing harmful viruses and bacteria.[58,59] The strength of the evidence supporting vitamin D's efficacy in reducing viral-borne infections, such as seasonal influenza, has convinced many physicians to begin boosting daily intakes in their patients to 5,000 IU per day or more during the flu season, rather than risk the questionable effectiveness of the flu shot.

> For years, we have known that vitamin D supplementation can effectively reduce the risk of developing MS and other autoimmune diseases. Now we are beginning to understand why.

A previously unexpected role for vitamin D in bolstering our natural immunity has now been documented. A 2007 study, conducted by researchers at the University of California at San Diego, showed that skin cells could independently activate vitamin D from within their cellular stores. Activated vitamin D was then able to switch on genes controlling the manufacture of *cathelicidin*, a specialized anti-microbial peptide (small protein) that specifically targets viruses, bacteria and other infectious agents.[60] This novel finding has immense implications for the use of vitamin D in treating wounds and infections.

As mentioned previously, vitamin D also expresses potent anti-inflammatory actions. These actions explain the vitamin's noted ability in the prevention and treatment of asthma and general allergic reactions. The hormone apparently activates several genes controlling the manufacture of an inflammation-suppressing chemical (Interleukin-10) produced in specialized white blood cells. Interleukin-10, in turn, dampens the body's over-response that can often precipitate allergic reactions. One recent study demonstrated an astounding 90% reduction in upper respiratory tract infections when supplementing with 2,000 IU/day of vitamin D, compared to the formerly prescribed recommended dietary intake of 400 IU/day.[61]

Vitamin D has even demonstrated protective effects against autoimmune dysfunctions that occur when the immune system begins to attack its own host. Diseases such as lupus, fibromyalgia, type-1 diabetes (an autoimmune disease of the pancreas), psoriasis, rheumatoid arthritis, chronic fatigue syndrome and multiple sclerosis are some of the common autoimmune diseases related to impaired vitamin D status.[62] Very recent studies reveal that the presence of activated vitamin D may help attenuate the over-response of our immune system to reduce *both* allergic and autoimmune responses. One of the mechanisms appears to be vitamin D's ability to inhibit the activation of Nuclear Factor kappa-Beta (NFkß), an important cellular signalling protein that acts as a sentinel in the body's inflammatory cascade.[63-65]

Multiple sclerosis (MS) is a neurological disorder of young people, caused by the formation of multiple lesions, or scars, in specialized nerve cells that control muscle function. MS has a genetic basis, its expression related to latitude and degree of exposure to sunlight. The disease is 500 times more likely to affect you if you live in a temperate zone than if you live in the tropics. For years, we have known that vitamin D supplementation can effectively reduce the risk of developing MS and other autoimmune diseases. Now we are beginning to understand why.

Early sun exposure or supplementation with vitamin D appears to activate the youthful thymus gland to seek out and destroy cells that can eventually attack the fatty myelin sheath surrounding motor neurons. Damage to this protective sheath, much like the fraying of an electrical cord, disrupts the electrical signal that controls muscular movement, resulting in the onset of MS. Vitamin D has been shown to regulate the expression of a class of genes that initiate the inflammatory process of MS, thus providing protection against onset of the disease.[61] For this reason, regular sun exposure and vitamin D supplementation early in life remain the best course of action for prevention of this debilitating disease.

Indeed, vitamin D's immunity-boosting talents make it one of our most reliable nutritional tools in bolstering comprehensive immunity. International experts throughout Europe and the United States have called for a global policy change on vitamin D, which they contend is crucial to reduce the risks of a host of degenerative diseases. The evidence is clear: you need to supplement year-round, especially during the winter months, to ensure that you maintain healthy levels of vitamin D. In particular, people living in the northern latitudes should supplement with higher levels of vitamin D to avoid the 'Vitamin D winter' that occurs between October to April anywhere north of the 37th parallel.

How Much is Enough?

In 1963, American and Canadian authorities drafted the Recommended Daily Allowance (RDA) for vitamin D intake; it was—admittedly—almost pure fabrication. There was little research data available to establish scientifically valid requirements for optimal health.[3,27] The only known deficiency in adults, at the time, was osteomalacia, a form of bone softening, and 200 IU/day of vitamin D was *just* enough to prevent this painful condition. It was also known that children who received less than 300-400 IU/day of vitamin D tended to develop rickets.

Consequently, the original recommendation for the daily intake of vitamin D in adults was based, in part, on providing *half* the recommended childhood dosage and, in part, on the avoidance of osteomalacia. In essence, the recommended intake for adults was an *arbitrary* figure based on a *disease* model, rather than any established data on optimal requirements.

In November 2010, the US Food and Nutrition Board and Health Canada, responding to the growing evidence on the importance of the vitamin D, revised their recommended daily intake for calciferol. The new reference standard adopted for vitamin D now calls for 600 IU/day, with a Safe Upper Limit of 4,000 IU/day. Convinced by the weight of recent supportive evidence, many experts in the field believe strongly that this new standard continues to fall far short of what is required for optimal health.

When you consider that just 10-20 minutes of full-body exposure to strong sunlight provides vitamin D blood levels equivalent to 10,000-15,000 IU/day taken orally, the new reference standard of 600 IU/day for adults appears scientifically indefensible.[66] Mother Nature is frugal—she would not have allowed for the manufacture of such prodigious levels of vitamin D in the skin if there was not an established biological need. While a marginal improvement over the previous standard, the new reference standard for vitamin D may still be 5 to 10 times too low for optimal health.[66,67]

So, the question remains: how much is enough?

It is important to understand that the *best* way to get your vitamin D is from the sun. Synthesis of vitamin D in the skin by strong sunlight produces a number of other important photoproducts not available through supplementation. Moreover, vitamin D made through solar synthesis lasts twice as long as vitamin D provided from the diet. That said, *everyone* living outside of the tropics, or living a predominantly indoor lifestyle, simply *must* supplement or they *will* become vitamin D deficient. Modern indoor lifestyles and seasonal variations in sun exposure do not provide us with sufficient natural stores of this important hormone.

> In essence, the recommended intake for adults was an *arbitrary* figure based on a *disease* model, rather than any established data on optimal requirements.

Table 1: Recommendations for Daily Intake of Vitamin D		
From: Holick MF, *The Vitamin D Solution*, Hudson Street Press, 2010, p 219		
AGE OR CONDITION	**INTAKE PER DAY**	**SAFE UPPER LIMIT**
Infants 0 to 1 yr	400-1,000 IU	2,000 IU
Children 1 yr to 12 yrs	1,000-2,000 IU	5,000 IU
Adolescents 13+ and adults	1,500-2,000 IU	10,000 IU
Obese individuals of any age	2-3 times the above	10,000 IU
Pregnant women	1,400-2,000 IU	10,000 IU
Lactating women*	2,000-4,000 IU	10,000 IU
* Lactating women who want to ensure their baby is getting sufficient vitamin D from their breast milk should supplement with 4,000 – 6,000 IU/day		

The objective in vitamin D supplementation is to raise your blood levels of vitamin D (measured as 25-hydroxyvitamin D) to between 40-60 nannograms per milliliter (40-60 ng/mL), as measured in the United States. In Canada, this is equivalent to a reference range of 100 to 150 nannomoles per liter (100-150 nm/L).

Holick suggests that a daily dose of between 2,000 – 5,000 IU/day is perfectly safe over the long term and contends that you can safely take up to 10,000 IU/day for at least five months without any signs of toxicity.[68] His recommendations for daily intake for particular individuals are provided in Table One (previous page).

Summary

Despite the rapid advancement in our knowledge about vitamin D, chronic insufficiency of this vital nutrient remains the most unrecognized and misdiagnosed nutritional deficiency in the world. Marginal improvements in the recommended daily intakes, issued recently by the United States and Canada, appear completely insufficient to address the problem.

More than one billion people worldwide and well over half of the North American population remain chronically vitamin D deficient. They will continue to be placed at considerable risk for serious chronic illness until substantive educational and preventive actions are taken. Around the world, calls for increasing the recommended daily intake of vitamin D to 1,000 IU/day for adults and up to 2,000 IU/day for teens have come from diverse health groups, including the Canadian Cancer Society and the American University of Beirut Medical Center in Lebanon. So far, these appeals appear to have fallen on deaf ears.

Life Extension Foundation, a leading advocate of anti-aging medicine in the Unites States, has called for the declaration of a national emergency to address the appalling vitamin D deficiency prevalent in the US population. Founder William Faloon contends that for cancer alone 275,000 lives could be saved each year if a nation-wide program of supplementation was developed to bring the nation's vitamin D status up to healthy levels. This same simple act of raising vitamin D to healthy levels in the people of Western Europe could save $260 billion a year and could reduce the death rate amongst Canadians by 18%. In light of these revelations, the socioeconomic consequences of further inaction become too stark to ignore.

Stop and consider the implications: a few minutes each day spent in the bright sun, or taking an inexpensive vitamin D supplement that costs mere pennies a day, can harness nature's powers to reduce our risks of dying from virtually *all* of today's major killers. Today, these chronic diseases contribute to nearly 90% of all non-accidental deaths in the modern world.[69]

Responsible medicine demands action when the evidence is so convincing, the protocol so simple and the results so dramatic. Not to act decisively shows a reckless disregard for public safety.

When you seek a new path to truth,
you must expect it to be blocked by expert opinion.

~ Albert Guérard

CHAPTER FOUR:

THE IODINE STORY

Iodine, much like its nutritional colleague vitamin D, is one of our most fundamental yet misunderstood essential nutrients. The element is found principally in the form of water-soluble iodide ions (I^-) in our oceans and deep subterranean water sources. Free iodine occurs mainly as a diatomic (two-atom) molecule I_2, and then only momentarily, after being oxidized from iodide. While a relatively rare element, its ubiquity in the world's oceans likely provided iodine with a fundamental biological purpose during early evolution.

As a water-soluble anti-oxidant, elemental iodide (I^-) was readily available as a potent biochemical weapon in early life forms. The ease with which it reacts with simple organic compounds and catalyzes cellular reactions likely explains why the element soon became an essential constituent in primitive cells. Cyanobacteria (blue-green algae), believed to be among the first photosynthetic life forms to evolve, developed a strong affinity for iodine, incorporating it as a membrane-bound antioxidant to protect against damaging free radicals* generated during photosynthesis.† Kelp, another ancient marine organism, is also known to actively scavenge iodine

Figure 5: Kelp

Ancient marine algae that appeared 5 to 23 million years ago, kelp sequesters iodine from surrounding ocean waters when placed under oxidative stress from strong sunlight.

---

* *Free radicals are molecules and molecular fragments with an unpaired electron, which are highly unstable and extremely short-lived. Free radicals are chemically volatile, reacting aggressively with other molecules at the instant of their creation. Oxygen-containing free radicals are called Reactive Oxygen Species (ROS) and include hydrogen peroxide, superoxide anion and the hydroxyl radical.*

† *Photosynthesis is a complex series of chemical reactions that use the energy of sunlight to manufacture sugars and other carbon-containing compounds. Before the evolution of photosynthetic plants in the ancient oceans, there was no available free oxygen in our atmosphere. It was only through photosynthesis that terrestrial oxygen-breathing life forms were capable of evolving.*

from the surrounding waters when placed under oxidative stress, presumably for the same reason.[1]

Iodine possesses another exceptional talent that helped secure its purpose in biological evolution: it is capable of spontaneously coupling with the amino acid[‡] tyrosine. This allowed the creation of a highly reactive and mobile chemical species called iodotyrosine. Advancing life forms soon integrated iodinated tyrosine into evolving biochemical pathways responsible for energy production, gene expression and DNA replication. The development of these complex biochemical pathways furthered the conversion of iodotyrosine into the iodine-containing hormones thyroxine (T4) and triiodothyronine (T3). Today, these powerful cell-signaling hormones are used by virtually all vertebrate life forms.[2] Considering iodine's early evolutionary role, it is not surprising that primitive invertebrates and algae continue to possess the ability to synthesize thyroxine.[3]

Iodine is the heaviest essential element to be utilized widely in biological functions (only tungsten, employed in enzymes by a few species of bacteria, is heavier). Its rarity in the earth's soils, due to its low abundance in mineral forms and the leaching of soluble iodide by rainwater, has led to widespread deficiency problems in both inland animal and human populations. The element is deposited in the earth's soils through evaporation of sea water and consequent precipitation in rainfall.[4] For this reason, land masses proximal to the earth's oceans contain much higher levels of iodine than do inland soils. Today, iodine deficiency affects about two billion people, particularly those in the developing world, and is the leading cause of preventable mental retardation.

Iodine's Discovery

For millennia, the peoples of the Pacific coasts of Asia and South America consumed seaweed for the cure of goitre, a swelling and dysfunction of the thyroid gland now known to be the direct result of chronic iodine deficiency. Numerous references to the treatment of goitre can be found in early Chinese medical writings dating as far back as 1500 BC. The ancient Greeks, including Galen, used marine sponge to treat swollen glands; but it was the Italian physicians of the School of Salerno during the 12th century that became the first to report the specific use of burnt sponge and dried seaweed to treat goitre.[5] Burnt sponge remained a goitre cure throughout the Middle Ages and into the modern era. No one knew what was in the seaweeds and sponges that could cure goitre—they simply knew it worked.

It was a serendipitous event in 1811 that led to the discovery of this unknown 'intrinsic factor.' French chemist Bernard Courtois, manufacturing saltpetre for armaments during the Napoleonic Wars, accidentally poured too much acid on the residue of seaweed ash. He immediately sublimated a beautiful and intensely violet vapour that crystallised on the sides of the reaction vessel. Analysis of the novel crystals by renowned French chemist Joseph Gay-Lussac and British chemist Sir Humphrey Davy confirmed the discovery of a new element—*iodine*. In 1813, Swiss physician Jean François Coindet hypothesized that the effectiveness of seaweed and sponges in the treatment of goitre was due to their high iodine content, a fact confirmed in 1819 by Andrew Fyfe of the University of Edinburgh.[6]

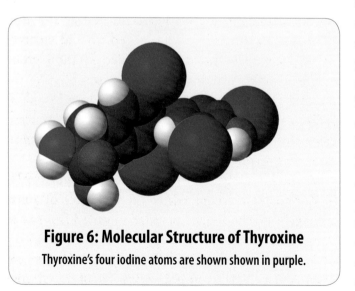

Figure 6: Molecular Structure of Thyroxine
Thyroxine's four iodine atoms are shown shown in purple.

‡ *Amino acids are the molecular building blocks of all proteins. Amino acids were plentiful in the primordial seas due to the intense electro-chemical activity of the earth's ammonia-rich early atmosphere. There are approximately 20 amino acids critical for cell life. Tyrosine is an essential amino acid for humans that, today, must be supplied through the diet.*

In 1895, the German chemist Eugene Baumann revealed that iodine is an invariable constituent of the thyroid gland, thereby establishing the causal link between diet and disease. Investigations in the early 1900s by Edward Kendall in Rochester, New York, next led to the isolation of an iodine-containing protein, which he named *thyroxine*. In 1930, Sir Charles Harington proved that the newly discovered hormone contained four atoms of iodine and devised a means for its chemical synthesis. By the mid-1900s, iodine, a rare element discovered little more than 100 years earlier by both accident and advent of war, was recognized as an essential nutrient in human biology.

The History of Iodine Use

Iodine as a listed medicine first appeared in the French pharmacopoeia in the year 1821 and soon came to be used for every conceivable pathology. The variety of diseases for which iodine was used was simply astonishing and included maladies such as chorea, scrofula, lacrimal fistula, deafness, syphilis, acute inflammation, gout, gangrene, dropsy, carbuncles, chilblains, burns, lupus, croup, asthma, ulcers and bronchitis—to mention but a few.

From 1820 to 1840, a series of monographs and essays provided a remarkable testament to the wide-ranging and extraordinary benefits attributed to the medicinal use of this novel nutritional *wunderkind*. The first British Pharmacopoeia of 1864 listed 14 iodine preparations. By 1894, *Martindale's Pharmacopoeia* listed 30 iodine preparations; by 1928, that number rose to 128 listings. In 1956, an International Index devoted exclusively to iodine preparations provided information on no less than 1700 approved pharmaceutical designations.[6] Regarding the use of potassium iodide salts, the 1911 edition of the *Encyclopedia Brittanica* effuses: "Their pharmacological actions, as obscure as their effects in certain disease conditions, are consistently brilliant."

According to Nobel Laureate Albert Szent-Györgyi, iodine in the form of potassium iodide (KI) was the *Universal Medicine* of the early 1900s. "Nobody knew what it did, but it did something and it did something good!" Iodine preparations were administered as a vapour; as nascent iodine; and in baths, pills, sweets, inhalants, soups, snuff, medicinal patches, ointments, creams, hair tonics, suppositories, plasters and even contraceptives. As a field dressing during the American Civil War, iodine simply had no peer. Tincture of iodine was declared requisite in all military field hospitals until Sir Alexander Fleming's discovery of penicillin ushered in the 'new age' of antibiotics following the close of the First World War.

By the early 1900s, iodine was well established in medical and surgical practices; daily therapeutic doses in the form of potassium iodide salt (KI) ranged from 300 to 1800 mg.[7] A 1940 review, published in the Harvard University Press, expressed amazement at the astounding therapeutic power of iodine in successfully treating difficult tertiary syphilitic lesions.[8] In the same year, iodine received wide acclaim as a principal treatment for hyperthyroidism.[9] Using iodine alone in patients with hyperthyroidism, Thompson and Starr independently confirmed high success rates (88-92%) with a solution of iodine/potassium iodide (commonly known as Lugol's solution) at doses ranging from 6 to 90 mg/day of iodide.[7]

Studies conducted by Marine and coworkers in the 1920s demonstrated iodine's safety and efficacy at higher doses. In a long-term study of adolescent school girls in Akron, Ohio, a region with a 56% incidence of goitre at the time, euthyroid (normal thyroid) students were given 2 g of sodium iodide twice yearly (equivalent to 11 mg of iodide/day or over 70 times the current recommended intake for adolescents). After 2½ years, 22% of the control group developed thyroid enlargement; conversely, the iodine supplementation group exhibited only 0.2% incidence of goitre. Despite the relatively high dose of iodine given, only 0.5% of the iodine supplementation group reported mild and transient iodine toxicity, which is characterized by runny nose, skin disruptions, brassy taste and dyspepsia.[10]

A similar study was conducted by Klinger (1921) in Zurich, Switzerland, where the incidence of goitre amongst the school-aged population varied from 82 to 95%. After 15 months of treatment with 10 to 15 mg of iodine weekly the incidence of goitre plummeted from 90% to 28%—a stunning example of the curative effects of iodine therapy. Moreover, in over 16 months of observation in more than 1,000 children, there were no reported cases of iodine toxicity. These findings support the argument that the danger of giving milligram amounts of iodine over a long period is negligible.

The Marine study was the first US study to demonstrate the decline of goitre with the use of iodine. In response to its findings, the US Food and Drug Administration (FDA) launched a national campaign to encourage the use of iodized salt,[11] an initiative which was also adopted by Canada. Americans and Canadians willingly complied by pouring the saltshaker over everything they ate, and soon overt iodine deficiency was but a memory and unsightly goitres became a rarity.

The thyroid needs only a 'whiff' of iodine (about 70 µg/day) to produce the requisite amount of thyroid hormone needed for good thyroid health; consequently, it was believed that the amount of iodine present in ½ teaspoon of fortified salt, as prescribed by the FDA, was more than sufficient to do the job. No consideration was given by the medical authorities of the day as to what daily requirement of iodine was necessary to assure the optimal health of *other* body tissues.

To the contrary, the prevailing wisdom of mid-twentieth century medicine was that iodine made a good antiseptic and a powerful disinfectant and that the thyroid needed it to make hormones—and that was it. Any suggestion of intakes above that needed for thyroid health was met with concern about the element's toxicity. Endocrinologists repeatedly warned that levels above 1-2 mg/day would be damaging to the thyroid;[1] however, their arguments ignored the empirical evidence that iodine had been used in *gram* amounts to treat chronic lung diseases, fungal infections, tertiary syphilis and arteriosclerosis—all with little untoward effect. In fact, primary care physicians, for years, used potassium iodide (KI) at doses from 1,500 to 10,000 mg/day to treat bronchial asthma and chronic obstructive pulmonary disorder (COPD) with excellent results and little evidence of adverse reaction.[1]

Today, dermatologists continue to use iodine to effectively treat inflammatory dermatoses (skin eruptions) at doses of 900 to 6,000 mg/day.[1] Isolated incidents of thyrotoxicosis following iodine repletion therapy,

used by some as evidence of harm, have generally been found to be mild transient responses amongst iodine-sensitized individuals and those suffering chronic and severe iodine deficiency.[12]

Iodine's Role in the Thyroid

The thyroid gland is a butterfly-shaped structure located at the base of the neck just below the Adam's apple. It controls our core metabolism and virtually every aspect of health including weight, mood, energy and circulation. As an endocrine gland, the thyroid is under the control of the body's master gland, the pituitary.

Thyrotropin-releasing hormone (TRH), secreted by the hypothalamus, causes the pituitary to release thyroid stimulating hormone (TSH) into the blood. In turn, TSH commands the thyroid gland to actively sequester iodine from the blood. Once within the thyroid, iodine is organified by combining it with the amino acid tyrosine to form the thyroid hormones *thyroxine* (T4) and *triiodothyronine* (T3). T4 contains four iodine atoms per molecule and is the predominant form of the hormone. It acts as a precursor to T3, which is generally regarded as the biologically *active* hormone. Once manufactured, the hormones are bound to thyroxine-binding globulin (TBG), a carrier protein responsible for transporting the hormones into the blood.

> The prevailing wisdom of mid-twentieth century medicine was that iodine made a good antiseptic and a powerful disinfectant and that the thyroid needed it to make hormones—and that was it.

Organified iodine has an intimate relationship with selenium, which explains why selenium deficiencies can quickly lead to thyroid dysfunction. A family of selenium-dependent enzymes called deiodinases converts T4 to the biologically active T3 form by removing an iodine atom from the outer tyrosine ring of the T4 molecule.

Until recently, medical science believed that the only tissue requiring iodine was the thyroid gland—we now know this view to be too parochial. Up to 70% of the body's iodine is stored in several other tissues, including the mammary glands, thymus gland, eyes, gastric mucosa, arterial walls, cervix and salivary glands. Iodine's presence in these tissues is so imperative, the body controls it by means of a cellular membrane pump known as the sodium-iodide symporter (NIS). There is good reason for this.

Iodine, in its ionic and molecular forms, is a powerful antioxidant, anti-inflammatory, anti-viral and anti-bacterial agent that plays a preventive role in fibrocystic breast disease; obesity; attention deficit disorder; psychotic disorders; fibromyalgia; and breast, prostate, endometrial, ovarian and gastric cancers. Deficiencies in maternal iodine intake place the developing foetus at extreme risk for hearing loss, learning deficits, brain damage and nerve myelination disorders.[13] One of the most devastating of these gestational iodine deficiency disorders is congenital hypothyroidism, which often leads to cretinism and irreversible mental retardation.[14]

Current DRIs for Iodine

The current daily Dietary Reference Intake (DRI) for iodine in both the United States and Canada is between 110 and 130 µg for infants up to 12 months, 90 µg for children up to eight years, 120 µg for children up to 13 years, 150 µg for adults, 220 µg for pregnant women and 290 µg for lactating mothers. The Tolerable Upper Intake Level (UL) for adults is 1,100 µg /day or 1.1 mg/day.

Most people mistakenly believe that these recommendations are derived from exhaustive research on efficacy and toxicity. In truth, the recommendations (first established in 1980) were based largely on uncorroborated findings in 1969 by Jan Wolff of the University of California, who suggested— but did not substantiate—that human intakes of iodine above 2 mg/day were "excessive and potentially harmful."[15] Later studies by Canadian researcher William Ghent rebuffed Wolff's assertion of harm, confirming that iodine at 5 mg/day was effective in normalizing diseased breast tissue caused by chronic iodine deficiency.[16] More recent reviews of human trials on the safety of iodine intake indicate that the upper limit of 2 mg/day proposed by Wolff has no firm basis.[17] In essence, the current dietary reference standards for iodine amount to little more than a 'shot in the dark.'

> Salt iodization programs undoubtedly reduced the national incidence of goitre by encouraging more liberal salt intakes; however, this introduced an unintended consequence— high blood pressure (hypertension).

While the thyroid gland needs only miniscule quantities of iodine, the slightly higher recommended levels in the DRIs amount to little more than a passing nod to our growing understanding that more iodine is needed for the health of other tissues. These newly discovered *extrathyroidal* roles of iodine have convinced many clinicians and researchers that the currently prescribed daily intakes for iodine remain far too modest.

Beyond the Thyroid

Iodine deficiency is considered to be the most common endocrine disorder and the most preventable cause of mental retardation worldwide. Fully one-third of the world's population—more than 2 billion people—live in iodine-deficient areas.[18, 19] Nowadays, about 800 million people are affected by iodine deficiency diseases that include goitre, hypothyroidism, mental retardation, and several other growth and developmental abnormalities.[20]

Iodine deficiency is defined as urinary iodine levels of less than 100 µg/day. World Health Organization (WHO) data from 1993 to 2003 indicate that, at the time, the global prevalence of deficiency in school-aged children exceeded 36%. Surprisingly, the highest prevalence of deficiency was in Europe, where 60% of the general population was found lacking in iodine.[21] Despite the fact that infant mortality rates have been shown to plummet by up to 65% wherever iodine deficiencies have been eliminated, maternal iodine deficiencies during pregnancy and post-natal development continue to place millions of the world's children at risk—a tragic situation that is easily and entirely preventable.[13]

Decades ago, as a public health measure to reduce the incidence of goitre, the United States, Canada and several other countries implemented national salt-iodization programs. Prior to this, people relied on iodine preparations from apothecaries (compounding pharmacists) to meet their daily iodine needs. Such preparations were generally compounded as Lugol's solution, a water-based solution of potassium iodide salt (KI) and molecular iodine (I_2) that contained a daily dose of 12.5 to 37.5 mg of elemental iodine—far above the average of 0.075 mg/day of iodine available through the discretionary consumption of table salt.

Salt iodization programs undoubtedly reduced the national incidence of goitre by encouraging more liberal salt intakes; however, this introduced an unintended consequence—high blood pressure (hypertension). Accordingly, in recent years public health bodies the world over have reversed course and now promote salt *restriction* as a means of reducing the incidence of heart disease and stroke. The resultant sharp decline in the use of table salt, particularly amongst health conscious individuals, has now created an inadvertent but dramatic decline in their iodine status. More and more, North Americans are again becoming iodine deficient— sometimes, it seems, we just can't win for trying.

Iodine intakes exhibit a marked decline in subjects placed on sodium restricted diets for treatment of cardiovascular disease.[22-24] A national survey conducted in the United States during the 1970s observed that only one person in 40 had urinary iodine levels suggestive of iodine deficiency. Twenty years later, largely due to the decreased salt usage encouraged by heart-health initiatives, *one in nine* study participants were deficient. Within two decades, salt reduction initiatives had effectively quadrupled the incidence of iodine deficiency and with it the risk of iodine-deficiency related disease.[25]

Public health initiatives for the avoidance of salt have also degraded the iodine status in Australia and New Zealand.[26, 27] A 1999 study, reported in the *Medical Journal of Australia*, found evidence of consistently low iodine intakes amongst ambulatory patients at a teaching hospital in Sydney that mirrored findings in both the US and France.[28, 29] The authors of the Australian study conclude that the prevalence of iodine deficiency demonstrates that dietary iodine sources for Australia are no longer adequate.[28]

Iodine deficiency is generally recognized as the most commonly preventable cause of mental retardation. Iodine deficiency becomes particularly critical in pregnancy due to the possibility of neuro-

> Within two decades, salt reduction initiatives had effectively quadrupled the incidence of iodine deficiency and with it the risk of iodine-deficiency related disease.

logical damage during foetal development as well as during lactation.[30] The 2001-2002 National Health and Nutrition (NHANES) survey found that 36% of US women of childbearing age may not receive sufficient dietary iodine to support foetal health.[31] Moreover, 15% had urinary iodine levels *below* 50 µg/L, a critical limit considered to be an indicator of moderate-to-severe deficiency.

These findings have serious implications: the hypothalamic/pituitary/thyroid axis begins to function at approximately 11 weeks gestation, its principal role to support the developing nervous system. Consequently, even *moderate* iodine deficiency at this critical stage can cause permanent neurological and mental defects in the developing foetus, including spasticity, ataxia and deaf-mutism.[32]

Recent research assessing iodine levels in the breast milk of lactating mothers confirms that only 47% of those surveyed contained levels of iodine sufficient to meet their infants' needs.[33] According to Jospeh Pizzorno, Editor-in-Chief of *Integrative Medicine:* "This growing deficiency may have resulted not only in an increase in thyroid dysfunction but also in an increase in fibrocystic breast disease, breast cancer and other malignancies, obesity, attention deficit disorder, psychotic disorders and fibromyalgia."[34]

While the debate about exactly *how much* iodine is essential for optimal general health is still very much a work in progress, one thing is very clear: iodine intakes well above the currently prescribed dietary reference standards appear to be necessary for good health, and we are simply not getting enough of it.

The Japanese Phenomenon

The Japanese have traditionally consumed copious amounts of seaweed, a reflection of their dietary lifestyle and their proximity to the ocean. More than 95% of the iodine consumed in the Japanese diet comes from seaweed, a rich source of this vital nutrient. Studies place the average consumption of seaweed in Japan at 4-7 g/day, with some estimates at 10 g/day. Data from the Japanese Bureau of Public Health indicate that during the 1960s intake of iodine averaged 13.8

mg/day, increasing to an average daily intake of 45 mg/day by 2006.[35, 36] In the case of the residents of Hokkaido, daily consumption of iodine was found to reach as high as 200 mg[37] (a 2008 study by Nagataki disputes these high levels).[38] Another study of 4,138 healthy euthyroid Japanese men and women found a daily intake of about 5.5 mg/day. Regardless of the discrepancy in these findings, the data show that the Japanese consume inordinately high levels of iodine in comparison to other cultures.

Despite these extremely high intakes, blood levels of the thyroid hormones in the Japanese population are maintained within a narrow range. Excess iodine appears to be excreted as a non-hormonal entity, mostly as inorganic iodide.[39] Moreover, with few exceptions, these inordinately high intakes do not appear to induce any untoward effects on thyroid function. To the contrary, based on evaluations of overall well-being, longevity and low incidence of cancer, the Japanese appear to be one of the healthiest and long-lived populations on earth.

With an age-adjusted incidence of 22 cases per 100,000, the United States has one of the highest rates of breast cancer in the world (Great Britain stands at 27 per 100,000). In contrast, the incidence of breast cancer in Japan is 6.6 per 100,000. In Canada, one in nine Canadian women is expected to develop breast cancer during her lifetime.

When Japanese, Chinese or Filipino women migrate to North America, breast cancer risk rises over several generations and approaches that amongst the indigenous population.[40, 41] This suggests that it is *diet*—not genetics—that is the major determining factor in breast cancer incidence. Many researchers argue that the markedly lower rates of breast cancer and fibrocystic breast disease enjoyed by Japanese women are likely due to the enhanced dietary intake of iodine in the traditional Japanese diet.[13] Several other studies support this argument and suggest that milligram amounts of iodine are safe and confer substantive health benefits beyond thyroid health.[42, 43] Although a period of increased thyroid activity may develop in individuals with long-standing

iodine deficiencies, this transient state normalizes over the longer term.[12, 44]

Iodine as an Antioxidant

Iodine is a powerful biological antioxidant. Painted on the skin, tincture of iodine will destroy 90% of the surface bacteria within 90 seconds. Recall that the ancient cyanobacteria sequestered iodine as a means of protecting themselves against the damaging free radicals that molecular oxygen breeds. While toxic to other bacteria, the development of iodine's protective antioxidant role in cyanobacteria likely made photosynthesis and the evolution of advanced life forms possible.

Hydrogen peroxide (H_2O_2) is an aggressive oxidizing agent that is a by-product of cellular respiration. Iodine has been shown to neutralize H_2O_2 by converting it to hypoiodous acid and then water, thereby preventing the formation of toxic hydroxyl radicals.[36] Iodine also has the capacity to directly scavenge hydroxyl radicals. Like vitamin C, the presence of iodine in the blood markedly enhances its antioxidant status.[45]

In breast and other tissues, elemental iodine (I^-) donates electrons to hydrogen peroxide to form iodinated proteins and lipids and reduce damaging free radical formation.[46] Within the blood, iodide actively scours free radicals. Within the salivary glands, a tissue known to selectively concentrate iodide, elemental iodine attaches itself to unsaturated fats in the cell membranes, protecting them from oxidative damage. As well, the high iodide concentration of the thymus gland, which sequesters iodide through the NIS pathway, supports the important antioxidant role of iodine in the immune system.[46]

Within the thyroid gland, iodine is not only involved in the manufacture of the cell-signalling thyroid hormones; its presence in sufficient amounts protects the thyroid from the oxidative burden that is the very *nature* of thyroid hormone synthesis. The manufacture of hydrogen peroxide (H_2O_2) is the hallmark of thyroid physiology and its production

> While toxic to other bacteria, the development of iodine's protective antioxidant role in cyanobacteria likely made photosynthesis and the evolution of advanced life forms possible.

during hormone synthesis places the thyroid under a significant oxidative load.[47]

With sufficient iodide present, the reactive oxygen species (ROS) produced are effectively removed and cellular damage is averted; however, the physiological need to sequester iodide for hormone synthesis in an *iodide-deficient* thyroid leaves little available to act as a protective antioxidant. The increased oxidative burden and consequent cellular damage that results likely set the course for the growth of goitrous nodules and the development of autoimmune thyroiditis (Hashimoto's disease) in chronically deficient individuals.[48, 49]

Iodine Deficiency and Disease

Iodine has numerous physiological roles independent of its actions on the thyroid. The body concentrates iodine in the salivary glands, breast, gastric mucosa, thymus, brain (choroid plexus) and other sites, including the joints, arteries and bones. In fact, iodine's concentration in these tissues is so critical the body has evolved a type of cellular membrane pump, called the sodium-iodide symporter, to actively transport iodine across a membrane concentration gradient as high as 50-fold.[50, 51]

While the primary manifestation of iodine deficiency is goitre, a nodular swelling of the thyroid gland, it is only the most visible sign. There are several other consequences, including hearing loss, learning deficits, brain damage and myelination disorders, that can occur during foetal development.[13] One of the most devastating of these iodine deficiency disorders (IDD) is congenital hypothyroidism, which often leads to cretinism and irreversible mental retardation.[14] In women, iodine deficiency can lead to overt hyperthyroidism, anovulation, infertility, gestational hypertension, spontaneous abortion and stillbirths.[52]

Mild hypothyroidism in pregnant women has been associated with marked cognitive impairment in their offspring.[32, 53] There is also a greater prevalence of attention deficit disorders (ADD) amongst the offspring of mothers from iodine-deficient regions compared to those in marginally deficient regions. Vermiglio (2004) showed that 69% of the offspring from iodine-deficient areas were diagnosed as attention deficit hyperactivity disorder (ADHD), an austere contrast to the 0% of those in marginally deficient areas.[54]

Deficiencies of this essential nutrient have also been associated with increased risk for thyroid carcinoma and prostate, endometrial, ovarian and stomach cancers.[55-60] Furthermore, there is a *strong* correlation between iodine insufficiency and the development of fibrocystic breast disease and breast cancer.[14] The strength of the evidence is so compelling that researchers hypothesize these diseases may, like goitre and cretinism, be iodine deficiency disorders.[36]

Researchers focusing on iodine's role in cardiovascular health have found that changes in thyroid status markedly influence cardiac contractile and electrical activity.[25] The iodine-containing hormones manufactured by the thyroid are important metabolic regulators of cardiovascular activity; they have the ability to exert action on myocardium (heart muscles), the vascular smooth muscles and the endothelium.* As well, recent evidence supports iodine's role in modulating insulin and blood-sugar levels in diabetics.[61-63]

The following will briefly review the role of iodine in three of our most serious degenerative disease processes: cancer, heart disease and diabetes. As well, because of its critical role in foetal and post-natal development, we will investigate the importance of iodine in breast health.

Iodine and Cancer

Iodine has been shown to induce apoptosis. This process of programmed cell death is essential for proper growth and development. In the foetus, apoptosis allows the degradation of non-essential tissues, such as the webbing between the toes and fingers that occurs during gestation. In the same manner, apoptosis destroys aberrant mature cells that have come to

---

* The endothelium is the thin layer of cells that lines the interior surfaces of blood vessels and lymphatic vessels. It forms a protective interface between circulating blood or lymph and the rest of the vessel wall.

represent a threat to the organism.[36] Several studies highlight the ability of iodine to induce apoptosis in both animal and human cancer cell lines.[64-66] This unique anti-cancer function of iodine may well prove to be its most important extra-thyroidal benefit.

Iodine's ability to induce cell death appears to be proportionally related to its molar concentration in cellular tissues. In the first report to demonstrate that a therapeutic dose of iodide is effective and highly selective against lung cancer, the authors found that a marked increase in intracellular levels of iodide in lung cancer cells induced apoptosis in greater than 95% of the aberrant cells.[66] Interestingly, it appears to be molecular iodine (I_2)—not iodide (I^-)—that has the greatest capacity to encourage apoptosis.

Breast Cancer

Animal studies have repeatedly shown that iodine prevents the development of breast cancer and argue for a causal relationship to the strong epidemiological findings in human populations. The ductal cells of the breast, the ones most likely to turn cancerous, are known to contain the sodium-iodide symporter (NIS). This molecular pump allows these cells to sequester iodine from the blood and maintain high levels of the nutrient against a steep concentration gradient. Presence of the NIS in the ductal cells indicates that iodine in high concentrations is a physiological imperative for breast health. A paucity of iodine likely renders these tissues vulnerable to oxidative damage and the onset of disease processes.

The potent carcinogens n-methyl-n-nitrosourea and 7,12-dimethylbenzyl anthracene can initiate cancers in animal models over 70% of the time. Laboratory rats given iodine, particularly in its molecular form (I_2), demonstrate a marked decrease in cancer incidence when exposed to these powerful carcinogens.[1] Studies show that iodine, at the physiological dose of 5 mg daily, can markedly reduce the size of both benign and malignant breast tumours, an effect credited to the nutrient's capacity to reduce damaging autocatalytic lipid peroxidation. Moreover, no toxic effects have been observed either on thyroid function or in other tissues at this dosage.[13, 67, 68]

Today, one in seven women in North America will develop breast cancer in her lifetime. Thirty years ago, when iodine consumption was double what it is now, only one in 20 women developed the disease.[1] In reviewing epidemiological studies of breast cancer, Wiseman and coworkers concluded that 92-96% of these cases are sporadic. It appears that there is a *single* putative agent protective against breast cancer— one that is lipid soluble and diminished by high fat intakes—the depletion of which is responsible for the vast majority of cases. The agent is a micro-nutrient or trace element present in soils and found in varying amounts in different localities. It is the considered opinion of several researchers that this protective factor is the element iodine, likely in its molecular form.[69]

Studies on iodine and breast cancer highlight a close correlation with insufficient iodine levels and malignant growth. Intervention studies conducted by Eskin and Ghent also indicate a facilitating role of iodine in reducing the carcinogenic effects of oestrogens and in maintaining the normalization of breast tissues.[70-72] Clinical studies confirm that breast cancer patients express markedly lower levels of iodine in the breast tissue than do healthy subjects.[73] Chronic iodine insufficiency has been found to alter both the *structure* and *function* of the mammary glands, especially the alveolar cells, which sequester iodine at high levels.

> It appears that there is a single putative agent protective against breast cancer— one that is lipid soluble and diminished by high fat intakes—the depletion of which is responsible for the vast majority of cases.

Stomach Cancer

People living in iodine deficient areas are not only prone to thyroid disorders, they also experience a higher incidence of stomach cancer. Like the thyroid and the breast, the cells lining the stomach contain a rich concentration of iodine, capitalizing on iodine's antioxidant talents. Increased iodine intake is strongly correlated with a reduction in the incidence of stomach cancer.[74] In Poland, which has one of the highest incidences of stomach cancer in the world, researchers observed a strong association between improved iodine supply and a decrease in the incidence of stomach cancer, suggesting a protective role of iodine prophylaxis in iodine deficient areas.[74] Recent findings by Abnet and coworkers, studying gastric cancer in China, are consistent with the antioxidant hypothesis that iodine deficiency is associated with an increased risk of gastric cancer.[55]

Hormone Sensitive Cancers

Hypothyroidism and low iodine intake are important contributing factors in oestrogen-dependent tumours of the breast, uterus and ovary.[75] As well, it has been recently reported that normal and cancerous prostate cells can take up iodine, which (depending on its chemical form) exerts dose-dependent, anti-proliferative and apoptotic effects.[76]

Evidence that iodine deficiency results in an elevated risk of these hormone-dependent cancers has been known since 1976, when it was first discovered that low iodine intakes result in a hyper-oestrogenic state that increases the onset of several cancers.[77] A 1986 study demonstrated a significant inverse correlation between iodine intake and the incidence of breast, endometrial and ovarian cancer in various geographic regions of the world.[78] More recent work by the Stoddard lab provides evidence that iodine also inhibits cancer promotion by regulating several genes involved in hormone metabolism, cell cycle progression and cellular growth and differentiation.[79]

Iodine and Heart Health

Iodine and iodine-rich foods have a long history of use in European and Asian cultures as natural remedies for cardiovascular disease and control of hypertension.[80-86] Textbooks from the mid-1900s advocate the use of iodides for the treatment of cardiovascular disorders, including arteriosclerosis, angina pectoris, aortic aneurism and arterial hypertension.[87-89]

The occurrence of iodine deficiency in cardiovascular disease is frequent. Because all cardiovascular abnormalities appear to be reversed by restoration of the euthyroid (normal thyroid) state,[90] Molnar and colleagues suggest that iodine supplementation might prevent the harmful cardiovascular consequences of chronic iodine deficiency.[91] The documented anti-microbial, anti-inflammatory and anti-proliferative activities of iodine appear to be important factors in determining overall cardiovascular health.[25, 92-94] The element possesses the unique ability to denature, polymerize and solubilize proteins. This latter attribute likely enables iodine to reduce blood viscosity, facilitating a reduction in blood pressure and the accompanying risk of thrombotic events.[94]

Recent studies substantiate that sub-clinical hypothyroidism contributes to cardiovascular disease and stroke. Mild thyroid failure, generally a consequence of iodine insufficiency, also independently contributes to the development of coronary artery disease.[95-97] In one study, individuals with subclinical hyperthyroidism exhibited a 41% increase in mortality from all causes, versus normal (euthyroid) subjects.[98] In a 1997 study published in the journal *Cardiology*, Fruhwald and coworkers recommend that patients with cardiovascular disease who are placed on sodium-reduced diets be screened for thyroid dysfunction. Based on clinical evidence of 61 patients with idiopathic dilated cardiomyopathy (a condition in which the heart becomes weakened and enlarged and cannot pump blood efficiently), only 3% of subjects had normal thyroid function. Moreover, the duration of the cardiomyopathy was strongly correlated with thyroid volume, which is considered a proxy for the severity of iodine deficiency. While iodine intake was not evaluated, the authors proposed that sub-clinical iodine deficiency was the underlying cause.[22]

Iodine deficiency-induced thyroid dysfunction can elevate low-density lipoproteins and total cholesterol and can raise the risk of atherosclerosis. As well, its effect on cardiovascular function can be characterized by decreased myocardial contractility and increased peripheral vascular resistance. Deficiency can also weaken the contractile function of the heart muscle and can create life threatening cardiac arrhythmias, an effect that may become dangerously pronounced during even moderate exercise.[96]

Relatively low thyroid function is also associated with more severe coronary and carotid atherosclerosis and impaired endothelial function.[99-102] Supporting studies also show that the iodine-containing hormones T3 and T4 influence the cardiovascular system through their direct actions on vascular smooth muscles, cardiac muscle, kidney function, haemostasis (blood clotting), oxidation of LDL lipoproteins and alteration of homocysteine* levels.[103-107] Consequently, restoring normal thyroid function through iodine repletion can help reverse a *multitude* of cardiovascular risk factors.[95, 108, 109]

Thyrotropin, also called thyroid stimulating hormone (TSH), is a glycoprotein secreted by the anterior pituitary gland that stimulates the manufacture of the iodine-containing hormones thyroxine (T4) and triiodothyronine (T3). A strong positive association between TSH levels and systolic and diastolic blood pressure has been noted that has long-term implications for cardiovascular health.[110] As well, elevated serum TSH levels are associated with an increase in the occurrence of obesity and less favourable lipid profiles.

High blood levels of TSH are indicative of an underactive or sluggish thyroid, which (barring disturbances in the hypothalamus or pituitary glands) is directly related to iodine insufficiency. Disturbances in TSH levels—even *within* the normal reference range—are associated with increased systolic and diastolic blood pressure, body mass index and serum lipid profiles, with harmful effects on the cardiovascular system.[110] Likewise, THS levels *within* the normal reference range were correlated with fatal coronary heart disease in women.[111] These results support the view that relatively low—but normal—thyroid function can significantly increase the risk of fatal cardiovascular events.

While a thorough review of the literature did not reveal any findings pertaining to *optimal* levels of iodine intake for healthy heart function, it is evident that iodine, through its actions as an active component of the thyroid hormones and its ability to directly influence cardiac-related events, plays a fundamental role in the maintenance of cardiovascular health.

> Recent studies substantiate that sub-clinical hypothyroidism contributes to cardiovascular disease and stroke. Mild thyroid failure, generally a consequence of iodine insufficiency, also independently contributes to the development of coronary artery disease.

Iodine and Metabolic Health

Unlike Type-2 diabetes (T2D), a metabolic disease that results from poor lifestyle choices and chronically high blood sugar, Type-1 diabetes (T1D) is a polygenetic disease that results from the destruction of insulin-producing beta cells in the pancreas of susceptible individuals. Although the cause of T1D is still not fully understood, it is believed to be of immunological origin. Environmental factors, in addition to genetic factors, can influence disease prevalence.

Iodine-containing hormones are known to regulate the immune system, influence metabolism and modulate insulin secretion. Consequently, the actions of these hormones in the development of T1D have recently attracted attention. In a 2009 study published in *Autoimmunity*, researchers investigated the effect of thyroid hormones on the development of T1D. They found that impairment of thyroid function in animal models during early development can profoundly influence the later development of T1D in genetically susceptible individuals.[112]

T1D patients display a larger thyroid volume compared to healthy individuals, and a large portion of T1D patients concurrently exhibit autoimmune thyroiditis (inflammation of the thyroid) and chronic iodine deficiency.[113] A 2005 study reports that the prevalence of thyroid diseases in diabetic patients is 200-300% higher than in non-diabetics.[114] This prevalence increases with age and is strongly influenced by gender and disease type (subjects with autoimmune diabetes have a greater prevalence of concurrent thyroid disorders).

Recent evidence also points to a congenital link in the expression of late onset (Type-2) diabetes. Researchers in Poland found that even moderate maternal iodine deficiency during pregnancy creates a risk of mental retardation, increased prenatal mortality,

---

* Homocysteine is a sulphur-containing amino acid that can elevate oxidative damage in the cardiovascular system. High levels of homocysteine are known to elevate the risks of cardiovascular disease and cardiac events.

and late-life onset of metabolic syndrome and T2D in the offspring.[115] Moreover, an increased prevalence of sub-clinical hypothyroidism has been described in pregnant diabetic women. In a study of insulin-dependent (T1D) pregnant diabetic women, Di Gilio and coworkers revealed that anti-thyroid antibodies were significantly more prevalent in diabetic than in non-diabetic expectant mothers.[116] In view of the health implications for both mother and child, this interplay between maternal iodine intake, pregnancy, diabetes and thyroid disturbances requires particular attention.

Iodine and Breast Health

Perhaps the most compelling evidence of an extrathyroidal role for iodine concerns its effects on breast health. Sufficient dietary intake of iodine is critical in maintaining breast health, a relationship that has been documented for well over a century. Normal breast architecture will not develop without sufficient iodine in the diet.[117] Chronic iodine deficiency causes fibrocystic breast disease (FBD), with characteristic nodules, cyst formation, pain and scarring. A 1928 US-based autopsy series reported a 3% incidence of FBD; by 1973, the incidence of this disease had exploded to 89% of the female population, plausibly in direct relation to decreasing levels of iodine intake.[63] According to a more recent report by the American Cancer Society, nine out of ten women exhibit benign breast changes, including lumps and tumours, when examined microscopically.[118]

The breasts are the second main glandular storage organ for iodine next to the thyroid gland. Breast tissue has a high affinity for iodine, which is required for normal growth and development of the breast. When tissue stores are replete, iodine acts as an antioxidant and antiproliferative agent, protecting the integrity of the breast tissue.[51] As an antioxidant, iodine acts as an electron donor in the presence of hydrogen peroxide, peroxidase and unsaturated membrane lipids, thereby decreasing oxidative damage to breast tissue cells.[119]

Human breast tissue and breast milk are rich sources of iodine, much greater than the thyroid gland itself.[13, 120] In fact, human breast milk contains a concentration of iodine four times greater than thyroid tissue, indicative of the high biological demand for iodine by the nursing infant. Breast tissue is also rich in the same globular iodine-transporting proteins used by the thyroid to sequester iodine from the blood; this indicates a clear evolutionary importance for iodine in neonatal care. As mentioned previously, the element is vital for the proper neurological development of the newborn; consequently, Mother Nature has developed a direct means of nourishing the infant with this essential nutrient.[40]

In 1966, Russian researchers first demonstrated that iodine repletion effectively relieves the signs and symptoms of FBD. Vishniakova and colleagues treated women with 50 mg of potassium iodide (KI) and reported beneficial healing in 71% of test subjects.[121] More recently, in a composite of three clinical studies, Canadian researchers confirmed the Russian findings. Ghent, Eskin and Low reported a 70% success rate in using iodine to treat fibrocystic breast disease.[42] A separate statistical review of one of these studies confirmed that iodine, at dosages of 3-6 mg/day, exerts a highly significant and beneficial effect on FBD, noticeably reducing breast tenderness and associated symptoms. Despite these strong findings, submission of this statistical review seeking FDA approval for a larger clinical trial was summarily denied.[122]

> Human breast milk contains a concentration of iodine four times greater than thyroid tissue, indicative of the high biological demand for iodine by the nursing infant.

The studies conducted by Ghent and colleagues also found that the molecular form of iodine was more effective and had significantly lower side effects than the ionic (iodide) form. Aqueous iodine solutions at 3-6 mg/day provided significant clinical improvements with a very low incidence of toxicity (0.1%). Side effects were minor (increased pain at onset and unpleasant taste) and were considered inconsequential.[36]

In 2004, a randomized, double-blinded, placebo-controlled, multicenter clinical trial—the 'gold standard' for clinical trials—evaluated the effects of varying doses of molecular iodine at 1.5, 3, and 6 mg/day on FBD. The study engaged 111 healthy women with normal thyroids but a history of breast pain. Both the 3 and 6 mg/day treatment groups, but not the 1.5

mg treatment group, reported significant improvements in clinical symptoms. All doses were associated with an acceptable safety profile and no dose-related increase in any adverse event was observed at any level.[123]

Molecular iodine appears to be the *principal* active form of iodine in the breast and is selectively concentrated in the tissue.[124] In animal-model studies of chemically induced breast cancer, researchers also confirmed that molecular iodine is significantly more effective at inhibiting cancer growth than is iodide. Further, only molecular iodine treatment was capable of quenching the damaging process of autocatalytic lipid peroxidation in breast tissue (oxidatively damaged fats are known to be involved in the initiation and promotion of cancer).[119]

> Iodine, at dosages of 3-6 mg/day, exerts a highly significant and beneficial effect on fibrocystic breast disease, noticeably reducing breast tenderness and associated symptoms.

Lastly, a 2005 report published in *The Original Internist* notes a strong correlation between dosage and the degree of improvement of symptoms of FBD with patients who received from 12.5 to 50 mg/day of Iodoral,® a tableted form of iodine containing 5 mg of molecular iodine and 7.5 mg of iodide (as the potassium salt). The course of treatment ranged from 6 months to one year and no clinically significant changes occurred to blood hormone profiles.

Despite the strength of this evidence, mainstream medicine's *'thyroid only'* view of iodine continues to discount the fact that this vital nutrient in larger amounts can provide profound extrathyroidal benefits—particularly in the case of breast health. Notably, a leading textbook on breast disease, *The Breast: Comprehensive Management of Benign and Malignant Disorders (2003)*, fails to even mention iodine anywhere in its 1766 pages.

How Much is Enough?

In attempting to parse the answer to the questions, "What level of daily intake constitutes an optimal level of supplementation with iodine—what is too much, what is not enough?" it soon becomes evident that the scientific consensus comes down firmly on both sides of the issue at once. According to Editor-in-Chief of *Integrative Medicine*, Joseph Pizzorno, there

is likely no other nutrient for which the integrative medical community holds such divergent views.[34] Much of the controversy stems from a fundamental misunderstanding of the putative actions of iodine.

A 2004 review of iodine toxicity and its amelioration, published in *Experimental Biology and Medicine*, observes that iodine toxicity is rare in animals and humans. All animal species appear to have a wide margin of safety for excess iodine consumption. According to the report, dietary iodine levels of 500–1,000 times the minimum dietary requirements are generally well tolerated in several animal species. While the report notes that a daily iodide intake of 10 times the adult requirement of 150 µg/day *may* cause adverse reactions in some people, it explains that most reported cases have occurred with very high iodine intakes (up to 1,000 mg) over an extended period of time.[125] According to Backer and Hollowell, the strongest research data show that levels of iodine intake in the physiological range of one to five mg/day are safe for most people for years.[126] This is *precisely* the order of magnitude where the protective effects of iodine repletion are seen in cancer prevention and fibrocystic breast disease.

However, a review of the literature regarding iodine toxicity does provide contrary evidence that iodine intakes well above recommended dietary limits can induce hypothyroidism and hyperthyroidism as well as autoimmune thyroid dysfunction. That said, many of these studies report changes in specific biochemical and physiological parameters that remain well within their clinically normal reference ranges and likely prove inconsequential in real life. Lastly, many of the studies reporting on the development of iodine-induced goitre and other thyroid perturbations have used *extremely* large doses of iodine (up to 2,000 mg/day) for prolonged periods of time.[127]

As Pizzorno correctly points out, research on the *optimum* intake of iodine in the absence of thyroid disease and for all health benefits appears to be non-existent in the literature.[34] As well, neither the maximum safe dietary dose of iodine nor the maximum safe period of consumption are firmly established.[126] Most of the available toxicity data comes from monitoring the effects of iodine repletion in iodine-deficient populations—that is, in people whose thyroids have *already* been damaged from long-standing iodine deficiencies.

Almost all such studies show a clear rise in the incidence of hyperthyroidism, the magnitude depending on dose and prior level of deficiency.[126, 128, 129] It appears that, upon repletion with iodine, hyperactive goitrous nodules that have developed during chronic iodine deficiency over-respond to the sudden availability of iodine and produce too much T3 and T4 hormone. In individuals with previously damaged thyroids, this sudden increase of serum thyroid hormone levels does not exert the normal dampening effect on thyroid activity that is witnessed in healthy thyroids.[130, 131] In most cases, this response is clinically inconsequential; the transient elevations in thyroid hormones and the presence of nodules resolve spontaneously after the long-standing iodine deficiency has been corrected.

Iodine-induced hypothyroidism appears to be much more common than iodine-induced hyperthyroidism, although the precise mechanism for its expression is not well understood.[132, 133] Individuals with iodine-induced hypothyroidism may or may not show clinical symptoms, such as mild swelling of the neck; however, all such individuals will express elevated levels of thyroid stimulating hormone (TSH). Iodine-induced hypothyroidism is most often of little significance, is only transient, and is generally sub-clinical (no signs or symptoms of hypothyroidism occur). According to Donald Miller, professor of Surgery at Seattle Hospital, "Some people taking milligram doses of iodine, usually more than 50 mg/day, develop mild swelling of the thyroid without symptoms. The vast majority of people, 98 to 99 percent, can take iodine in doses ranging from 10 to 200 mg a day without any clinically adverse effects on thyroid function."[1]

Interestingly, in a 2011 randomized controlled trial on older people in New Zealand, two groups *accidentally* received greater than 50 mg iodine per day for 8 weeks because of a supplement formulation error.[134] Ten of forty-three study participants expressed elevated thyroid stimulating hormone levels (elevated TSH is a clinical marker for *hypo*thyroidism). By the twelfth

> Most of the available toxicity data comes from monitoring the effects of iodine repletion in iodine-deficient populations—that is, in people whose thyroids have *already* been damaged from long-standing iodine deficiencies.

week, 80% of those expressing elevated levels of TSH had returned to normal. In three of the participants, TSH levels declined marginally (depressed TSH is a clinical marker for *hyper*thyroidism). No other adverse effects or toxicities were noted. In other words, while about 30% of the study population reacted mildly to this very high level of supplementation, the increase or decrease in serum TSH was transient and clinically inconsequential, returning to baseline within three months. Furthermore, it is expected that many of these elderly subjects who reacted had long-standing but undiagnosed nodular goitres. While embarrassing to the authors—and the findings contrary to the conventional wisdom of mainstream medicine—this serendipitous event served to elucidate the benign nature of supplementation with iodine at multi-milligram levels.

Expert Opinion

In a 1983 review of iodine-induced thyroid toxicity, Fradkin and Wolff [135] highlighted two reports of experience using potassium iodide at doses ranging from 1.6-6.4 g/day in large cohorts of pulmonary patients. Neither study revealed any significant evidence of hyperthyroidism. Furthermore, they observed that the few scattered case reports of thyroid toxicity after the use of potassium iodide supplementation must be viewed in light of the one-hundred million iodine (10^8) tablets prescribed annually in the United States. The authors concluded that, in view of the large exposure to iodine in the United States, the occurrence of thyroid toxicity must be considered a *rare* complication.

In a commentary in the 10th edition of the *Pharmacological Basis of Therapeutics* (2001), Farwell and Braverman note: "In euthyroid individuals, the administration of doses of iodine from 1.5-150 mg daily results in small decreases in plasma thyroxine and triiodothyronine concentrations and small compensatory increases in serum TSH values, with all values remaining in the normal range."

In a June, 2012 editorial in *Integrative Medicine*, Editor-in-Chief Joseph Pizzorno concludes that, in the absence of thyroid disease, the safe dosage of iodide appears to be at least 1.0 mg/day; however, the safe intake of iodine is "unclear but definitely much higher."

Showing less vicissitude than her husband, medical researcher and writer Lara Pizzorno acknowledges that, while a dosage range of 400µg/day to 1mg/day of iodine is safe and beneficial to most individuals—even those at risk of thyroiditis—supplementation in the range of 3-6 mg/day should be considered for women with breast disease. She also suggests that, with appropriate monitoring, doses from 12.5-50 mg/day should be considered.[51]

For iodine's harmful potential to be realized, other contributing factors must be present. This includes selenium deficiency: dietary selenium is required to activate the enzymes glutathione peroxidase and superoxide dismutase, and the thioredoxin and deiodinase enzymes, all of which are essential to safely metabolize iodine. Sufficient iron is necessary for the proper function of thyroid peroxidase enzyme, which oxidizes iodine for organification into the thyroid hormones. As well, exposure to environmental pollutants, such as heavy metals, industrial solvents and polychlorinated biphenyls (PCBs) can increase the oxidative burden of the thyroid and can interfere with iodine transport. Pizzorno contends that, for everyone, the critical caveat of iodine supplementation is to provide the necessary co-factors for proper iodine metabolism.

"While selenium, iron and vitamin A play roles highlighted in cancer research, a number of other nutrients, including zinc, copper, vitamin E, vitamin C and the B vitamins riboflavin (B2), niacin (B3) and pyridoxine (B6), are involved in the manufacture of thyroid hormone or as cofactors of the deiodinases that convert T4 to the far more active T3. Deficiencies of any of these nutrients can negatively impact the response to prophylactic iodine."[51]

Conclusions

There is convincing evidence that iodine's potential for harm is *only* actuated when it is used *singularly* and in very high doses in individuals with extreme sensitivity or in those with previous undisclosed thyroid disorders (most often caused, ironically, by long-standing deficiencies of the same nutrient). In healthy populations, the evidence supports iodine intakes at levels one to two magnitudes greater than the current DRIs—a dosage that can be safely tolerated with scant adverse effects.

To review:

✓ There is a *single* putative factor protective against breast cancer—one that is lipid soluble—the depletion of which is responsible for the vast majority of cases; the weight of the evidence indicates this factor is iodine.

✓ Iodine at 5 mg daily reduces the size of both benign and malignant breast tumours, an effect credited to the nutrient's capacity to reduce autocatalytic lipid peroxidation.

✓ At 3.0 mg, 6.0 mg and higher, iodine has been found to exert a beneficial and highly significant effect on fibrocystic breast disease (FBD); the efficacy of iodine supplementation on reduction of cystofibrotic breast pain is dose-related, with the higher doses providing the greatest benefit.

✓ Iodine exerts a dose-dependent apoptotic effect on hormone sensitive cancers; its ability to induce cell death is proportionally related to its molar concentration in cellular tissues.

✓ Even moderate maternal iodine deficiency during pregnancy creates a risk of mental retardation, increased prenatal mortality, and late-life onset of metabolic syndrome and type-2 diabetes in the offspring.

✓ The documented anti-microbial, anti-inflammatory and anti-proliferative activities of iodine appear to be important factors in determining overall cardiovascular health.

✓ Three generations of clinicians have found iodine/iodide solutions in amounts from 12.5-37.5 mg to be the safest and most effective approaches to treating symptoms of iodine deficiency and reducing the risk of other iodine deficiency-related diseases.

A daily intake of iodine in the range of 1 to 10 mg—one to two magnitudes greater than the current DRIs—is admittedly a level of intake well above that necessary to support healthy thyroid function.

However, as we have seen, iodine is so much more than *'just about the thyroid.'* Furthemore, it is a level that research shows is inherently safe and will provide significant extrathyroidal health benefits for those interested in optimal health and disease prevention.

In reviewing the evidence, NutriSearch asserts that the current DRIs for iodine, as established by the US Food and Nutrition Board and Health Canada, are inadequate and not reflective of the dietary needs required for optimal extrathyroidal benefits. The current recommended dietary intakes of iodine urgently need to be revised in light of the established extra-thyroidal roles of iodine, its recognized importance in disease prevention, and the growing level of iodine insufficiency in the North American population.

Accordingly, NutriSearch has enhanced the daily requirement for optimal supplementation with iodine *from our previous recommended daily intake of 150 μg/day to 1,000 μg/day.* This new higher level of intake is now reflected in our revised *Blended Standard*.

Facts are the air of scientists. Without them you can never fly.

— Linus Pauling (1901-1994)

CHAPTER FIVE:

COMPARING SUPPLEMENTS

Every nutritional supplement included in the *NutriSearch Comparative Guide to Nutritional Supplements™* is assigned a rating based on a comprehensive analytical model developed by NutriSearch. This model is based on a compilation of the recommended daily nutritional intakes of 12 independent nutritional authorities.

Each of the 12 authorities cited has published one or more works that recommend specific daily nutritional intakes deemed important for long-term health. Each author, listed below, is acknowledged within his or her respective scientific, medical and naturopathic field:

Robert Atkins, MD: The late Robert Atkins was the founder and medical director of the Atkins Center for Complementary Medicine in New York City. An early proponent of the value of nutritional supplementation, Dr Atkins' bestselling book, *Dr Atkins' Vita-Nutrient Solution,* stresses the importance of daily supplementation in overcoming nutritional deficiencies found in our foods today. A practising physician and a professor of medicine at Capital University of Integrative Medicine, Dr Atkins gained recognition in 1972 with the publication of his first book, *Dr Atkins' Diet Revolution.* Subsequent to this, he wrote *Dr Atkins' Nutrition Breakthrough* and *Dr Atkins' Health Revolution.*

Phyllis Balch, CNC: Until her death in 2004, Phyllis Balch was a leading nutritional consultant, recognized for her expertise in nutrition-based therapies. She authored several best-selling books, including: *Prescription for Dietary Wellness: Using Foods to Heal; Prescription for Herbal Healing: An Easy-to-Use A-Z Reference to Hundreds of Common Disorders and Their Herbal Remedies;* and *Prescription for Nutritional Healing: the A-to-Z Guide to Supplements,* co-authored by **Dr James Balch**, a certified urologist, a member of the American Medical Association, and a Fellow of the American College of Surgeons. Because of the co-authorship of *Prescription for Nutritional Healing [2002],* on which we base their recommendations, we recognize the authors as a single reference source.

Michael Colgan, PhD, CCN: Dr Colgan is a best-selling author and internationally acclaimed speaker on anti-aging, sports nutrition and hormonal health. His first public book, *Your Personal Vitamin Profile,* was considered a definitive guide for accurate, scientifically researched nutritional information. He has subsequently authored *Hormonal Health: Nutritional and Hormonal Strategies for Emotional Well-Being and Intellectual Longevity* and *The New Nutrition: Medicine for the Millennium.* Dr. Colgan has served as a consultant to the US National Institute on Aging and to the US, Canadian and New Zealand governments as well as to many corporations. His professional memberships include the New York Academy of Sciences, the American Academy of Anti-Aging Medicine, the American College of Sports Medicine and the British Society for Nutritional Medicine. In 2002, Dr Colgan was inducted into the Canadian Nutrition Hall of Fame. In 2011, Dr Colgan partnered with Isagenix International to join with their scientific research team to find nutritional products that would help slow aging.

Terry Grossman, MD and Ray Kurzweil are co-authors of *Fantastic Voyage,* an insightful book on the science behind radical life extension. Dr Grossman is the founder and medical director of Frontier Medical Institute in Denver, Colorado. A diplomat of the

American Board of Chelation Therapy (ABCT) and a member of the American Academy for Advancement of Medicine (ACAM), the International Oxidative Medicine Association (IOMA) and the American Academy of Anti-aging Medicine (A4M), Dr Grossman is a licensed homeopathic and a naturopathic medical doctor; he now runs the Grossman Health and Wellness Center in Denver, Colorado. **Ray Kurzweil** is one of the world's leading inventors, thinkers and futurists. He is the author of three previous books, *The Age of Spiritual Machines*; *The 10% Solution for a Healthy Life*; and *The Age of Intelligent Machines.* Kurzweil received the 1999 National Medal of Technology; in 2002, he was inducted into the National Inventor Hall of Fame. Named Honorary Chairman for Innovation of the White House Conference on Small Business by President Reagan in 1986, he has received additional honours from former Presidents Clinton and Johnson.

Jane Higdon, PhD: With over 13 years of experience as a certified family nurse practitioner, Jane Higdon also held a Master of Science in nursing, a Master of Science in exercise physiology, and a Doctorate in nutrition. Until her tragic death in 2006, Jane Higdon was a Research Associate at the Linus Pauling Institute, Oregon State University. The Linus Pauling Institute's mission is to determine the function and role of micronutrients and phytochemicals in promoting optimum health and in preventing and treating disease. The Institute conducts research to determine the role of oxidative stress and antioxidants in human health and disease.

Philip Lee Miller, MD and Life Extension Foundation are co-authors of *The Life Extension Revolution: The New Science of Growing Older Without Aging* (2005). Dr Miller is the founder and medical director of the California Age Management Institute, Los Gatos, California. A practising physician for over 30 years, he is a diplomat of the American Board of Anti-Aging Medicine and serves on the Medical Advisory Board of **Life Extension Foundation (LEF)**, the world's largest organization dedicated to the science of preventing and treating degenerative disease and aging. In addition to developing unique disease treatment protocols, LEF funds pioneering scientific research aimed at achieving an extended healthy lifespan. At the heart of Life Extension's mission are its research programs for identifying and developing new therapies to slow and reverse the deterioration associated with aging.

Earl Mindell, RPh, MH has written 48 books on nutrition and health, including the best-seller, *Dr Mindell's Vitamin Bible*, published in the mid-1980s. Subsequent publications include *Earl Mindell's Vitamin Bible for the 21st Century*; *Dr Mindell's What You Should Know About Creating Your Own Personal Health Plan*; *Earl Mindell's Herb Bible*; *Earl Mindell's Food as Medicine*; *Shaping up with Vitamins*; and *Earl Mindell's Anti-Aging Bible*. Mindell received a Bachelor of Science in Pharmacy in 1964, earning his Master's in Herbal Medicine in 1995. He is a registered pharmacist and a Fellow of the British Institute of Homeopathy.

Michael Murray, ND is one of the world's leading authorities on natural medicine. He has published over 30 books featuring natural approaches to health. In addition to his private practice as a consultant to the health food industry, he has been instrumental in bringing many effective natural products to North America. His research into the health benefits of proper nutrition is the foundation for a best-selling line of dietary supplements from Natural Factors, where he is Director of Product Development. He is a graduate, former faculty member, and serves on the Board of Regents of Bastyr University in Seattle, Washington.

Richard Passwater, PhD has been a research biochemist since 1959. His first areas of research interest were in the development of pharmaceuticals, spectrophotoluminescence and analytical chemistry. He has continued to research nutritional supplements and has now published over 42 books and booklets, as well as over 500 articles on nutrition and nutritional supplements. Twice honoured by the Committee for World Health, his scientific contributions have garnered him worldwide recognition. His discovery of biological antioxidant synergism in 1962 has been the focus of his research since that time. In 1973, Dr Passwater's article *Cancer: New Directions* was the first to report that a synergistic combination of antioxidant nutrients significantly reduces cancer incidence. His pioneering work with Drs Linus Pauling and James Enstrom highlighted the protective effect of vitamin E against heart disease. His best-selling book, *Supernutrition: Megavitamin Revolution*, legitimized megavitamin therapy. Dr Passwater's most recent public books include *The Antioxidants; The New Supernutrition;* and *Cancer Prevention and Nutritional Therapies*. He is the nutrition editor for *The Experts Journal of Optimal Health* and the scientific editor for *Whole Foods*, and he serves on the editorial board of the *Journal of Applied Nutrition*. Dr Passwater is also the Director of the Solgar Nutritional Research Center.

Nicholas Perricone, MD is a board-certified clinical and research dermatologist. An internationally recognized anti-aging expert, award-winning inventor and a respected scientific researcher, Dr Perricone is an Adjunct Professor of Medicine at the Michigan State University's College of Human Medicine. Certified by the American Board of Dermatology, he is also a Fellow of the New York Academy of Sciences, the American College of Nutrition, the American Academy of Dermatology, and the Society of Investigative Dermatology. Dr Perricone has served as Assistant Clinical Professor of Dermatology at Yale School of Medicine and as Chief of Dermatology at Connecticut's Veterans Hospital. He is author of *The Perricone Weight-loss Diet* and *The Acne Prescription* and has written three New York Times bestsellers: *The Wrinkle Cure; The Perricone Prescription;* and *The Perricone Promise*.

Ray Strand, MD has practised family medicine for four decades, focussing over the past 20 years on nutritional medicine. An articulate advocate for the integration of optimal nutrition and advanced nutritional therapies in preventive healthcare, he is a member of the Scientific Advisory Board of Ariix, a premier health and wellness company. Dr Strand has lectured on nutritional medicine across the United States, Canada, Australia, New Zealand, and England. His publications include *Bionutrition: Winning the War Within; Death by Prescription; Healthy for Life; What Your Doctor Doesn't Know About Nutritional Medicine*

May Be Killing You; Preventing Diabetes; and *Living by Design*.

Julian Whitaker, MD is the author of several popular books, including *Reversing Diabetes; Reversing Heart Disease;* and *Dr Whitaker's Guide to Natural Healing*. Board certified in anti-aging medicine, Dr Whitaker belongs to the American College for Advancement in Medicine and is a founding member of the American Preventive Medicine Association. He became fascinated early in his career by the preventive and healing powers of nutrition and natural therapies. In 1974, along with four other heathcare professionals and two-time Nobel Prize winner Linus Pauling, Dr Whitaker founded the California Orthomolecular Medical Society. In 1976, he joined the staff at the Pritikin Longevity Center, and in 1979 he founded the Whitaker Wellness Institute. Today, Whitaker Wellness is the largest alternative medicine clinic in the United States, where patients participate in an intensive program of diet, exercise, nutritional and herbal supplementation and lifestyle change.

In borrowing from the preceding authors' scientific insights to construct our analytical standard, we recognize the immense contribution that they have made, individually and collectively, to the advancement of scientific knowledge and the pursuit of optimal health.

Constructing the *Blended Standard*

The individual recommendations for daily nutrient intakes from the 12 authorities cited above are pooled to construct the *Blended Standard*, the yardstick by which every product in the *NutriSearch Comparative Guide to Nutritional Supplements™* is compared. While each author's recommendations may have characteristics not recognized by the others, we have exploited their substantial commonality. Unless otherwise noted, for a nutrient to qualify for inclusion in the *Blended Standard*, three of the 12 authorities must cite a recommended daily intake for the specified

Continued on page 51

Table 2: Table of Recommended Daily Intakes (Blended Standard)

Nutritional Components	Amt	Atkins Average	Balch/Balch Average	Colgan Average	Higdon/LPI Average	Grossman/Kurzweil Average	Miller/LEF Average	Mindell Average	Murray Average	Passwater Average	Perricone Average	Strand Average	Whitaker Average	Blended Standard Median	NOTES	Upper Limits (UL)
Vitamins																
Vitamin A	IU	2,250	7,500	6,250	5,000	5,000	5,000	NR	5,000	17,500		NR	5,000	5,000	†	10,000 IU
Vitamin D	IU	135	400	400	600	1,300	400	300	250	650		625	250	1,000		2000 IU
Vitamin K	ug		300	75	no amt	105	7,500	180	180			75	180	180		ND
B-Complex Vitamins																
Biotin	ug	338	600	500	30		300	200	200	63		650	200	250		ND
Folic Acid	ug	3,000	600	400	400	600	800	350	400	600		900	300	600		1000 ug
Vitamin B1 (thiamin)	mg	45	75	50	2	105	100	38	55	63		25	55	55		ND
Vitamin B2 (riboflavin)	mg	36	33	45	2	55	50	63	30	63		38	55	45		ND
Vitamin B3 (niacin)	mg	23	33	50	20	60	50	63	55	150		53	55	[28]		35 mg
Vitamin B3 (niacinamide)	mg	45	75	80			150		20				20	60		ND
Vitamin B5 (Pantethine)	mg	113												ID		ND
Vitamin B5 (Pantothenic acid)	mg	113	75	150	10		400	63	63	150		140	63	75		ND
Vitamin B6 (pyridoxine)	mg	45	75	50	2	75	50	100	63	63		38		63		100 mg
Vitamin B6 (pyridoxyl-5-phosphate)	mg	9												ID		ND
Vitamin B12 (cobalamin)	ug	210	300	100	18	18	100	550	400	88		175	300	175		ND
Antioxidant Vitamins and Nutrients																
Coenzyme Q10	mg		65	30		130	125	60	100	35	30	25		60		ND
alpha-Lipoic acid	mg		30	100		150	375		35		28	23		100		ND
Para-Aminobenzoic Acid	mg	450					50			63				NR		ND
Vitamin C	mg	750	2,000	2,000	200	1,250	3,000	2,000	1,000	7,000		1,500	175	1,500	^^^	2000 mg
Vitamin E (as alpha tocopherol)	IU	225	500	400	299	600	1,000	400	600	700		600	600	600		1467 IU (1000 mg)
Vitamin E (as gamma tocopherol or mixed tocopherols)	mg			200										200	^^^	ND
Bioflavonoid Complex																
Bioflavonoids (mixed/citrus)	mg	525	350	350				no amt	4,000					540	!	ND
Hesperidin	mg		75											ID		ND
Phenolic compounds (see comment in legend)	mg											no amt		NR	^^	ND
Pinus Epicatechins	mg			900	300				350					ID		ND
Procyanidolic Oligomers	mg			10		150			50	100		100		100		ND
Quercetin	mg	105	105	185					900			no amt		ID		ND
Resveratrol (3,4',5-trihydroxystilbene)	mg													ID		ND
Rutin	mg		25			400						no amt		ID		ND
Carotenoids																
Astaxanthin (marine carotenoid)	mg										3			ID		ND
beta Carotene	IU	4,500	15,000	11,250			15,000	6,250	15,000	17,500		12,500	15,000	13,750	***	ND
carotenoids (mixed)	IU		0				5,000	6,250				542		5,625		ND
Lutein/Zeaxanthin	mg		6	6		6						4		5		ND
Lycopene	mg		15	15		20						2		15		ND
Glutathione Complex																
Acetyl-l-cysteine	mg	90	300	50								63		76		ND
Cysteine	mg		75							150				ID		ND
Glutathione	mg	23		100								15		NR		ND

Table 2: Table of Recommended Daily Intakes *(Blended Standard)* (continued)

	Units													Blended Standard		Upper Limit
Lipid Metabolism																
Acetyl-l-Carnitine	mg		300								500			500		ND
Carnitine	mg		500		750			750			500		55	500		ND
Choline	mg	450	125	200			150		55	138		150	55	94		3500 mg
Inositol	mg	360	125				50	63	55	63		200		125		ND
Lecithin	mg		350	250				200		63				350	* ^	ND
alpha Linolenic Acid (an omega-3 essential fatty acid)	mg		no amt						6,000	2,500		no amt		3,125		ND
Conjugated linoleic acid (CLA)	mg										2,500			ID		ND
Linoleic Acid (an omega-6 essential fatty acid)	mg								2,000			no amt		ID		ND
gamma Linolenic Acid (GLA)	mg		150								300			ID		ND
Omega-3 fish oil (EPA/DHA)	mg		25	25		3,350	1,304	no amt		360	978	no amt		1,141	* ^	ND
Phosphatidylcholine	mg		200											ID		ND
Phosphatidylserine	mg		180						300					ID		ND
Minerals																
Boron	mg		5	3			2	3	4	3		3	2	3		20
Calcium	mg	300	1,750	800	1,100	1,250	1,000	600	750	350		1,150	500	800		2500 mg
Chromium (trivalent)	ug	225	275	200	120	160	200	300	300	300	100	250	300	238		ND
Copper	mg	1	3	1	1	2	2	3	2	3		2	2	2		10 mg
Fluorine (as fluoride)	mg				NR									ID		10 mg
Iodine	ug		163	100	NR		150		100	100		150	100	1,000	†	1100 ug
Iron	mg		NR	10	NR	!!!	!!!	NR	23	15		NR	23	NR	**	45 mg
Magnesium	mg		875	600	100	500	500	525	375	400		650	375	[280]	!!	350 mg
Manganese	mg		7	6	2	4	20	10	13	4		5	13	7		11 mg
Molybdenum	ug		65	60	75		150		18	150		75	18	65		2000 ug
Potassium	mg		300	100			99		350	130			350	215		ND
Selenium	ug		150	250	128	175	200	38	150	150		200	150	150		400 ug
Silicon	mg		600						13			3	1	8		ND
Vanadium	ug	68						113	75	53		65	75	75		75
Zinc	mg	36	40	13	15	23	40	13	30	28		25	23	25		40 mg
Other Nutritional Factors																
Arginine	mg					7,500		no amt						ID		ND
Betaine (trimethylglycine or TMG)	mg													350		ND
Bromelaine (digestive enzymes)	mg													ID		ND
Carnosine	mg													1,000		ND
Dimethylglycine (DMG)	mg					1,000								ID		ND
Dimethylaminoethanol (DMAE)	mg					1,600								ID		ND
Garlic extract (standardized)	mg										75	350		ID		ND
Gingko Biloba	mg			80		1,000	1,000					no amt		ID		ND
Glucosamine	mg							no amt			0.5 tsp			ID		ND
Glutamine	mg							no amt		100				ID		ND
Indole-3-Carbinol	mg					200			1,500					ID		ND
Lysine	mg							2		100				ID		ND
Melatonin	mg		75											ID		ND
Methionine	mg								3					ID		ND
Octacosanol	ug		75											ID		ND
Taurine	mg		300							50				ID		ND
Tyrosine	mg	675	500							50				ID		ND
Vinpocetine	mg													ID		ND

Notes for Table 2: Recommended Daily Intakes *(Blended Standard)*

Upper Limits (UL)

The upper level of intake considered safe for use by adults, incorporating a safety factor, as determined by the Food and Nutrition Board of the Institute of Medicine

References by author

Balch, PA. *Prescription for Nutritional Healing*, Avery Books, New York, NY, 2002.

Colgan, M. *Hormonal Health*, Apple Publishing, Vancouver, BC, 1996.

Mindell, E. *What You Should Know about Creating Your Personal Vitamin Plan*, Keats Pub., New Canaan, CT, 1996.

Murray, M and Pizzorno J. *Encyclopedia of Natural Medicine*, Prima Publishing, Rocklin, CA, 1998.

Murray, M. *Encyclopedia of Nutritional Supplements*, Prima Publishing, Rocklin, CA, 1996.

Passwater, RA. *The New Supernutrition*, Simon and Schuster Inc. New York, NY, 1991.

Strand, R. *What Your Doctor Doesn't Know about Nutritional Medicine May Be Killing You*, Thomas Nelson Inc. Nashville TN, 2002.

Whitaker, J. *Dr. Whitaker's Guide to Natural Healing*, Prima Publishing, Rocklin CA, 1996.

Perricone, N. *The Perricone Weight-loss Diet*, Ballantine Books, New York, 2005.

Kurzweil, R and Grossman, T. *Fantastic Voyage*, Holtzbrinck Publishers, 2004.

Atkins RC. *Dr. Atkins' Vita-nutrient Solution*, Fireside Printers, New York, 1999.

Miller, PL. and the Life Extension Foundation, *The Life Extension Revolution*, Bantam Dell, New York, 2005.

Higdon J. and the Linus Pauling Institute. *An Evidence-based Approach to Vitamins and Minerals*, Thieme Publishers, New York, 2003.

Legend

*   Colgan: lecithin specified in form of phosphatidyl-choline

**   Balch: only if an iron deficiency exists

*** Strand: conversion from mg to IU provided by Murray MT, *Encyclopedia of Nutritional Supplements*, page 25

^   Passwater: 1-2 caps estimated at 1000 mg/cap as lecithin

^^   Level of Phenolic Acids adapted from: Visioli F et al. *Atheroclerosis* 1995, 117: 25-32

^^^ Based on the recommended 2:1 ratio of alpha tocopherol to gamma tocopherol
see Helzlsouer KJ et al, *J Nat Canc Inst*. 2000;92(24):2018-2023

!   Also includes values for hesperedin, quercetin, rutin, and pinus epicatechins

!!   350 mg represents the Upper Limit for a pharmacological agent only

!!! pre-menopausal women only

†   Vitamin D and Iodine amounts adapted to reflect emerging science and/or changes to DRI amounts by Health Canada and the US Institute of Medicine. Safe Upper Limits also increased to reflect the new recommendations of the Food and Nutrition Board, Institute of Medicine

ID   Insufficient Data

NR   Not Recommended

[ ] daily recommended intake truncated at 80% of Upper Safe Limit for that nutrient

continued from page 47

nutrient. In all, 47 nutrient categories, consisting of 19 vitamins or vitamin-like factors, 13 minerals, five phytonutrient complexes, three omega fatty acids, and seven other nutritional factors are identified and incorporated into the standard.

The recommended daily intake for each nutrient is determined, wherever possible, by calculating the median (middle) value from those authors who provide a specific dosage recommendation. In some cases, where recent scientific evidence has eclipsed the recommendations, *NutriSearch* provides a recommended daily intake—or removes a previously recommended nutrient—based upon these new findings. Since the 2007 (4th Edition) of the guide, modifications have been made to the pooled recommendations in two key areas based upon new scientific findings. This includes changes to the daily levels of intake of the following:

✓ Vitamin D has been increased from 400IU/day to 1,000 IU/day

✓ Iodine has been increased from 100 µg/day to 1,000 µg/day

With the exception of Passwater's recommendations (which are based on diet, level of health and physical activity), the recommended daily intakes published by each author are presented for the general adult population. Passwater's lower two categories (C and D) are selected for inclusion in the *Blended Standard*. These categories represent individuals who have poor-to-average diets, poor-to-average health, take little or no exercise and live a sedentary lifestyle, reflecting today's general profile of the North American adult population.

The recommendations for daily intake compiled in the *Blended Standard* prescribe appropriate levels of intake for each of the 18 Health Support criteria developed for the rating of each product. In turn, these 18 criteria are used to provide an overall product rating, represented on a five-star scale. Details of each criterion are discussed in Chapter Six.

The *Table of Recommended Daily Intakes*, shown on pages 48-49, provides the daily nutritional recommendations of each authority, along with the median value for each nutrient incorporated into the *Blended Standard* derived from these recommendations.

Limitations of the Study

The products reviewed in this comparison represent a vast range of nutritional options available in the marketplace today. By necessity, *NutriSearch* has limited the selection to include only those products that meet specified criteria.

A qualifying product:

✓ must comprise a broad-spectrum nutritional supplement formulated for general preventive maintenance rather than a specified therapeutic use;

✓ must contain a comprehensive assortment of both minerals and vitamins;

✓ may contain assorted antioxidants and plant-based nutrients;

✓ must be formulated in tablet, capsule, powder or liquid form and have a specified daily dosage; and

✓ must provide a comprehensive list of ingredients, along with specified amounts (in µg, mg or IU) for each nutrient in the formulation.

Individual products may contain nutrients other than those listed in the *Blended Standard*. With the exception of iron,* nutrients are *not* included in the comparison if those nutrients are not identified in the *Blended Standard*. In addition, while a manufacturer may list a nutrient identified in the *Blended Standard*, **the nutrient is not included in the comparison if the exact amount (µg, mg or IU) of the nutrient is not provided or cannot be determined.** For example, if vitamin A in a product is shown as "5,000 IU of vitamin A with beta carotene" the entire amount is entered as vitamin A because the precise amount of beta carotene cannot be determined.

---

* *Due to findings on its potential toxicity, we have eliminated iron as a component of the* Blended Standard; *however, because of its continued use in many supplements, iron continues to be included in the criterion for potential toxicity.*

A Note on Proprietary Blends

Some manufacturers list a collection of nutrients, usually those plant-based nutrients that comprise the flavonoids and polyphenols found in food-based sources, as a *Proprietary Blend*. **In such cases, where the specified amounts of the individual nutrients are not described on the label, it is not possible for NutriSearch to give credit for each nutrient in the blend.** Instead, NutriSearch will endeavour to provide credit for the major nutrient *type* only, if this can be determined from the labelling information, based on the milligram amounts of the general category as described on the label.

Manufacturing Quality

Our *initial* product rating does not consider compliance with current Good Manufacturing Practices (cGMP), nor does it reflect an analysis of product content. **The five-star rating is based solely on label claim.**

However, those manufacturers whose products achieve the maximum five-star rating are invited by *NutriSearch* to demonstrate their commitment to quality by providing proof of their level of GMP compliance and by furnishing a notarized certificate of analysis for their product(s). This requires submission of evidence of an independent audit of current manufacturing practices (GMP) and an independent laboratory analysis of product content, including identity and potency. Manufacturers who provide such standards of evidence qualify for the *NutriSearch Medal of Achievement Program.*™ Details of this program are discussed in Chapter Seven.

Qualifying the Products

All nutritional products considered for inclusion in this comparative guide are initially screened for excessive potency of specific nutrients, according to the Upper Limit of daily intake (UL) established by the US Food and Nutrition Board. The UL (shown in the right-hand column of the Table of Recommended Daily Intakes on pages 48-49) represents the upper level of intake for a specific nutrient deemed safe for use by adults.*

Any product containing three or more nutrients with potencies exceeding 150 percent of the Upper Limit is eliminated from further consideration. Disqualified products are listed in the Product Rating Tables with an appropriate notation.

The Final Product Rating (Star Rating)

Using the 18 Health Support criteria described in Chapter Six, all qualifying products are evaluated using a series of algorithms (mathematical procedures) to arrive at a *Final Product Rating*. The development of each criterion is based on the scientific evidence available in the literature. Nutrient potencies are based on the median values of the pooled recommendations for intake established in the *Blended Standard*.

A five-star scale divided into half-star increments represents the *Final Product Rating*. A rating of five stars highlights those products possessing health support characteristics that are clearly superior to the majority of products on the market. Conversely, a rating of one star or less represents products possessing few, if any, of the health support characteristics reflected in the *Blended Standard*.

---

* *The Food and Nutrition Board, Institute of Medicine, Washington, DC has recently established the ULs for a number of vitamins and minerals. These values are shown in The Table of Recommended Daily Intakes, pages 48-49.*

*There are, in fact, two things, science and opinion;
the former begets knowledge, the latter ignorance*

~ Hippocrates (460BC-377 BC)

CHAPTER SIX:

PRODUCT RATING CRITERIA

This chapter explains the *Health Support Profile,* a set of mathematical models based on the 18 Health Support criteria described below. The *Health Support Profile* provides an overall ranking for each product included in this guide in accordance with the nutrient intake recommendations as described in the *Blended Standard.* Together, the NutriSearch *Blended Standard* and the 18 Health Support criteria form the basis of our analysis. For a detailed explanation of the *Blended Standard,* please refer to the previous chapter.

To evaluate a product, its rating for each Health Support criterion is calculated mathematically. This rating is determined by the nutrients and their potencies present in the product in relation to the requirements for each criterion.

Next, these 18 individual ratings for each product are pooled to provide a raw product score for that product. These scores, separated into a percent rank scale, represent a product's rating relative to all products evaluated. Final product ratings are displayed as star ratings, shown in half-star increments from zero to five stars.

The five-star scale is, at once, both visual and intuitive: a five-star rating represents a product of the highest quality relative to all products evaluated in accordance with the NutriSearch *Health Support Profile* used in our analysis. Conversely, a one-star rating or less represents products possessing few, if any, of the characteristics for optimal nutrition as reflected in the *Blended Standard.*

This *Health Support Profile* is described in detail below.

The NutriSearch Health Support Profile

To receive a full point for any single Health Support criterion, the product must *meet or exceed* the benchmark established for that criterion. Each criterion uses a sliding scale, from 0% to 100%, where partial points are awarded for the partial fulfillment of the criterion. The last criterion, *Potential Toxicities,* penalizes the product if the formulation exceeds defined limits of daily intake for those nutrients (vitamin A and iron) that demonstrate potential cumulative toxicities.

The following discussion provides an overview of each criterion used in our *Health Support Profile.* For each criterion, we address the fundamental question posed; in turn, each question presents the logical argument that forms the basis of our mathematical model for that criterion.

1. Completeness

The human body requires several vitamins and vitamin-like substances, a diverse group of plant-based antioxidants, numerous trace elements and minerals, and several essential fatty acids. Most, but not all, of these substances can only be obtained through the diet. In all, 47 essential nutrients and nutrient categories comprise our *Blended Standard*—the benchmark upon which our analysis is built.

This criterion assesses whether the product contains all of the *Blended Standard* nutrients.

Does the product contain the full spectrum of nutrients and nutrient categories listed in the Blended Standard and considered essential for optimal health? To qualify, a nutrient or nutrient category must be present at a dosage that is at least 20% of the value in the Blended Standard.

2. Potency

Epidemiological evidence reveals that there is considerable genetic variation in the functionality of several key coenzymes* in human cells. In many instances, these genetic variations (polymorphisms) will hinder the ability of a coenzyme to bind to the active site of other enzymes, thus impairing the reactions that these enzymes control. This, in turn, can increase susceptibility to disease. Individuals affected with a gene polymorphism will likely require supplementation with those nutrients serving as precursors for the affected coenzymes at a daily intake substantially greater than recommended for that nutrient. Consequently, the potencies for the 47 essential nutrients and nutrient categories used in our *Blended Standard* reflect the need for supplementation with some of these nutrients at levels significantly higher than their Dietary Reference Intakes (DRIs) recommended by the US Food and Nutrition Board and Health Canada.

For more information on gene polymorphisms, please refer to page 63, *Methylation Support*, in this guide and to pages 31-32, *Genetic Polymorphisms Common*, in the *NutriSearch Comparative Guide to Nutritional Supplements*, 4th (Professional) Edition

This criterion assesses how much of each nutrient the product contains compared to the *Blended Standard*.

For each nutrient in the product, what is the level of potency relative to the potency for that nutrient in the Blended Standard?

3. Mineral Forms

Minerals are essential components of our cells and serve as cofactors in the thousands of enzyme-controlled reactions that power the machinery of the cell. Throughout the body, minerals also form critical structural components, regulate the action of nerves and muscles, maintain the cell's osmotic (water) balance, and modulate the pH (acidity) of the cell and extracellular fluids. While minerals comprise only 4% to 5% of our total body weight, life would not be possible without them. This criterion examines mineral forms (mineral salts, chelated minerals and organic-acid/mineral complexes), which affect the ability of the minerals to be absorbed into the blood, making them available to our cells.

During the digestive process, minerals separate from the food and dissociate into ions (electrically charged atoms in solution). Ionized minerals can then pass freely through the intestinal wall and into the blood. They also attach themselves to amino acids or other organic acids and 'hitch a ride' with these carriers, which are preferentially absorbed by the cells lining the small intestine. From here, the carriers and their attached minerals enter the blood and then travel to the liver to be readied for use by the cells of the body.

When nutritional supplements are consumed, the minerals are naturally conjugated (joined) to amino acids available in the gut during the digestive process.[1] This is why it is best to consume your supplements with a meal. This suggests that there should be no differences in mineral bioavailability† between supplements that use chelated mineral complexes and those that use less expensive inorganic mineral salts. However, such is not the case. For one thing, as people age, they lose their ability to produce sufficient stomach acid, making it increasingly difficult to absorb common mineral salts. Complex mineral interactions can further inhibit absorption and influence mineral bioavailability.

Many components of our daily diet, including other minerals, can interfere with the absorption of certain minerals and make them unavailable to the body.[2] For example, natural fibre found in fruits and cereals has a depressing effect on the absorption of minerals supplied as inorganic mineral salts. Surprisingly, recent

---

* *Coenzymes (helper enzymes) are small organic non-protein molecules that carry chemical groups between enzymes. Many coenzymes are activated water-soluble vitamins that have a phosphate group attached to the vitamin. Non-vitamins, such as ATP—the energy currency of the cell—can also act as coenzymes. While coenzymes are consumed in the reactions in which they assist, they are constantly regenerated; their concentration is maintained at a steady level within the cell.*

† *Bioavailability is the ability of a given nutrient to be absorbed by the gut and to be utilized by the cells of the body.*

evidence shows that a fibre-rich diet can even *deplete* the body's mineral stores when minerals are provided as mineral salts, resulting in a *negative* mineral balance.[3,4] Considering the ready availability of dietary supplements that use mineral salts, these mineral-mineral and mineral-substrate interferences take on considerable importance. Imagine taking a mineral supplement in good faith and going into a negative mineral balance—actually *losing* ground for the very minerals you consumed!

The short of it is this: avoid the use of supplements that provide minerals principally in the form of inorganic mineral salts (such as oxides, carbonates, sulphates and phosphates). While less expensive to manufacture, supplements using mineral salts do not provide optimal nutritional value.

To resolve mineral-mineral interferences and increase the overall bioavailability of minerals, quality manufacturers chemically bond the mineral to an amino acid or organic acid carrier. These chelated minerals are believed to mimic the natural mineral chelates formed during the digestion process. Beyond their reported superior bioavailability, chelated minerals have lower absorptive interference and better tolerance in the gut than mineral salts.[5] Moreover, minerals delivered in chelated form avoid the competitive inhibitions to absorption and the mineral-mineral interactions experienced by mineral salts.

While not chelates in the true sense of the word, minerals joined to organic acids, such as citrate, malate, succinate, alpha ketoglutarate and aspartate—known collectively as Krebs cycle intermediates—are also preferentially absorbed. These organic acids, essential to the central metabolic pathway of the cell, appear to be *selectively* absorbed through the gut. The attached mineral simply piggybacks along for the ride.

Both Krebs cycle intermediates and amino-acid chelates fulfill all the requirements for an optimal

> **Beyond their reported superior bioavailability, chelated minerals have lower absorptive interference and better tolerance in the gut than mineral salts.**

carrier molecule:[6] they are easily metabolized, non-toxic, helpful in increasing the absorption of the mineral carried, and efficiently degraded and employed in other areas of the cell's metabolism. Organic-acid complexes also provide needed acidity to promote absorption in the gut. Moreover, both the mineral/amino-acid chelates and the mineral/organic-acid complexes appear to be better tolerated by the human gut than mineral salts.[7]

This criterion poses the following question:

For those minerals included in a formulation, how many are found in their most bioavailable forms as amino-acid chelates or organic-acid complexes?

4. Vitamin E Forms

Regular consumption of natural vitamin E has long been known to lower the risk of degenerative disease. A good deal of laboratory evidence and data from epidemiological and retrospective studies show that a high dietary intake of vitamin E can ward off heart disease[8-11] and keep several cancers at bay.[12-14] Vitamin E is a fat-soluble vitamin that exists in eight different structural forms (four tocopherols and four tocotrienols). Each form (isomer)* has its own biological activity, which is the measure of its potency or functional use in the body. Two of these isomeric forms have particular importance when it comes to supplementation.

Alpha Tocopherol

Alpha tocopherol is the most prevalent form of vitamin E in humans and the most common type of vitamin E used in nutritional supplements. It is the only form of vitamin E actively maintained by the human body and is, therefore, the form found in the largest quantities in the blood and tissues. As well as showing the highest level of biological activity, natural

---

* *Isomers are molecules with the same chemical formula and often with the same kinds of bonds between atoms, but in which the atoms are arranged differently to provide either a different structural formula (structural isomerism) or a different three-dimensional shape (stereoisomerism).*

alpha tocopherol appears to be quickly absorbed into human cells. In contrast, the synthetic form (discussed below) is quickly metabolized and excreted in the urine.

Alpha tocopherol functions as a chain-breaking antioxidant that prevents the propagation of autocatalytic lipid peroxidation* within the cell membrane. Found in leafy green vegetables, vegetable oils and nuts, intakes of small quantities of this fat-soluble vitamin—as little as 100 IU per day—have been associated with a significantly reduced risk of heart disease in both men and women.[15]

Natural alpha tocopherol is called *d*-alpha tocopherol. Synthetic alpha tocopherol, also known as *d/l*-alpha tocopherol or all-rac tocopherol, is produced commercially in a process that yields both the *d*- (right handed) and *l*- (left handed) isomers. These isomers are mirror images of each other. Evidence regarding the biological activity of synthetic vitamin E has prompted the National Academies of Science to recognize synthetic *d/l*-alpha tocopherol as possessing only half the biological activity of natural *d*-alpha tocopherol.[16] According to researchers at the Linus Pauling Institute synthetic *d/l*-alpha tocopherol is *less* bioavailable and only about half as potent as natural *d*-alpha tocopherol.

It is important to note that the use of high-dose synthetic *d/l*-alpha tocopherol can cause adverse effects, including hemorrhagic toxicity—an effect not reported with natural vitamin E. This may explain why several studies on the health benefits of vitamin E supplementation have been ambiguous.[17-21] Most such studies have used synthetic vitamin E, rather than the natural form of vitamin E found in the diet.[22]

Gamma Tocopherol

While alpha tocopherol has been the primary form of vitamin E used in the manufacture of dietary supplements, researchers at Johns Hopkins University report that the benefits of alpha tocopherol supplementation may be unintentionally compromised by a concurrent *decrease* in the levels of gamma tocopherol, known to occur during high-dose supplementation with the alpha form.[23]

Gamma tocopherol possesses distinctive chemical properties that differentiate it from its alpha analogue and may explain the observed differences in the physiological effects of the two vitamin E forms. For example, gamma tocopherol has been shown to be more effective than alpha tocopherol in:

✔ reducing prothrombotic events associated with oxidative stress;[24,25]

✔ reducing platelet aggregation and clot formation;[24]

✔ enhancing the activity of the antioxidant enzyme, superoxide dismutase (SOD), and inhibiting the proinflammatory COX-2 enzyme;[26,27]

✔ regulating the activity of genes that can influence cancerous growth; and [28,29]

✔ subduing nitric oxide-induced oxidative stress by removing nitrogen radicals.[30]

Not surprisingly, gamma tocopherol is emerging as an important partner to alpha tocopherol in the science of preventive health. Both forms of vitamin E are recognized nutritional thoroughbreds, each possessing protective talents based on their individual chemistries; however, *it is their work as a team*—at once both complementary and synergistic—that is the likely 'power behind the punch' of vitamin E observed in epidemiological, retrospective and laboratory studies.

The Bruce Ames research group at the University of California, Berkeley, contends that consumers taking vitamin E supplements containing an imbalance of the two principal forms of vitamin E are depriving themselves of the protection afforded by a mixture of tocopherols. Accordingly, the researchers argue that vitamin E supplements should contain a ratio of alpha/gamma tocopherol that is closer to that found in nature.

This criterion assesses the product for the various forms of vitamin E and their bioactivity.

Does the product contain the natural (d) isomer of alpha tocopherol or does the product contain the less useful synthetic (d/l) isomers of alpha tocopherol?

---

* *Lipid peroxidation refers to the oxidative degradation of unsaturated lipids, which results in structural damage to the cell membrane. The process proceeds by a free radical chain-reaction mechanism.*

Does the product contain gamma tocopherol (or a mixture of gamma, beta and delta tocopherols) at a potency of up to one-half the potency of alpha tocopherol in the same product? What is the potency of gamma tocopherol or mixed tocopherols in the product, compared to the potency for gamma tocopherol in the Blended Standard?

5. Immune Support

An explosion of research over the past decade has uncovered vitamin D as a vital component of our immune system. Working in conjunction with other micronutrients, vitamin D can help protect us against many of the most common degenerative diseases, including heart disease, stroke, cancer, multiple sclerosis, dementia and many others. Unfortunately, this new research coincides with a dramatic downturn in vitamin D intake amongst North Americans.

Another nutrient recently discovered as vital to immune support is iodine. The high iodine concentration of the thymus gland is *prima facia* evidence of the important role played by iodine in the immune system—a role likely related to the element's innate antioxidant powers.[31-33]

Many other nutrients, including vitamin A, vitamin C, vitamin E, zinc, selenium and the B-vitamins B_1, B_2, B_5 (pantothenic acid), B_6, B_{12} and folic acid, are also essential to a healthy immune system.[34] This criterion assesses the product for vitamin D and iodine levels and for the presence of these other nutrients that boost the immune response.

Does the product contain vitamin D and iodine at the potencies described in the Blended Standard? Does the product also contain beta carotene and vitamin A, vitamin C, vitamin E, zinc, selenium and the B-vitamins B_1, B_2, B_5 (pantothenic acid), B_6, B_{12} and folic acid at the potencies established in the Blended Standard?

6. Antioxidant Support

The weight of scientific evidence supports supplementation with antioxidants in the prevention and treatment of many of today's common ailments. As was anticipated decades ago by leading researchers,[35] high-dose supplementation with antioxidants has gained a significant role in the prevention and treatment of many of today's common ailments. However, antioxidants do not work in isolation. When an antioxidant neutralizes a free radical it is depleted and must be replenished, often by another antioxidant, before it can be used again. For this reason, it is vital to supplement with a wide spectrum of antioxidants—an approach that is reflective of what occurs in nature.

Of all the antioxidants, vitamin E may offer the greatest protection against heart disease because of its ability to imbed itself into the LDL-cholesterol molecule and protect it from oxidative damage.

As an aqueous-phase antioxidant, vitamin C (ascorbic acid) is the principal sentry against oxidative attack in the extra-cellular fluids and within the cytoplasm of the cell. Further, vitamin C is a cofactor or substrate for eight separate enzyme systems involved in various cellular functions, including collagen synthesis, ATP synthesis in the mitochondria and hormone biosynthesis. Its primary antioxidant partners include vitamin E and beta carotene, which help regenerate vitamin C.

Of all the antioxidants, vitamin E may offer the greatest protection against heart disease because of its ability to imbed itself into the LDL-cholesterol molecule and protect it from oxidative damage. Its solubility in lipids (fats) makes the vitamin an important component of the cell membrane, where it works to protect the cell against lipid peroxidation and reduce oxidation-induced inflammatory events. More recently, the gamma analogue of vitamin E has shown great promise in reducing the risks of several cancers. Researchers at the University of Uppsala, Sweden, found that gamma tocopherol proved more effective than alpha tocopherol in reducing several prothrombotic events associated with oxidative stress.[36]

Beta carotene, a member of a diverse group of auxiliary photosynthetic pigments, plays a dual role in human nutrition. As an antioxidant, its extensive conjugated double bond structure reacts effectively with singlet oxygen radicals, absorbing and diffusing their destructive energies.[37] As a precursor for vitamin A (retinol), beta carotene supplies a portion of the body's requirement for the vitamin, which plays a central role in the chemistry of vision. Both beta carotene and vitamin A prevent the oxidation of cholesterol, reduce oxidative damage to DNA and disable oxygen free radicals produced by exposure to sunlight and air pollution.[38] The yellow carotenoid is also involved in the activation of gene expression and the control of cell differentiation (cell specialization). Together, vitamin C, vitamin E and beta carotene form an important antioxidant triad that plays a central role in attenuating oxidative and inflammatory events.

Iodine, much like its fat-soluble colleague vitamin E, possesses the ability to quench autocatalytic lipid peroxidation in cellular membranes. Iodine attaches itself to the carbon-carbon double bonds of membrane-bound polyunsaturated lipids, thereby rendering them less vulnerable to free radical degradation.[39,40] Similarly, the iodothyronines (precursors to the thyroid hormones) have been found to quench the propagation of the free-radical chain reactions involved in lipid peroxidation by becoming oxidatively deiodinated.[41] In breast and other tissues, iodide (I⁻) acts as an electron donor, transferring an electron to the oxygen of hydrogen peroxide, forming iodinated proteins and lipids, thereby decreasing the damage caused by free radical formation.[39,42]

Several other antioxidants play synergistic roles to the vitamin C, vitamin E, beta carotene triad. These include vitamin A, alpha lipoic acid, lycopene, coenzyme Q_{10} and the antioxidant mineral selenium.

This criterion examines the nutrients that help to prevent or repair cellular damage caused by oxidation.

> *Does the product contain vitamin C, vitamin E (including alpha tocopherol and gamma tocopherol, or mixed tocopherols), vitamin A, beta carotene, alpha lipoic acid, lycopene, coenzyme Q_{10}, selenium and iodine at potencies up to 100% of the potencies for these nutrients in the Blended Standard?*

> Too much phosphorus, from soft-drink consumption or high protein intake, will suck calcium out of the bone and weaken its integrity.

7. *Bone Health*

As living tissue, healthy bones require at least 24 bone-building materials, including trace elements and protein. The most important minerals are calcium, magnesium, phosphorus and potassium. Equally important is the balance between these minerals. Strong bones need lots of calcium, but calcium supplementation also requires the presence of magnesium, which increases calcium retention in the bone. Phosphorus, another important component in bone formation, must be in proper balance with calcium. Too much of it, from soft-drink consumption or high protein intake, will suck calcium out of the bone and weaken its integrity. Vitamins D and K are also vital for enhanced calcium deposition,[43] while silicon, boron and zinc are required to strengthen the bone's mineral matrix.[44] Vitamin C stimulates formation of the collagen matrix, an important protein component that creates a framework for calcium crystallization.[43]

Silicon increases bone-mineral density and appears to have a role in the prevention and treatment of osteoporosis. Silicon deposition is found in areas of active bone growth, suggesting that it may be involved in the growth of bone crystals and the process of bone mineralization. Zinc is essential for the proper action of vitamin D; its status plays a central role in bone health. Increased zinc excretion, common in osteoporosis sufferers, is a likely consequence of accelerated depletion of bone mineral content. Diets low in zinc have been shown to slow adolescent bone growth.[45] Last but not least, vitamins B_6, B_{12} and folic acid reduce mineral loss by modulating blood homocysteine levels.[43]

The scientific evidence supports the need for long-term supplementation with several key nutrients in the maintenance of bone health. This is particularly true for women in their peri- and post-menopause years. Accordingly, supplementation with vitamins D, K, C, B_6, B_{12}, folic acid and the minerals boron, calcium, magnesium, silicon and zinc, at levels deemed suitable for optimal nutritional health, is included as an important component of our product-rating criteria.

The criterion for Bone Health poses the following question:

Does the product contain vitamin D, vitamin K, vitamin C, vitamin B$_6$, vitamin B$_{12}$, folic acid, boron, calcium, magnesium, silicon and zinc at potencies up to 100% of the potencies for these nutrients in the Blended Standard?

8. Heart Health

Epidemiological research has consistently revealed that individuals with a high dietary intake of antioxidant vitamins have a lower-than-average risk of cardiovascular disease.[46] This evidence is particularly consistent for vitamin E.[47] As well, many clinical studies show magnesium supplementation to be of significant benefit in the treatment of cardiac arrhythmias (irregular heart beat) and in reversing the depletion of potassium that accompanies a magnesium deficit. Many cardiovascular events, such as angina pectoris (chest pain), congestive heart failure (failure to pump blood efficiently) and cardiomyopathy (weakening or damaging of the heart muscle), are related to low magnesium status.[48]

Vitamin E's cardio-protective effects appear to stem from its ability to bind to LDL cholesterol, protecting it from free-radical-induced oxidative damage and the consequent buildup of atherogenic plaque. Low levels of vitamin E in the blood are predictive of a heart attack almost 70% of the time.[49] A large study, conducted by the Harvard School of Public Health, showed that men who consumed at least 67 mg (100 IU) of vitamin E per day for at least two years had a 37% lower risk of heart disease than those who did not take supplements.[50]

Iodine and iodine-rich foods have long been used in European and Asian cultures as traditional treatments for cardiovascular disease and control of hypertension.[51-57] Textbooks from the mid-1900s advocated the use of iodides for the treatment of cardiovascular disorders, including arteriosclerosis, angina pectoris, aortic aneurism and arterial hypertension.[58-60] Iodine has numerous physiological roles independent of its actions on the thyroid. The documented anti-microbial, anti-inflammatory and anti-proliferative activities of iodine appear to be important factors in determining overall cardiovascular health.[61-64] The element possesses the unique ability to denature, polymerize and solubilize proteins. This latter attribute may enable iodine to reduce blood viscosity, thereby facilitating a reduction in blood pressure and the accompanying risk of thrombotic events.[63]

Population studies suggest a link between calcium intake and blood pressure.[65] While results have not been consistent, several studies show that calcium supplementation can lower blood pressure in hypertensive individuals.[66] A review on the effects of mineral intakes in reducing hypertension concludes that a decrease of sodium and concurrent increase of calcium, along with increased potassium and magnesium intakes (modifications characteristic of the Dietary Approaches to Stop Hypertension [DASH] diet), have a dramatic impact in lowering blood pressure.[67] Regulation of intracellular calcium appears to play a key role in hypertension, as well as obesity.[68] Overall, sub-optimal calcium intakes contribute to the aetiology of hypertension. Dietary calcium appears to reduce blood pressure by normalizing intracellular calcium levels.

Supplementation with magnesium is of benefit in the treatment of cardiac arrhythmias and the prevention of potassium depletion; both minerals play an important role in the proper functioning of the heart.[69-72] Deficiency in magnesium has been observed in cardiomyopathy and mitral valve prolapse. In fact, over 85% of patients with mitral valve prolapse exhibit a chronic magnesium deficiency, which is relieved through supplementation.[73,74] Several studies confirm improvement in heart function in patients with cardiomyopathies when supplemented with magnesium.[70-72,75] Because the mineral acts in so many ways to enhance cardiac function and optimize cellular metabolism, magnesium is widely recognized as a critical nutrient for general cardiac support.

Coenzyme Q$_{10}$ (CoQ$_{10}$), an antioxidant manufactured by the body and an essential component in cellular energy production, is also prevalent in the heart muscle. Low tissue levels of CoQ$_{10}$ in the heart muscle have been associated with several cardiovascular complications, including angina, congestive heart failure, cardiomyopathy, hypertension (high blood

> Low levels of vitamin E in the blood are predictive of a heart attack almost 70% of the time.

pressure) and mitral valve prolapse (failure of the valve to close properly).

Several double-blind studies in patients with various cardiomyopathies show the benefits of CoQ_{10} supplementation. Langsjoen and co-workers reported an 89% improvement rate in 80 cardiomyopathy patients treated with CoQ_{10}.[76] The coenzyme also appears to moderate blood pressure through an unusual mechanism; by lowering cholesterol levels and stabilizing the vascular system through its antioxidant properties, it is able to reduce vascular resistance. Several studies confirm a lowering of both systolic (pumping) and diastolic (resting) pressures in the range of ten percent through CoQ_{10} supplementation.[77-79]

Other nutrients play important roles in optimizing cardiovascular health and reducing hypertension. These include gamma tocopherol, calcium, magnesium, l-carnitine and acetyl-l-carnitine, procyanidolic oligomers (PCOs), phenolic compounds and lycopene.

The criterion for Heart Health poses the following question:

> *Does the product contain vitamin D, iodine, vitamin E (including alpha tocopherol and gamma tocopherol, or mixed tocopherols), beta carotene, coenzyme Q_{10}, calcium, magnesium, l-carnitine or acetyl-l-carnitine, procyanidolic oligomers (PCOs), phenolic compounds and lycopene at potencies up to 100% of the potencies for those nutrients and nutrient categories in the Blended Standard?*

9. *Liver Health (detoxification)*

Glutathione (GSH) is a small protein that consists of three amino acids: glutamic acid, cysteine and glycine. Because of the chemical nature of sulphur-containing cysteine, glutathione effortlessly donates electrons, accounting for its powerful antioxidant properties. Intracellular glutathione status is a sensitive indicator of cellular health and of the cell's ability to resist toxic challenges. An important water-phase antioxidant, glutathione is an essential component

in the glutathione peroxidase system, one of three vital free-radical scavenging mechanisms in the cell. Glutathione peroxidase enzymes serve to detoxify peroxides, including hydrogen peroxide (H_2O_2), generated within cellular membranes and lipid-dense areas of the cell, particularly the mitochondrial membrane. Severe glutathione depletion quickly leads to cell death; experimental glutathione depletion has been found to induce cellular apoptosis.[80,81]

Glutathione depletion at the cellular level invokes extensive damage to the mitochondria, the energy centres of the cell. Depletion of mitochondrial glutathione, in fact, may be the ultimate factor determining a cell's vulnerability to oxidative attack.[82] Nowhere is glutathione's presence more vital than in these cellular 'furnaces,' where a cascade of oxidation-reduction reactions complete the final steps in respiration—a process known as oxidative phosphorylation. Throughout this process, electrons invariably escape and react with ambient oxygen to generate toxic free radicals.[83] It is estimated that two percent to five percent of the electrons that enter the cell's mitochondria are converted to reactive oxygen species (oxygen-based free radicals),[83] generating considerable oxidative stress for the cell.[84,85] These free radicals, like sparks from a fire, pose an immediate threat to other cellular components, such as the DNA, enzymes, structural proteins and lipids.

The cumulative structural damage wrought by oxygen and other free radical species is now recognized as a principal contributor to the degenerative disease process and the progressive loss of organ function commonly recognized as aging.[85] Consequently, the cell is constantly challenged to destroy these free radical 'sparks' before they can inflict lasting damage. Minimizing such oxidative assaults may prove to be the ultimate challenge of being alive. For this reason, the formidable reducing power of glutathione is of profound importance to the cell.

Glutathione helps regenerate other antioxidants that are, themselves, depleted from their task of fending off free radical challenges. Glutathione-induced regeneration, in fact, may be the mechanism used

> The glutathione status of a cell … will perhaps turn out to be the most accurate single indicator of the health of the cell. That is, as glutathione levels go, so will go the fortunes of the cell.
> ~ Parris Kidd, PhD

by the cell to conserve the lipid-phase antioxidants, vitamin A, vitamin E and the carotenoids.[86] Dietary vitamin C can protect against tissue damage resulting from glutathione depletion; likewise, supplementation with glutathione or its metabolic precursors can quickly replenish vitamin C deficiencies.[87,88] Thus, glutathione and ascorbic acid—two of the pre-eminent cellular antioxidants—are tightly linked: glutathione can replenish vitamin C and vitamin C can replenish glutathione. Together, these two antioxidant powerhouses protect an entire spectrum of biomolecules within the cell and facilitate the cell's optimal performance.[82] According to Dr Parris Kidd: "The glutathione status of a cell … will perhaps turn out to be the most accurate single indicator of the health of the cell. That is, as glutathione levels go, so will go the fortunes of the cell."

While dietary glutathione is efficiently absorbed in the gut, the same may not be the case for nutritional supplementation. Oral dosing appears to raise glutathione levels, albeit with great variability between subjects.[89,90] Accordingly, supplementation with glutathione precursors and with those nutrients involved in the glutathione peroxidase pathway, including vitamin C, cysteine and n-acetyl-cysteine, selenium, vitamin B_2 (riboflavin) and vitamin B_3, is necessary to optimize cellular glutathione levels.

Iodine is another important nutrient for liver health and detoxification. Iodine's ability to staunch the potential damage of hydrogen peroxide (H_2O_2) provides support for the work of the glutathione peroxidase enzyme system in helping to remove these toxic agents from the body. Iodine also has the capacity to directly scavenge hydroxyl radicals and has been shown to neutralize H_2O_2 by converting it to hypoiodous acid and then water, thereby preventing the formation of toxic hydroxyl radicals.[91] As well, in target tissues such as the liver, the iodine-containing and physiologically active thyroid hormone, T3, can bind to thyroid receptors in the nuclei of cells to help regulate gene expression and control metabolism.

This criterion examines those nutrients that optimize levels of glutathione and enhance liver function.

Does the product contain iodine, vitamin C, n-acetyl-cysteine (including cysteine), selenium, vitamin B_2 and vitamin B_3 (including niacin and niacinamide), at potencies up to 100% of the potencies for these nutrients in the Blended Standard?

10. Metabolic Health (glucose control)

Diabetes, now the seventh leading cause of death in the United States and Canada, is a chronic disorder of carbohydrate, fat and protein metabolism. The disease first appears as a constellation of metabolic changes associated with hyperinsulinemenia (elevated insulin levels) and hyperglycaemia (elevated blood-sugar levels). This condition, a precursor to full-blown diabetes, is called Insulin Resistance Syndrome. Untreated, insulin resistance will develop into full-blown diabetes; with it comes greatly magnified risks of heart disease, stroke, eye, and kidney disease and loss of nerve function. Frank diabetes is the principal cause of adult blindness and limb amputation.

Non-insulin-dependent (type-2) diabetes mellitus is a disease strongly associated with a sedentary lifestyle and the modern western diet. Inadequate physical activity, combined with a diet high in refined sugars, saturated fats and proteins, and low in dietary fibre, has resulted in an epidemic of obesity throughout Canada and the United States—and with it, the prevalence of type-2 diabetes. Obesity is, in fact, a hallmark of the disease: almost 90% of those diagnosed with type-2 diabetes are obese at the time of diagnosis.[92,93] While there is disagreement as to whether obesity causes type-2 diabetes or whether diabetes begets obesity, one thing is clear: the disease involves a profound disturbance in the metabolic balance of the body, with dramatic consequences for the individual.

To reduce the risk of frank type-2 diabetes, one must prevent the onset of insulin resistance. However,

> Diabetes, now the seventh leading cause of death in the United States and Canada, is a chronic disorder of carbohydrate, fat and protein metabolism. The disease first appears as a constellation of metabolic changes associated with hyperinsulinemenia (elevated insulin levels) and hyperglycaemia (elevated blood-sugar levels).

millions of North Americans suffer unknowingly from this syndrome, placing them at an increased risk for cardiovascular and neurological dysfunctions. The development of insulin resistance is multi-factorial; however, research shows that complications associated with this pre-diabetic disorder may be mitigated effectively through conscientious dietary and lifestyle changes.

Vitamins B_3, B_6, B_{12}, C, E, biotin, coenzyme Q_{10} and the elements, iodine, chromium, magnesium, manganese and zinc are all essential for proper metabolic support and the regulation of glucose metabolism. Accordingly, supplementation with these nutrients, at levels deemed suitable for optimal nutritional health, is included as an important component of our product-rating criteria.

The criterion for Metabolic Health poses the following question:

Does the product contain vitamin B_3 (including niacin and niacinamide), vitamin B_6, vitamin B_{12}, vitamin C, vitamin E (including alpha tocopherol and gamma tocopherol, or mixed tocopherols), vitamin D, iodine, biotin, coenzyme Q_{10}, chromium, magnesium, manganese and zinc at potencies up to 100% of the potencies for these nutrients in the Blended Standard?

11. Ocular Health

Vitamin A is best known for its effects on the visual system. There are four types of photopigments produced from vitamin A, which are present in the retina of the eye: Rhodopsin is found in the retinal cells responsible for night vision, and three iodopsins (sensitive to red, yellow and blue wavelengths) regulate colour vision during daylight. These four analogues of vitamin A are isomers of retinal, an active (aldehyde) form of the vitamin.[94] Poor adaptation to changes in light intensity and poor night vision are indicative of a low vitamin A status. In developed countries, vitamin A deficiency usually results from malabsorption; supplementation with vitamin A induces a rapid restoration of vision.[95] Beta carotene, once it is converted into the active form of vitamin A by the enzyme beta carotene mono-oxygenase, also contributes to the chemistry of vision.[96]

People who eat foods rich in lutein and zeaxanthin (including broccoli, collard, kale, spinach and turnip greens) are much less likely to suffer from age-related cataracts* than those who do not. These carotenoid pigments are also effective in reducing the incidence of macular degeneration;† this is a likely consequence of their ability to quench oxidative damage within the eye. Recent studies show that these auxiliary photosynthetic pigments may also slow age-related increases in lens density.[97]

Low circulating levels of vitamins C, E and beta carotene are implicated in the development of cataracts in the eye;[98] conversely, high serum levels of these nutrients reduce the prevalence of cataract formation.[99,100] Beta carotene also acts as a natural biological solar filter, protecting against light-induced UV damage to the eye.[101] There is substantial evidence that, when used in combination, the actions of these antioxidant partners are synergistic, providing a level of protection that strikingly exceeds the sum of their individual contributions.[102]

The criterion for Ocular Health poses the following question:

Does the product contain the antioxidants, vitamin C, vitamin E (including alpha and gamma tocopherol, or mixed tocopherols), vitamin A (including beta carotene) and the carotenoids, lutein and zeaxanthin at potencies up to 100% of the potencies for these nutrients in the Blended Standard?

---

* *A cataract is a clouding of the eye's natural lens, which focuses light onto the retina at the back of the eye. The lens is mostly made of water and protein, with the protein fibres arranged in a precise way to keep the lens clear and transparent. Oxidative damage to these proteins causes them to clump together and cloud the lens, forming cataracts. In time, the cataract may grow larger and cloud more of the lens, making it translucent or milky. The consequence is blurred and darkened vision.*

† *Macular degeneration is the development of blurred or distorted central vision due to degeneration of the macula of the eye. This small area in the center of the retina makes sharp-detail vision possible from the central portion of the eye.*

12. *Methylation Support*

Over 40 major clinical studies confirm that homocysteine levels are a predictive marker for heart disease, stroke and peripheral artery disease. A powerful oxidizing agent, homocysteine is believed to be responsible for the initial damage to the inner walls of the arteries and subsequent initiation of atherosclerotic plaque formation. Twenty to 40 percent of patients with heart disease have elevated levels of homocysteine.[103,104] Deficiencies in vitamin B_6, vitamin B_{12} and folic acid can increase circulating levels of homocysteine; conversely, these nutrients—working together—reduce circulating homocysteine levels by helping to convert homocysteine to methionine, a harmless amino acid used by the cell for other functions.

Most individuals with high levels of homocysteine respond well to supplementation with vitamins B_6, B_{12} and folic acid; however, a significant proportion of the North American population is resistant to this nutritional intervention. Such individuals suffer from a common gene polymorphism that impairs the enzyme, methylene tetrahydrofolate reductase (MTHFR). A defect in this enzyme creates a metabolic bottleneck that limits the conversion of homocysteine to methionine and results in elevated levels of homocysteine in the blood. Supplementing with vitamins B_6, B_{12} and folic acid cannot effectively alleviate this bottleneck; however, studies by Bates and coworkers (1986) showed that the defective enzyme is sensitive to riboflavin deficiency.[105] Consequently, it has been suggested by the Ames group of Berkeley that mega-dose therapy with vitamin B_2 (riboflavin), the precursor vitamin to the flavin adenine dinucleotide (FAD) coenzyme that is required by the defective enzyme, would prove beneficial.[106]

When provided as a dietary supplement, trimethylglycine (TMG), commonly known as betaine, can also address homocysteine resistance, experienced in about 15% to 20% of the general population. Supplementation with TMG creates a bypass to the metabolic bottleneck, providing an alternate route for the methylation of homocysteine. By donating one of its three methyl (CH_3-) groups to homocysteine, TMG effectively regenerates methionine and lowers homocysteine levels.[107] The subsequent decrease in blood homocysteine can be maintained as long as the supplement is taken.[108]

A high level of homocysteine in the blood is a primary risk factor for cardiovascular disease and warrants supplementation with vitamins B_2, B_6, B_{12}, folic acid and trimethylglycine as a prudent preventive measure. This holds particularly true for the elderly, who commonly suffer from an age-related decline in vitamin B_{12}.

The criterion for Methylation Support poses the following question:

Does the product contain vitamin B_2, vitamin B_6, vitamin B_{12}, folic acid and trimethylglycine at potencies up to 100% of the potencies for these nutrients in the Blended Standard?

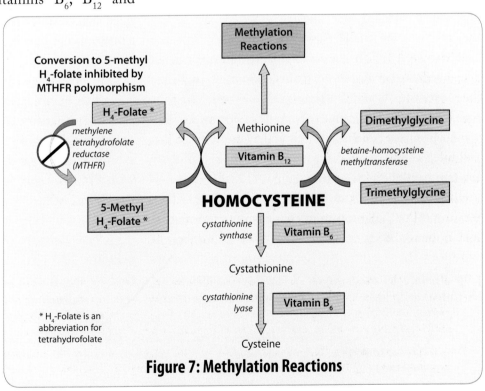

Figure 7: Methylation Reactions

13. Lipotropic Factors

In our toxic world, we are exposed to ever-increasing levels of contaminants and harmful chemicals that, once ingested, accumulate in fatty deposits within the body. The liver and the brain are two primary targets for the bioaccumulation of lipid-soluble toxins, such as pesticides and metals. Vitamins C, E and beta carotene, the water-soluble B-complex vitamins and some of the trace minerals consumed in the diet play important roles in protecting these tissues from the damage caused by oxidative assault from such toxins.[109,110] However, it is the liver—the body's filtration and purification unit—that does most of the heavy lifting here.

First in line to deal with the contaminants consumed in our foods and drinking water, the liver is subject to a daily onslaught of noxious challenges. In addition to the external toxic load (a function of lifestyle and environment), the liver must also deal with a range of endogenous (internal) toxins produced by the metabolic processes of our body. Normally, the liver can cope quite handily; however, when things go wrong, the workload for the liver can increase dramatically.

Fortunately, proper diet, nutritional supplementation and treatment with herbal remedies can fortify the liver to withstand this toxic stress. Within the liver, choline and inositol assist with the elimination of exogenous and endogenous toxins, helping to mobilize the fatty deposits and remove metals and other noxious compounds. Such agents are known as lipotropic (fat-moving) factors because of their ability to mobilize fats and bile (a secretion from the liver that helps emulsify fats during the digestive process).

Lipotropic factors have a long history of use within the naturopathic community, helping to restore and enhance liver function and treat a number of common liver ailments. Dietary lipotropic factors work by increasing the levels of S-adenosylmethionine (SAM-e), the liver's in-house lipotropic agent and glutathione, the premier detoxicant in the body. They have been used preferentially because, until recently, dietary SAM-e has not been widely available, and because oral glutathione is not well absorbed in the digestive tract.

The criterion for Lipotropic Factors poses the following question:

> *Does the product contain the important lipotropic factors, choline or lecithin (phosphatidylcholine) and inositol at potencies up to 100% of the potencies for these nutrients in the Blended Standard?*

14. Inflammation Control

Chronic inflammation is a principal mechanism by which degenerative disease takes root. Reducing oxidative stress and changing the balance within the body to favour the production of anti-inflammatory chemical messengers is, therefore, important in lowering the levels of inflammation. This can be attained through conscious changes to diet and lifestyle, including appropriate supplementation.

Consuming foods rich in the omega-3 essential fatty acids, eicosapentaenoic acid (EPA) and docosahexaenoic acid (DHA), derived from fish oil, has a profound impact on reducing inflammation. When an appropriate balance of omega-3 to omega-6 essential fats is consumed, production of anti-inflammatory signalling chemicals, called prostaglandins,* is favoured and inflammation is kept in check.[111] Increasing the consumption of foods rich in omega-3 fats, such as salmon and other cold-water fish, or supplementing with a high quality ultra-refined fish oil, suppresses the formation of inflammation promoting prostaglandins while stimulating the synthesis of the beneficial ones.[112,113] Because the modern North American diet contains 10 to 20 times the amount of omega-6 oils that we need, the most sensible dietary approach is to reduce sources of omega-6 oils and supplement with

> Alpha linolenic acid can be found in a variety of other plant sources, such as pumpkin seeds, walnuts and other nuts; however, flaxseed—by far the richest source of this important omega-3 oil—contains a whopping 58% by weight.

---

* *Prostatglandins belong to a large class of oxygenated fatty acids called the eicosanoids. They are derived from the essential fatty acids supplied through our diet. Eicosanoids are actually primitive hormones from our evolutionary past that act as localized cellular signalling molecules.*

high-dose omega-3 oils to bring us back to an optimal 4:1 ratio of omega-6/omega-3.[114]

Supplementing with flaxseed oil is another effective means of optimizing your omega-6/omega-3 ratio. Anti-inflammatory EPA can actually be manufactured in the body through the conversion of alpha linolenic acid, another omega-3 fat prevalent in flaxseed oil. Supplementation with the oil, along with restriction of omega-6 fatty acid intake, raises tissue EPA levels to those comparable with the use of fish-oil. In fact, flaxseed oil contains more than *twice* the omega-3 fats as fish oil. Alpha linolenic acid can be found in a variety of other plant sources, such as pumpkin seeds, walnuts and other nuts; however, flaxseed—by far the richest source of this important omega-3 oil—contains a whopping 58% by weight.[114]

Gamma tocopherol is another nutrient that plays a pivotal role in quenching inflammation.[115] Acting through a mechanism unavailable to alpha tocopherol, gamma tocopherol reacts with and neutralizes toxic reactive nitrogen oxide (RNO) radicals, thereby subduing inflammation.[116] Gamma tocopherol can also reduce inflammation by inhibiting cyclooxygenase-2 (COX-2), an enzyme central to the inflammatory process. COX-2 controls the synthesis of inflammatory prostaglandin E2. Administration of gamma tocopherol has been found to reduce several other powerful inflammatory protagonists at the site of inflammation.[117]

Lipoic acid (LA) is both a water-soluble and fat-soluble antioxidant. Capable of preventing oxidative damage in the cytosol (the fluid portion) of the cell and within the cell membranes, LA is able to neutralize reactive nitrogen oxide and oxygen species, including one of the most damaging free radicals of all—the hydroxyl (OH) radical.[118] While all antioxidants possess some anti-inflammatory properties, LA's aptitude as an anti-inflammatory agent is highly regarded. LA is a potent inhibitor of nuclear factor kappa beta (NFkß), the nuclear transcription factor that is activated in response to oxidative stress. NFkß, once activated, switches on genes that manufacture several pro-inflammatory chemicals. For this reason, the presence of lipoic acid is critical to the cell's ability to reduce inflammation.[119]

There is substantial evidence that supplementation with physiological doses (doses in the range provided in a normal diet) of vitamin C can also depress clinical markers of inflammation, including tumor necrosis factor-beta (TNF-ß)[120] and C-reactive protein.[121] In an investigation of the effect of antioxidant therapy in the recurrence of atrial fibrillation, vitamin C dramatically lowered the rate of recurrence from 36.3% to 4.5% and attenuated the associated low-level inflammatory response.[122] Importantly, intracellular vitamin C can inhibit the activation of NFkß.[123] High-dose supplementation with vitamin C can also reduce dysfunction of the endothelial lining of blood vessels, caused by acute inflammation,[124] and it can suppress apoptosis (cell death) of endothelial cells damaged from an inflammatory response.[125]

New research has revealed that the plant-based flavonoids not only serve as effective antioxidants, they also modulate cell-signalling processes that influence inflammatory events.[126] Several recent studies reveal

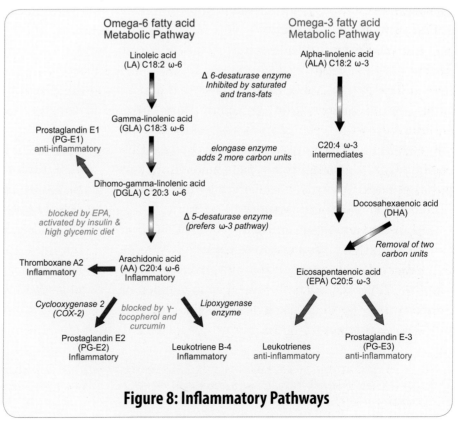

Figure 8: Inflammatory Pathways

that, as a group, flavonoids possess remarkable anti-inflammatory abilities, including the ability to subdue the generation of prostaglandin E2.[127-129] Numerous studies report that flavonoids inhibit the activity of the dangerous inflammation-promoting enzyme cyclooxygenase-2,[128,130] calm the inflammation-signalling molecule NFkß and inhibit the synthesis of the inflammatory mediator nitric oxide (NO).[131] Resveratrol, a type of polyphenol found in grapes, has been shown to inhibit the expression of inflammatory cytokines* in vivo (within the body)[132] and block the activation of other cell-signalling molecules, including NFkß.[133] Through its ability to inhibit NFkß activation, resveratrol, along with other flavonoids, can effectively control inflammation at a critical choke point, thereby influencing a wide variety of inflammatory pathways.

Similar to resveratrol, green tea polyphenols can inhibit the activation of NFkß and, through this mechanism, control a wide variety of inflammatory pathways. They are also believed to be neuroprotective, invoking a spectrum of cellular mechanisms, including the chelation of metals, scavenging of free radicals, activation of anti-inflammation signalling pathways and modulation of mitochondrial function in nervous tissues.[134] Green tea polyphenols are now being considered as therapeutic agents to alter brain processes and to serve as neuroprotective agents in progressive neurodegenerative disorders, such as Alzheimer's and Parkinson's disease.[135]

A review by Bengmark (2006) shows that almost 1500 papers dealing with curcumin have been published in recent years—an indication of the level of interest this nutrient is attracting within the scientific community.[136] Curcumin is completely non-toxic and possesses potent antioxidant activity; a natural phenol, it is found in the South Asian spice turmeric. It has been shown to inhibit such mediators of inflammation as NFkß, phospholipase, cyclooxygenase-2 (COX-2), lipoxygenase (LOX) and inducible nitric oxide synthase (iNOS). Moreover, studies show that a number of inflammation-signalling cytokines (proteins) are also inhibited by curcumin.

Recent studies have examined the anti-inflammatory nature of virgin olive oil and of the olive-vegetation water expressed from the processing of the oil. The findings show that, similar to the polyphenols found in green tea, grapes and turmeric, olive oil phenols can reduce the expression of a key inflammatory cytokine, tumor necrosis factor alpha (TNF-alpha) and decrease the production of the inflammation-promoting enzyme, inducible nitric oxide synthase (iNOS).[137] In several recent studies, olive oil phenols have demonstrated protective anti-inflammatory effects by reducing atherosclerotic lesions,[138] thereby reducing major risk factors for cardiovascular disease, including endothelial dysfunction.[139] They are also effective in lowering the expression of inflammation-signalling molecules in human inflammatory bowel disease.[140] Several researchers consider the consumption of virgin olive oil and olive extracts a valued strategy in the prevention of inflammation.

There are, indeed, a wide variety of nutrients that are involved in fighting systemic inflammation, and we have included these in our Inflammation Control criterion. These nutrients and nutrient categories include eicosapentaenoic and docosahexaenoic acids; linolenic acid; gamma tocopherol; alpha lipoic acid; vitamin C; flavonoids; procyanidolic oligomers; and the phenolic compounds found in green tea, turmeric (curcumin) and olive extracts. All are proven inflammation antagonists.

The criterion for Inflammation Control poses the following question:

Does the product contain eicosapentaenoic and docosahexaenoic acids, linolenic acid, gamma tocopherol, alpha lipoic acid, vitamin C, vitamin D, iodine, flavonoids, procyanidolic oligomers and the phenolic compounds from green tea, olive and turmeric extracts at potencies up to 100% of the potencies for these nutrients or nutrient categories in the Blended Standard?

---

* Cytokines are proteinaceous signalling compounds, similar to hormones and neurotransmitters, which are used extensively for localized inter-cellular communication.

15. *Glycation Control*

Aging—the outcome of the conflict between chemistry and biology in living systems—introduces chronic cumulative chemical modifications that compromise the structure and function of important biomolecules within our cells. We now know that changes to these molecular structures, driven by oxidative stress, can render them dysfunctional. Their accumulation, the detritus of an ongoing oxidative war within the cell, is a hallmark of the aging process.

Proteins with long life spans serve as convenient molecular repositories for cumulative oxidative damage, which is detectable in the form of advanced glycation and lipoxidation end-products (AGEs and ALEs).[141] A telltale sign of protein oxidation is the addition of carbonyl groups ($>C=O$) to particular amino acids within a protein's structure. Carbonylation is an irreversible process;[142] just as you cannot unscramble an egg, carbonylated proteins, once formed, must be destroyed and expunged from the cell. Normally, they are marked for degradation by the cell's proteolytic enzymes; however, they can also escape to form aggregates within the cell that accumulate with age. Carbonylation of proteins occurs through direct oxidative attack from free radicals and metal ions, from reactions with oxidized sugars and lipid peroxides (oxidized fats), and through the process of glycation.[143]

Glycation (also called glycosylation) is the complexing of a protein with a sugar to form a molecular arrangement that irreversibly alters the structure of the protein and destroys its functionality. The effects of glycation can be seen in the browning of a glazed ham or turkey during the cooking process. Essentially, the same things happen in the human body, which acts much like a low-temperature oven (37°C) with a 76-year cooking cycle.[144] Over time, non-enzymatic reactions between sugars and proteins generate a 'browning' of our cells with an inexorable accumulation of dysfunctional glycosylated proteins.

Excessive glycation is a common occurrence in diabetes. Fuelled by high blood-sugar levels, glycation is responsible for much of the damage to tissues and organs that is a hallmark of the disease, including disruption of the transport of blood gases, development of cataracts and diabetic retinopathy, destruction of the myelin sheath of nerve cells and the development of diabetic neuropathies. For the diabetic, the consequences of uncontrolled glycation can prove deadly.

The build-up of glycosylated proteins also leads to molecular cross linking and further oxidative modifications, resulting in the formation of AGE deposits. These high-molecular-weight aggregates can become toxic to the cell.[145] A growing body of evidence suggests that AGEs and similar toxic rubble (ALEs) from ongoing lipid peroxidation contribute to the progress of several degenerative diseases, including Parkinson's disease, Alzheimer's disease and cancer. [141,146-149]

Carnosine, a simple dipeptide of the amino acids beta alanine and l-histidine, has emerged as the most promising broad-spectrum shield to date against the damaging oxidative modification of proteins.[150] In multiple studies, the peptide has been shown to inhibit lipid peroxidation, free radical induced oxidative damage, protein glycation, AGE formation and protein-protein cross linking.[151-154] As an antioxidant, it reduces carbonylation; as a chelator of metal ions, it interrupts their ability to catalyze other forms of oxidative protein modification. Carnosine acts as a natural scavenger of toxic reactive aldehydes produced from the degradation of fats, sugars and proteins. As well, carnosine inhibits the cross linking of proteins that leads to the formation of AGEs.[152] Senile plaque formation of amyloid-beta protein is stimulated in the presence of metal ions, such as copper and zinc. As a chelator of these metals, carnosine helps prevent the formation of these plaques.

Most importantly, carnosine shields normal proteins from the toxic reach of AGEs already present in the cell.[155] By offering itself as a sacrificial target and binding preferentially to glucose, carnosine spares important cellular proteins from oxidative

> The effects of glycation can be seen in the browning of a glazed ham or turkey during the cooking process. Essentially, the same things happen in the human body, which acts much like a low-temperature oven (37°C) with a 76-year cooking cycle.

degradation.[156] In the process, carnosine sacrifices itself, becoming glycosylated and forming a non-mutagenic derivative that can be safely degraded by the cell.[157] Some researchers have observed that carnosine's ability to address the challenges of protein modification fits the bill so well, it appears that the molecule was designed by nature to address this unique need.[150]

While carnosine is available in the US market, it is restricted in products manufactured for the Canadian market. Regardless of this, our Health Support criteria are evidence-based and do not consider the regulatory question. Consequently, we have included carnosine as a critical component of our Glycation Control criterion.

High doses of vitamin C and E, separately and in combination, have also been found to confer protection against glycation.[158,159] The combination of vitamins C and E was found to block the formation of protein cross links and delay collagen aging in young mice.[160] As well, these nutrients can reduce levels of glycosylated haemoglobin and low-density lipoproteins in diabetic animals.[161] A cross-sectional study investigating the association of diet and lifestyle with levels of glycosylated blood proteins in non-diabetic adults demonstrated that a high intake of these antioxidants strongly correlated with a reduced level of glycation.[162]

In animal-model studies, alpha lipoic acid has also been found to prevent glycation and the inactivation of proteins.[163] It has been proposed that supplementation with alpha lipoic acid and vitamin E may directly strengthen the anti-glycation defense mechanisms in the brain to protect against Alzheimer's disease.[164] When human blood cells are treated with alpha lipoic acid, they demonstrate a marked reduction in lipid peroxide levels.

The criterion for Glycation Control poses the following question:

Does the product contain l-carnosine, vitamin E (including alpha tocopherol and gamma tocopherol or mixed tocopherols), vitamin C and alpha lipoic acid at potencies up to 100% of the potencies for those nutrients or nutrient categories listed in the Blended Standard?

16. Bioflavonoid Profile

Polyphenols are a diverse class of compounds found naturally in the leaves, bark, roots, flowers and seeds of plants. Citrus fruits, grapes, olives, tea leaves, bark, vegetables, dark berries, whole grains and nuts are particularly rich sources of these natural antioxidants. Polyphenol pigments are largely responsible for the brightly coloured hues of ripened fruits and vegetables. Within the plant, they guard the cells from disease, filter out harmful ultraviolet light and protect the delicate plant seeds until germination. When consumed in the diet, polyphenols become prodigious free radical scavengers, conferring numerous health benefits. There is evidence that some phenolic compounds also help detoxify the body by chelating with metals and facilitating their removal.[165,166]

There are two major groups of polyphenols, differentiated on the basis of their structural formula: the flavonoids and the phenolic compounds (derived from phenolic acids). The flavonoids are known as 'nature's biological response modifiers' because of their ability to alter the body's reactions to allergens, viruses and carcinogens and to protect cellular tissues against oxidative attack. Flavonoids, found in the edible pulp of many fruits and vegetables, impart a bitter taste when isolated. Citrus fruits, such as oranges, lemons, limes, grapefruit and kiwi, are particularly rich sources of flavonoids. Rose hips, cherries, black currents, grapes, green peppers, broccoli, onions and tomatoes are also high in these compounds, as are many herbs, including bilberry, ginkgo, yarrow, Hawthorne berry and milk thistle. Other flavonoid compounds are found in the leaves, bark and seeds of various plant species. The leaves of *Camellia sinensis* (dried to make green and black tea), the bark of the maritime (*Landes*) pine and the seeds of ripened grapes are excellent sources of a variety of flavonoid compounds. As well, soybeans, nuts and whole grains are replete with a class of flavonoids known as isoflavones.

Flavonoids are important for the health and integrity of blood vessels. Through their ability to decrease permeability, flavonoids can reduce microvascular haemorrhaging and enhance capillary strength. The flavonoids confer cardio-protective benefits specifically through their ability to prevent oxidation of cholesterol.

This ability is reported to be similar to, and possibly more potent than, the antioxidant powers of vitamins C and E. The scientific literature is filled with studies reporting the beneficial effects of dietary flavonoids in human health. Flavonoids, along with beta carotene, vitamin C and vitamin E, may be the cell's principal cancer chemopreventive agents. Their abundance in fruit and vegetables underlies the strong correlation between high fruit and vegetable consumption and reduced cancer risks.[167,168]

Citrus flavonoids, also called bioflavonoids, are, perhaps, the largest of the flavonoid groups. Studies indicate they can relax smooth muscles in the arteries, reduce vascular permeability and enhance the strength of capillaries, thereby lowering blood pressure and improving circulation. As well as possessing anti-inflammatory properties, citrus flavonoids exhibit powerful antioxidant properties and protect the cardiovascular system from harmful lipid peroxidation. Quercetin, one of the most biologically active of the flavonoids, serves as the backbone for many of the citrus flavonoids. Quercetin is indicated in the prevention of diabetes, due to its ability to enhance insulin production, protect the insulin-producing beta cells in the pancreas and inhibit platelet aggregation (a principle cause of blood clotting in diabetics).[169] In animal studies, quercetin has proved effective against a wide variety of cancers.[170] Unfortunately, there is little human research available to assess its efficacy. Other important citrus flavonoids, including rutin, quercitrin and hesperidin, are derivatives of quercetin. The subtle differences in the chemistry of these compounds are a consequence of the various sugar molecules attached to the quercetin backbone.

According to Bagchi,[171] the flavonoids found in grape seed extract (GSE) are highly bioavailable. Proanthocyanidins, the active components of GSE, form a complex of bioflavonoid compounds, known as procyanidolic oligomers (PCOs). This unique

group of flavonoids appears to confer the cardio-protective benefits noted by consumers of red wine. PCO compounds also exhibit cytotoxicity (cell-killing ability) against several types of cancer cells, increase intracellular levels of vitamin C, enhance capillary stability and inhibit the destruction of collagen.[172,173]

The antioxidant actions of flavonoids appear to protect blood lipids from oxidative damage by quenching lipid peroxidation.[174,175] These properties complement and enhance the antioxidant powers of vitamin C, vitamin E and the carotenoids. Flavonoids also possess several other important pharmacological properties: they are anti-bacterial, anti-viral, anti-inflammatory, anti-allergic, anti-hemorrhagic and vasodilatory.[176-180]

The criterion for the Bioflavonoid Profile poses the following question:

Does the product contain a mixture of bioflavonoids (including citrus and other flavonoids, billberry flavones and related extracts, hesperidin, quercetin, quercitrin, rutin, soy isoflavones, and silymarin and related milk thistle extracts) and PCOs (including grape seed and grape seed extract, Hawthorne berry and Hawthorne berry extract, pine bark and

Figure 9: Vegetable Stall
Brightly coloured and green leafy vegetables are an excellent source of bioflavonoids, phenolic compounds and other vital nutrients.

pine bark extract, pycnogenol and resveratrol) at potencies up to 100% of the recommended potencies for mixed bioflavonoids and PCOs in the Blended Standard?

17. *Phenolic Compounds Profile*

Phenolic compounds are derivatives of the phenolic acids, hydroxycinnamic acid and hydroxybenzoic acid. These compounds differ from the flavonoids in that they are composed of a single six-carbon ring, known as an aromatic or cyclic ring, which provides them with a strong electron-donating ability. The many different phenolic compounds found in nature are variations of these basic structures, with a wide variety of different groups attached to this basic hydrocarbon skeleton. The difference in the ring structure in the phenolic compounds, compared to the flavonoids, provides for a slightly different (but equally valuable) chemical nature.

The most intensely studied of the phenolic compounds include:

- ✓ turmeric, a perennial herb of the ginger family and a major ingredient in curry. Long used in Chinese and Ayurvedic (Indian) medicine as an anti-inflammatory, it is an effective antioxidant, anticarcinogenic, cardiovascular and hepatic agent.
- ✓ green tea, a rich source of a class of polyphenolic compounds called catechins. These antioxidant compounds possess powerful anti-mutagenic properties, protecting cellular DNA from oxidative damage.[181]
- ✓ olive extracts containing tyrosol, hydroxytyrosol and the oleuropeine glycosides, found in the fruit of the olive tree. Extra Virgin olive oil, extracted from the first cold press of the olive, derives its unique aroma, pungent taste and high thermal stability from these complex aromatic compounds.[166]

The weight of scientific evidence supporting the health benefits of the dietary consumption of polyphenols is immense. Their power as free radical antagonists, their recognized efficacy in reducing cardiovascular and cancer risks and their demonstrated pharmacologic properties as anti-inflammatory, anti-viral, anti-bacterial, anti-allergic, anti-hemorrhagic and immuno-enhancing agents, make an exceptionally

strong case for their inclusion in nutritional supplementation. The International Consensus Statement, issued by the European Commission in 1997, promoting the adoption of the Mediterranean diet, echoes the scientific findings: the consumption of olive oil and the phenolic compounds derived from the fruit of the olive tree confers significant health benefits.

The biochemistry of polyphenols is an emerging area of nutritional research; because of its novel nature, there is not yet a quantitative consensus among our cited nutritional authorities with respect to daily intake. While there is recognition that supplementation with polyphenols is highly desirable, no median recommended daily intake specific to phenolic compounds is yet available. For this reason, NutriSearch has turned to the available scientific literature (Visioli et al)[165,182] in order to establish a recommended daily intake of 25 mg of phenolic compounds as the basis for our *Blended Standard*.

The criterion for the Phenolic Compounds Profile poses the following question:

Does the product contain phenolic compounds (polyphenolic acids and their derivatives, including cinnamon bark and cinnamon bark extract, cranberry and cranberry extract, curcumin, fenugreek, ginger and gingerols, green tea leaf and green tea extracts, olive fruit and olive extracts, papaya, pomegranate fruit and pomegranate extract, rosemary and turmeric rhizome) at the potency for this nutrient category established in the Blended Standard?

18. *Potential Toxicities*

In order to optimize preventive-health benefits, the strategy of nutritional supplementation is to encourage long-term use. Consequently, there exists a potential risk for consumers with regard to the cumulative toxicity of particular nutrients. It would be foolish to supplement with high levels of certain nutrients only to find down the road that your investment, instead of promoting wellbeing, has jeopardized your health. Most nutrients used in nutritional supplements have a high degree of safety; however, some nutrients require a degree of prudence when it comes to long-term use.

Vitamin A (retinol), because of its solubility in fatty tissues, can become toxic when taken in high doses over a long period. As well, chronic iron overload can significantly increase the level of oxidative damage to cells. Accidental overdose of iron-containing supplements is, in fact, a leading cause of fatal poisoning in children. This is not to say that vitamin A and iron are not important to the health of our cells; both nutrients play crucial roles in cellular metabolism. However, it is important to be aware that there exist safe and effective alternatives for meeting the daily requirements for these nutrients without compromising one's health through imprudent use. Because of their importance in cellular health and their potential for cumulative damage, either too much or too little vitamin A and iron is problematic.

> Excessive iron supplementation in any form can create problems for the cell. Iron overload can cause deterioration of the gut lining, vomiting and diarrhoea, abdominal and joint pain, liver damage, loss of weight and intense fatigue.

Vitamin A

Despite the prevalence of vitamin A deficiency, retinol toxicity is a common occurrence. As many as 5% of those who supplement with vitamin A unknowingly suffer from toxicity symptoms.[183] Supplementation at 5,000-10,000 IU per day of pre-formed vitamin A—a dose well within the range offered in many popular vitamin supplements—may lead to a cumulative toxic overdose.[184] As well, accidental ingestion of a single large dose of vitamin A can produce acute toxicity in children. One study of over 22,000 pregnant women who supplemented with vitamin A during early pregnancy found that, among the babies born to women who took more than 10,000 IU of preformed vitamin A per day in the form of supplements, about 1 infant in 57 had a malformation attributable to the supplement. [185,186]

Consumption of more than 10,000 IU of vitamin A carries a five-fold greater risk of birth defects than does consumption of less than 5,000 IU per day. Rothman and co-workers[186] found that the prevalence of birth defects appears greatest in those women who consume high levels of the pre-formed vitamin within the first seven weeks of their pregnancy. The authors conclude that women who might become pregnant should limit their retinol intake to below 5,000 IU. An alternative is to supplement, instead, with beta carotene.

Beta carotene, the orange/yellow-coloured pigment found in many garden vegetables, is a retinol precursor. The body easily converts beta carotene into vitamin A by cleaving the carotene molecule into two molecules of retinol as needed, thereby avoiding the toxic accumulation of pre-formed vitamin A. Once transformed into active retinol, beta carotene confers the same beneficial effects. Other than occasional loose stools or slight discoloration of the skin, even high doses of beta carotene do not exhibit toxicity. As an added benefit, beta carotene is a much more potent antioxidant than retinol and provides even greater protection against oxidative challenge.

Iron

Iron plays an important role in the physiology of the body. As a central part of the haemoglobin and myoglobin molecules, iron is indispensable to the body's ability to transport gases into and out of the cell. It is also needed in several important enzymes involved in energy production, metabolism and DNA synthesis. Some iron is lost through the breakdown of red blood cells and excretion in the bile. However, due to its importance, the body conserves iron at all costs; the kidneys do not eliminate the metal.

The dark side of iron supplementation arises when it is consumed in amounts excessive to the body's needs. While unbound (non-haeme) iron is more likely to generate oxidative challenges through free radical generation, excessive iron supplementation in any form can create problems for the cell. Iron overload can cause deterioration of the gut lining, vomiting and diarrhoea, abdominal and joint pain, liver damage, loss of weight and intense fatigue.[187] Acute doses as low as three grams can cause death in children.

Approximately one out of every 250 North Americans suffers from haemochromatosis, a gene polymorphism common in those of northern European descent. The disorder causes the body to accumulate and store abnormally high levels of iron. People with haemochromatosis store twice as much iron as others, placing themselves at increased risk for iron-related diseases. Symptoms generally occur after 50 years of age and include fatigue, abdominal pain, achy joints, impotence and symptoms that mimic diabetes. Evidence from several studies suggests that high levels of iron contribute to a noticeable increase in the risk for cardiovascular disease, likely due to non-haeme iron's aggressive pro-oxidant nature. Serum ferritin (iron) levels are, in fact, one of the strongest biochemical markers for the progression of atherosclerosis, a consequence of dramatically increased oxidation of LDL cholesterol.[188] A 1995 study, conducted on Finnish men, found that those with high body stores of iron had a substantially increased risk of heart attack. Men with the highest levels of stored iron showed a level of risk three times that of men with the lowest levels.[189]

Iron accumulation disorders contribute to a variety of other disease states, all of which are degenerative in nature. Studies reveal that chronic iron overload contributes to increased infections, cancer, arthritis, osteoporosis, diabetes and various cognitive dysfunctions.[190,191] Data obtained from the first National Health and Nutrition Examination Survey (NHANES I), linking body-stores of iron and cancer, found an elevated risk was associated with high iron levels.[192] Unless you are a woman with regular menses (menstrual periods), the only way to remove excess iron is through bloodletting. That is why, for men, iron overload can prove quite problematic. Research conducted in 2004 found evidence that long-term supplementation in dialysis patients with iron at doses less than 5 mg/day can lead to iron-overload toxicity.[193] Consequently, this guide has adopted an upper limit of iron intake at 5 mg/day when considering a product's rating. Any product containing iron at a daily dose greater than this limit is penalized in this rating criterion.

The criterion for Potential Toxicities poses the following questions:

Does the nutritional supplement contain vitamin A and iron (which is no longer included in the Blended Standard)? Does the potency of vitamin A exceed 100% of the potency for that nutrient in the Blended Standard? Does the potency of iron exceed 5 mg/day?

Summary

The 18 individual Health Support ratings, as described above, are pooled for each product to provide a raw product score. These scores are then categorized by percent rank, which represents a product's rating relative to all products evaluated.

Final product ratings are displayed as star ratings, shown in half-star increments from zero to five stars. The five-star scale is, at once, both visual and intuitive: a five-star product represents a product of the highest quality relative to all products evaluated in accordance with our analysis model. Conversely, a one-star rating or less represents products possessing few, if any, of the characteristics for optimal nutrition as reflected in this analysis.

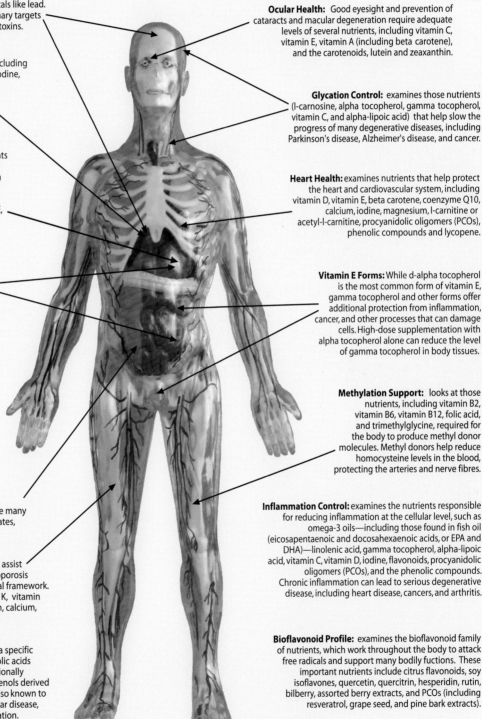

Completeness: looks to see if the product contains all the Blended Standard nutrients.

Potency: looks to see how much of each nutrient the product contains compared to the Blended Standard amounts.

Antioxidant Support: examines the nutrients that help to prevent or repair cellular damage caused by oxidation, including vitamin C, vitamin E, vitamin A, beta carotene, alpha-lipoic acid, lycopene, coenzyme Q10, iodine, and selenium.

Immune Support: Recent scientific research confirms the vital roles that vitamin D and iodine play in maintaining our long-term health. This new criterion examines the many nutrients, including vitamin D and iodine, which help to ward off many of the most common degenerative diseases that shorten our lives.

Lipotropic Factors: examines those nutrients, including choline, lecithin, and inositol, that help remove toxins, including heavy metals like lead. The liver and the brain are two primary targets for the accumulation of fat-soluble toxins.

Ocular Health: Good eyesight and prevention of cataracts and macular degeneration require adequate levels of several nutrients, including vitamin C, vitamin E, vitamin A (including beta carotene), and the carotenoids, lutein and zeaxanthin.

Liver Health: examines those nutrients (including vitamin C, cysteine and n-acetyl cysteine, iodine, selenium, vitamin B2, and vitamin B3) that enhance liver function and optimize levels of glutathione, which helps cells to fight off toxic challenges.

Glycation Control: examines those nutrients (l-carnosine, alpha tocopherol, gamma tocopherol, vitamin C, and alpha-lipoic acid) that help slow the progress of many degenerative diseases, including Parkinson's disease, Alzheimer's disease, and cancer.

Metabolic Health: examines those nutrients that help the body handle its daily sugar load, keeping systems responsive to insulin and restoring lost insulin sensitivity. These nutrients include vitamin B3, vitamin B6, vitamin B12, vitamin C, vitamin D, vitamin E, biotin, coenzyme Q10, chromium, iodine, magnesium, manganese, and zinc.

Heart Health: examines nutrients that help protect the heart and cardiovascular system, including vitamin D, vitamin E, beta carotene, coenzyme Q10, calcium, iodine, magnesium, l-carnitine or acetyl-l-carnitine, procyanidolic oligomers (PCOs), phenolic compounds and lycopene.

Potential Toxicities: examines those nutrients that can build up in the body, possibly leading to toxic levels with long-term intake. This includes vitamin A and iron. Accidental overdose of iron-containing supplements is, in fact, a leading cause of fatal poisoning in children. Vitamin A is available, safely, as beta carotene, while adequate iron is easily obtainable for most people from foods.

Vitamin E Forms: While d-alpha tocopherol is the most common form of vitamin E, gamma tocopherol and other forms offer additional protection from inflammation, cancer, and other processes that can damage cells. High-dose supplementation with alpha tocopherol alone can reduce the level of gamma tocopherol in body tissues.

Mineral Forms: examines the molecules that minerals are bound with to help them cross into the bloodstream. Amino acid chelates and organic acid complexes (such as citrates and gluconates) mimic the natural mineral chelates that form during the digestive process. Chelated minerals also appear not to block other minerals from being absorbed, unlike many of the less expensive mineral salts (carbonates, sulphates, and chlorides).

Methylation Support: looks at those nutrients, including vitamin B2, vitamin B6, vitamin B12, folic acid, and trimethylglycine, required for the body to produce methyl donor molecules. Methyl donors help reduce homocysteine levels in the blood, protecting the arteries and nerve fibres.

Bone Health: examines the nutrients that assist in bone remodeling, vital to ward off osteoporosis and other diseases that weaken the skeletal framework. These nutrients include vitamin D, vitamin K, vitamin C, vitamin B6, vitamin B12, folic acid, boron, calcium, magnesium, silicon, and zinc.

Inflammation Control: examines the nutrients responsible for reducing inflammation at the cellular level, such as omega-3 oils—including those found in fish oil (eicosapentaenoic and docosahexaenoic acids, or EPA and DHA)—linolenic acid, gamma tocopherol, alpha-lipoic acid, vitamin C, vitamin D, iodine, flavonoids, procyanidolic oligomers (PCOs), and the phenolic compounds. Chronic inflammation can lead to serious degenerative disease, including heart disease, cancers, and arthritis.

Phenolic Compounds Profile: examines a specific group of phenolic compounds (polyphenolic acids and their derivatives), known to be exceptionally potent defenders against free radicals. Phenols derived from olives, green tea, and curcumin are also known to improve major risk factors for cardiovascular disease, including lowering the impact of inflammation.

Bioflavonoid Profile: examines the bioflavonoid family of nutrients, which work throughout the body to attack free radicals and support many bodily fuctions. These important nutrients include citrus flavonoids, soy isoflavones, quercetin, quercitrin, hesperidin, rutin, bilberry, assorted berry extracts, and PCOs (including resveratrol, grape seed, and pine bark extracts).

Figure 10: Eighteen Important Health Support Criteria

> Quality means doing it right when no one is looking.
>
> — *Henry Ford (1863 – 1947)*

CHAPTER SEVEN:

MEDALS OF ACHIEVEMENT

In the production of nutritional supplements, the use of appropriate manufacturing standards (Good Manufacturing Practices) and laboratory verification of the finished product are the consumer's best assurances of quality and safety. These assurances are provided by federal regulations that can differ markedly from country to country.

Australia undoubtedly has some of the toughest product manufacturing regulations in the world, requiring all manufacturers of dietary supplements to register their products as listed medicines. All nutritional products manufactured in or sold into the Australian market must manufacture to Good Manufacturing Practices (GMP), based on pharmaceutical standards of quality and safety. Similar to Australia, Canada requires all manufacturers of natural health products (NHPs)* sold in or into Canada to comply with federally mandated manufacturing and product-quality standards that approach the level of oversight required for pharmaceutical products. The United States, on the other hand, eschews such rigorous regulatory oversight; compliance with pharmaceutical-model manufacturing and quality standards is entirely voluntary. In the US, it is up to the manufacturer, not any government agency, to determine if their products are safe. Moreover, unlike Canada and Australia, which require certification audits prior to obtaining a product license, the US FDA does not require manufacturers to register or licence their products prior to marketing.

On June 25, 2007, the US FDA established regulations entitled *Current Good Manufacturing Practice (cGMP) In Manufacturing, Packaging, Labeling, Or Holding Operations For Dietary Supplements.* These regulations oblige companies who manufacture, package, label or hold dietary supplements to establish and follow current good manufacturing practices (cGMP) to ensure the quality of the products manufactured. These regulations, which were phased in over the last several years, are now in full effect. While a step in the right direction, the new regulations are based on far less stringent *food-grade* GMP, rather than *pharmaceutical-grade* GMP.

With respect to post-market surveillance, Australia conducts regular post-market audits of manufacturing sites and products, both domestically and world-wide, for every manufacturer who sells in or into the country. Canada, while it has the statutory authority to do so, falls woefully short on providing assurances of post-market manufacturing quality. The United States lacks any post-market surveillance program whatsoever; in the US, the FDA only investigates products *after* problems are found. It is because of this lack of post-market oversight that the purchase of nutritional supplements in both Canada and the United States continues to remain an issue of *buyer beware.*

Assessing Product Quality

How a nutritional product is made—what's in it and what's not *supposed* to be in it—is critical to the quality and safety of the finished product. That is why NutriSearch has introduced a level of product assessment, called the *NutriSearch Medal of Achievement Program,*[TM] that looks beyond product content and

---

* *In Canada, vitamins, minerals and herbal products are commonly known as natural health products (NHPs) or nutritional supplements. Conversely, in the United States, such products are commonly known as dietary supplements.*

investigates how a product is manufactured (level of GMP compliance). Through independent laboratory testing, we also look at what is actually in the finished product.

This higher standard of evidence incurs considerable cost and effort on the part of the selected manufacturers; consequently, it is offered only to those manufacturers whose products merit a five-star rating, based upon our initial content analysis. For these top-rated products, each manufacturer must provide notarized certification showing:

✔ a level of GMP compliance modelled on pharmaceutical standards;

✔ 3rd-party laboratory verification of product identity, potency and purity according to label claim.

Together, GMP certification and laboratory-based content analysis provide assurance to the consumer that the product meets established standards for manufacturing safety and product quality, and that what is on the label is really in the bottle.

Currently, in the United States there are two independent, non-government programs that NutriSearch recognizes for the evaluation of GMP compliance for nutritional (dietary) supplements. Each program has its own standard of GMP compliance.

These programs are:

✔ NSF International Dietary Supplement Verification Program;

✔ USP Dietary Supplement Verification Program.

For US-based companies who sell dietary supplements into Canada or Australia, two additional standards of evidence are recognized by NutriSearch. Both Health Canada's NHPD and the Australian TGA will license US-based manufacturers in accordance with their respective national standards. Accordingly, NutriSearch will accept evidence of compliance with either of these manufacturing standards as verification of GMP compliance for both US and Canadian products. Such products will bear a Health Canada Natural Product Number (NPN) or will be listed in the Australian Register of Therapeutic Goods.

> When a manufacturer or supplier contacts the NSF Dietary Supplements Certification Program Office, an NSF representative will assist the manufacturer through a five-step certification process.

Overview of the Available Certification Programs

The following discussion will provide the reader with an overview of the various government and non-government programs available in the United States and Canada that provide certification for dietary (nutritional) supplements.

The USP Dietary Supplement Verification Program

The USP Dietary Supplement Verification Program (DSVP) sets GMP standards that approach pharmaceutical-model GMP. Although the organization does not claim to address all safety issues, USP will not accept a supplement into its program that contains an ingredient with known safety concerns.

Even before USP begins its verification of a product, the applicant must pass three criteria:

✔ A detailed checklist for USP GMP compliance;

✔ verification of validated analytical methodologies for each ingredient in the product;

✔ validation of finished product shelf-life.

Once a supplement has been accepted, USP conducts a three-day site audit based on its GMP model for dietary supplements, published in its General Chapter 2750 *Manufacturing Practices for Dietary Supplements*. The detailed audit examines personnel, document management, equipment, facilities, component control, maintenance, record keeping, laboratory controls, label control, quality control and performance reviews.

Product verification includes laboratory testing for ingredient identity and potency. Testing for contamination with microbes, heavy metals, pesticides and other toxins is also conducted. The USP product verification program quantitatively evaluates all active ingredients, where possible, in a product. Product performance characteristics, including dissolution and disintegration, weight variation and content uniformity, are also examined. Post-market surveillance, self-audits and mandatory reporting of changes to the product or production processes are all part of the ongoing participation in the DSVP. If critical product deficiencies are detected, USP may recommend a recall of the product or demand removal of the DSVP certification mark.

NutriSearch considers the USP DSVP to be the definitive standard for both facility and product verification. For further information on the USP Dietary Supplement Certification Program, contact the United States Pharmacopoeia, 12601 Twinbrook Parkway, Rockville, Maryland 20852-1790, USA. You can also contact the program by calling 1-301-816-8273 or by e-mail at uspverified@usp.org.

NSF Dietary Supplements Certification Program

The NSF Dietary Supplements Certification Program includes both facility audits and laboratory-based product verification; each step of the program uses third-party agents selected by NSF. When a manufacturer or supplier contacts the NSF Dietary Supplements Certification Program Office, an NSF representative will assist the manufacturer through a five-step certification process. This process includes application, formulation review, facility audit, product testing, documentation-report registration and certification. Initial facility inspections for certification are conducted by trained NSF field auditors and include a GMP audit and assessment of conformity to NSF policies. Products are then tested at NSF laboratories to verify conformity to the NSF Dietary Supplement Standard - NSF 173-2001.

Product assessment includes testing of raw materials as well as the finished product. Testing includes identity, quantity, consistency and purity, where analytical criteria can be established. Tolerances for purity of ingredients and contamination standards are adopted from several sources, including the World Health Organization, the NSF International Standards, USP, British Pharmacopeia, European Pharmacopeia and Health Canada. Certification is awarded after all of the requirements for listing have been successfully completed. Annual audits and product testing are conducted to ensure ongoing compliance.

NutriSearch considers the NSF Dietary Supplements Certification Program a dietary supplement-model GMP that approaches the rigours of a pharmaceutical-model GMP. However, NSF has chosen to accept products into its program that have received only NPA-GMP (food-model) certification. NutriSearch is of the opinion that the qualification of products manufactured to food-model GMP without the need for an NSF-GMP audit compromises the rigour of the NSF certification criteria.

Consequently, for such products, NutriSearch treats the NPA-GMP certification as a food-model standard. Products bearing an NSF-GMP certification will not be awarded a NutriSearch Medal of Achievement unless the manufacturer can verify that the product was subjected to a full NSF facility audit for GMP.

NHPD and TGA Certification

Health Canada's NHPD oversees the manufacture, distribution and sale of natural health products, including vitamin, mineral and herbal supplements. Until the mid-2000s, nutritional supplements sold in Canada were treated the same as prescription drugs, requiring pharmaceutical standards for ingredients, processing and distribution. Health Canada's former Therapeutic Products Program issued a Drug Identification Number (DIN), which still applies to pharmaceutical products, to accepted natural health products. Awarding a DIN required manufacturers to comply with site-licensing and product-licensing requirements before receiving pre-market product approval.

Responsibility for site and product licensing for the sale of natural health products was transferred to the new Natural Health Products Directorate (NHPD) in 2004. As in the past, all natural health products sold in Canada under the new NHPD regulations continue to be subject to rigorous levels of compliance. Pre-market site and product licensing continue to be mandatory prior to the awarding of a Natural Product Number (NPN). Not only must the product formulator meet Health Canada's GMP for natural health products; so, too, must the label printers, distributors, packagers, importers and ingredient manufacturers.

Unfortunately, Health Canada does not necessarily conduct a physical audit of the manufacturing plant, nor does it conduct a laboratory analysis of product content before issuing GMP and product approval; it relies, instead, on extensive documentation to demonstrate compliance. It is illegal to offer for sale in Canada a natural health product that does not bear a current NPN. Products sold in or into Canada, which bear a Health Canada NPN, are recognized by NutriSearch as providing sufficient evidence of compliance with Canadian NHP-model GMP.

Widely considered one of the toughest regulators in the world, Australia's TGA is responsible for controlling the manufacturing, distribution and sale of vitamin/mineral products in that country. TGA-approved supplements, which are classified in Australia as Listed Medicinal Products must bear an AUST-L numerical identifier and must meet pharmaceutical-model GMP. The TGA strictly regulates not only the specific ingredients in nutritional supplements, but also the source, amounts and forms of those ingredients. TGA regulations require all manufacturing facilities to pass a GMP site audit based on the Australian Code of Good Manufacturing Practice for Medicinal Products. In addition, pre-market evaluation of a product includes a close look at potential toxicity, product dosage, potential side effects, long-term effects and more. The TGA continues to monitor products long after they enter the Australian market, requiring ongoing evidence of compliance with its regulations and GMP requirements.

NutriSearch considers both the Canadian NHPD and Australian TGA approvals to be an accredited level of GMP compliance. Products approved for sale in these countries and that bear the respective NPN (Canada) or AUST-L (Australia) numerical identifier are eligible to apply for a NutriSearch GOLD Medal of Achievement.

The NutriSearch GOLD Medal of Achievement is awarded once the manufacturer completes a third-party laboratory analysis of product content.

Independent ISO 17025 Analysis

In order to facilitate the laboratory verification required for qualification in the NutriSearch *Medal of Achievement Program*, manufacturers may also use an independent ISO/IEC-17025-certified third-party laboratory. ISO 17025 certification ensures that the laboratory chosen to conduct the analysis follows accepted calibration and analytical procedures.

ISO, the International Standards Organization, is best known for its ISO 9000 certifications, recognized globally as an assurance of quality. The ISO/IEC-17025 standard is the laboratory equivalent of ISO 9000. It applies to any analytical service that wants to assure its customers of precision, accuracy and reproducibility of results.

NutriSearch will accept, as a standard of evidence, a notarized certificate of analysis from an ISO/IEC-17025 certified laboratory. The certificate of analysis must show identity and potency of all active ingredients (where possible); product stability and dissolution; and potential contaminants, such as heavy metals and microbials.

Summary

Together, GMP certification and laboratory analysis demonstrate that the product meets recognized standards for manufacturing safety and product quality. Most importantly, it is the consumer's assurance that **what is on the label is really in the bottle.**

For this Fifth Professional Edition, only four manufacturers have completed the necessary steps to earn a NutriSearch GOLD Medal of Achievement. These companies have invested significant time, resources and money to ensure their products are manufactured to the highest standards possible, and they have submitted all the necessary documentation, including notarized copies of GMP compliance and independent laboratory analysis of the finished product.

Deservedly so, NutriSearch recognizes these companies and their products as the *Best of the Best*. Graphs of each company's highest-scoring product, along with contact information, are included on the following page.

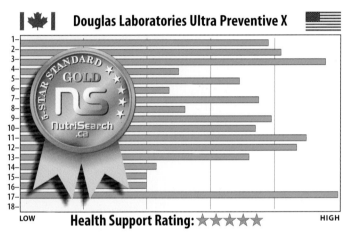

Blueberry Health Sciences Essentials Premium

Health Support Rating: ★★★★★

LOW HIGH

Headquarters:
56 Lehigh Aisle,
Irvine, CA 92612
USA

www.blueberryhealthsciences.com

Tel: (949) 864 -6108
Fax: (949) 423-0168

Skype: bhs.info
E-Mail: bhs.customerservice@
gmail.com

Hong Kong Office:
Suite 16, 6/F, Hong Leong Plaza,
No.33 Lok Yip Road,
Fanling, NT, Hong Kong

Tel: +852 8192-7188
Fax: +852 3171-6516

Douglas Laboratories Ultra Preventive X

Health Support Rating: ★★★★★

LOW HIGH

Douglas Laboratories U.S.A.
600 Boyce Road
Pittsburgh, PA 15205 USA

www.douglaslabs.com
nutrition@douglaslabs.com

Phone: (412) 494-0122
Fax: (412) 494-0155
   or (888) 245-4440
Toll-free: 1-800-245-4440
   or 1-888-DOUGLAB (368-4522)

Douglas Laboratories Canada
552 Newbold Street
London, Ontario
CANADA N6E 2S5

Phone: (519) 439-8424
Toll-free: 1-866-856-9954
Fax: (519) 432-0071

www.douglaslabs.ca
info@douglaslabs.ca

Truestar Health TrueBASICS Solo

Health Support Rating: ★★★★★

LOW HIGH

Truestar Health
2 Bloor Street West
Suite 700
Toronto, ON M4W 3R1

1-888-448-8783

www.truestar.com
Email: cs@truestar.com

USANA Health Sciences Essentials

Health Support Rating: ★★★★★

LOW HIGH

3838 West Parkway Boulevard
Salt Lake City, UT 84120

Associate & Customer Inquiries
Toll-free Order Express
English: 1-888-950-9595
French: 1-888-782-8282
Chinese: 1-888-805-2525
Chinese Fax line: 801-954-7240
Spanish: 1-888-683-8383
24-hour fax (toll-free):
   1-800-289-8081

Distributor Services
English: 1-801-954-7200
Spanish: 1-801-954-7373
French: 1-801-954-7272
Chinese: 1-801-954-7878
Chinese Fax line: 801-954-7240
Japanese: 1-801-954-7773
Korean: 1-801-954-7231
Fax: 1-801-954-7300

E-mail: distserv@usana.com
www.usana.com

CHAPTER EIGHT

HEALTH SUPPORT PROFILE GRAPHS

In this 5th Professional edition of the Comparative Guide, we take a slightly different approach to our product graph section by providing you with a close look at the top 30 leading brands by market share in North America, according to the findings of the global market research company Euromonitor International.

For each top-selling US and Canadian brand listed by Euromonitor, we have selected the highest rated broad-spectrum multivitamin/mineral product, according to our research criteria. These products are graphically portrayed in the following pages, allowing you to visually examine how they perform in relation to our 18 Health Support criteria, shown in the legend on the top left of each even-numbered page. Each graph displays the flag of the country in which the product is sold, along with the product's star rating. Ratings are indicated on a scale of five stars, in half star increments.

Where a particular brand manufactures gender-specific products, both the men's and women's products are shown. Where a particular brand manufactures a product with the same name but differing formulations in each country, both products are shown. In two instances, no qualifying product was found within the brand lineup. (Please refer to page 51 for our qualifying criteria.) Where a NutriSearch Gold Medal of Achievement has been earned, the five stars shown in the product graph are depicted in gold.

Table 3: Leading Brands by Market Share*

Brand Name	Market Share	Top-Rated Product for this Brand	Star Rating
Nature Made	5.1%	Multi for Her 50+	★½ ☆☆☆
		Multi for Him 50+	★★ ☆☆☆
Centrum	4.4%	Advantage	★★ ☆☆☆
GNC	3.1%	Mega Men Liquid	★★★★ ☆
		Women's Ultra Mega Energy & Metabolism	★★★½ ☆
One-A-Day	1.9%	Men's 50+ Advantage	★½ ☆☆☆
		Women's 50+ Advantage	★½ ☆☆☆
Nature's Bountry	1.9%	Mega Vita-Min	★★½ ☆☆
Nature's Way	1.9%	Alive! (No Iron Added)	★★★★½
Sundown	1.6%	Whole Food Multivitamin	★★½ ☆☆
Nutrilite	1.5%	Daily Free	★½ ☆☆☆
Herbalife	1.5%	Multivitamin Complex	★★ ☆☆☆
Shaklee	1.5%	Vita-Lea Gold with Vitamin K (CA & US versions)	★★½ ☆☆
Nature's Sunshine	1.1%	Super Supplemental	★★★ ☆☆
Forever Living	1.1%	- *No Qualifying Products* -	
Jamieson	1.1%	Mega-Vim	★★★ ☆☆
Puritan's Pride	1.0%	Mega Vita-Min	★★★ ☆☆
Melaleuca	1.0%	Vitality Men's	★★½ ☆☆
		Vitality Women's	★★ ☆☆☆
Douglas Laboratories	0.7%	Ultra Preventive X	☆☆☆☆☆
Twinlab	0.7%	Allergy Multi Caps	★★★½ ☆
Schiff	0.7%	Single Day	★★★ ☆☆
USANA Health Sciences	0.6%	Essentials (CA & US versions)	☆☆☆☆☆
Vitamin World	0.5%	Mega Vita-Gel	★★½ ☆☆
Life Extension	0.5%	Life Extension Mix Extra Niacin without Copper	★★★★★
Solgar	0.5%	Male Multiple	★★★★½
		Female Multiple	★★★★ ☆
Sunrider	0.4%	- *No Qualifying Products* -	
Garden of Life	0.4%	Vitamin Code Liquid Formula	★★★ ☆☆
Pure Encapsulations	0.4%	Men's Nutrients	★★★★½
		Women's Nutrients	★★★★½
Enrich	0.4%	- *No Qualifying Products* -	
Natrol	0.3%	My Favorite Multiple Iron Free	★★★½ ☆
Unicity	0.3%	Core Health Basics	★½ ☆☆☆
Pharmanex	0.3%	Vitox	★★½ ☆☆
Theragran	0.1%	Theragran-M Premier 50 Plus	★★ ☆☆☆

*   Vitamins in North America, *Euromonitor Passport*
   © 2013 Euromonitor International, a market research company. www.euromonitor.com

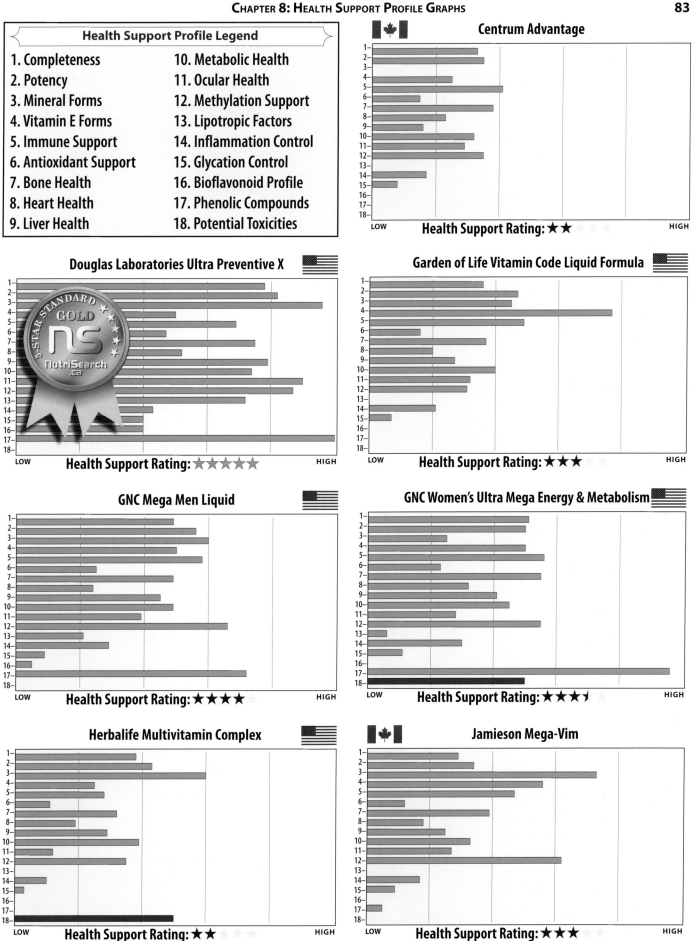

Health Support Profile Legend

1. Completeness
2. Potency
3. Mineral Forms
4. Vitamin E Forms
5. Immune Support
6. Antioxidant Support
7. Bone Health
8. Heart Health
9. Liver Health
10. Metabolic Health
11. Ocular Health
12. Methylation Support
13. Lipotropic Factors
14. Inflammation Control
15. Glycation Control
16. Bioflavonoid Profile
17. Phenolic Compounds
18. Potential Toxicities

Centrum Advantage
Health Support Rating: ★★☆☆☆

Douglas Laboratories Ultra Preventive X
Health Support Rating: ★★★★★

Garden of Life Vitamin Code Liquid Formula
Health Support Rating: ★★★☆☆

GNC Mega Men Liquid
Health Support Rating: ★★★★☆

GNC Women's Ultra Mega Energy & Metabolism
Health Support Rating: ★★★✦

Herbalife Multivitamin Complex
Health Support Rating: ★★☆☆☆

Jamieson Mega-Vim
Health Support Rating: ★★★

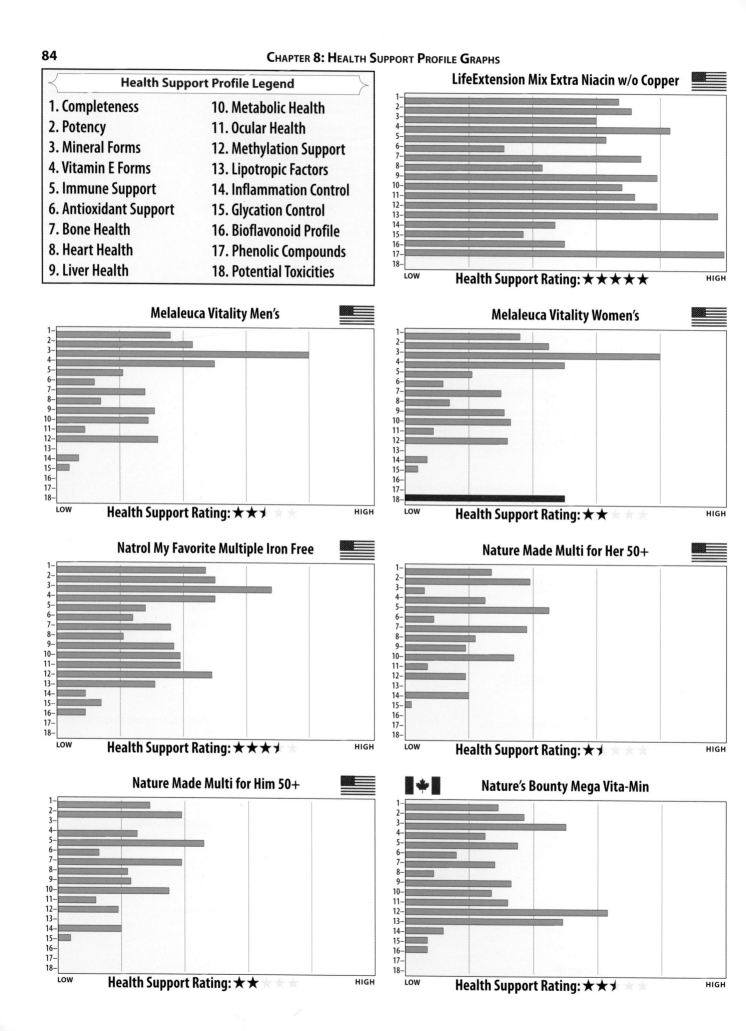

Health Support Profile Legend

1. Completeness
2. Potency
3. Mineral Forms
4. Vitamin E Forms
5. Immune Support
6. Antioxidant Support
7. Bone Health
8. Heart Health
9. Liver Health
10. Metabolic Health
11. Ocular Health
12. Methylation Support
13. Lipotropic Factors
14. Inflammation Control
15. Glycation Control
16. Bioflavonoid Profile
17. Phenolic Compounds
18. Potential Toxicities

LifeExtension Mix Extra Niacin w/o Copper

LOW   Health Support Rating: ★ ★ ★ ★ ★   HIGH

Melaleuca Vitality Men's

LOW   Health Support Rating: ★ ★ ◢ ☆ ☆   HIGH

Melaleuca Vitality Women's

LOW   Health Support Rating: ★ ★ ☆ ☆ ☆   HIGH

Natrol My Favorite Multiple Iron Free

LOW   Health Support Rating: ★ ★ ★ ◢ ☆   HIGH

Nature Made Multi for Her 50+

LOW   Health Support Rating: ★ ◢ ☆ ☆ ☆   HIGH

Nature Made Multi for Him 50+

LOW   Health Support Rating: ★ ★ ☆ ☆ ☆   HIGH

Nature's Bounty Mega Vita-Min

LOW   Health Support Rating: ★ ★ ★ ◢ ☆   HIGH

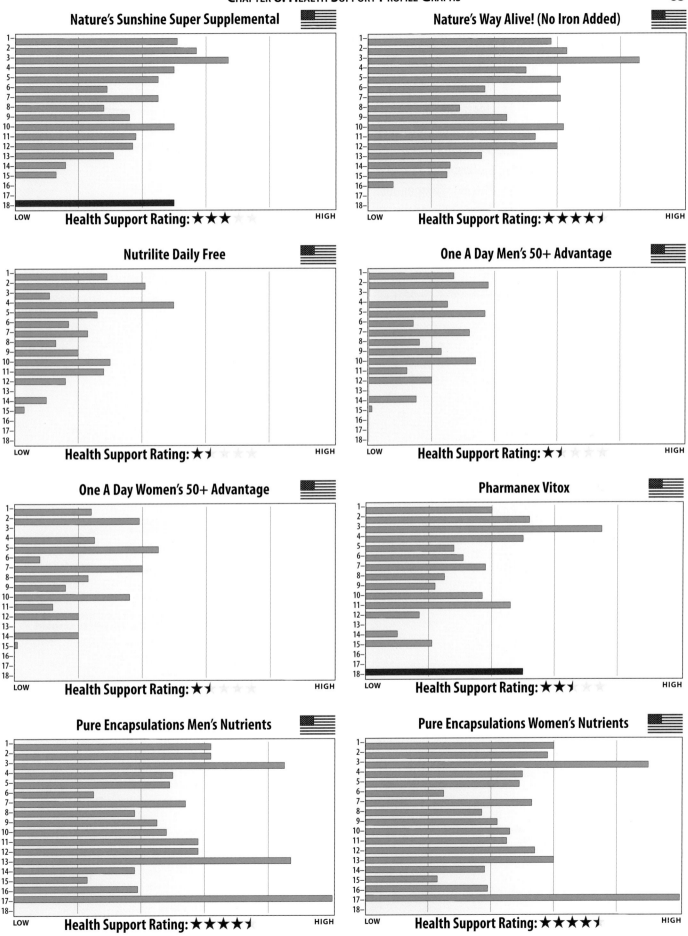

Nature's Sunshine Super Supplemental
Health Support Rating: ★ ★ ★

Nature's Way Alive! (No Iron Added)
Health Support Rating: ★ ★ ★ ★ ✒

Nutrilite Daily Free
Health Support Rating: ★ ✒

One A Day Men's 50+ Advantage
Health Support Rating: ★ ✒

One A Day Women's 50+ Advantage
Health Support Rating: ★ ✒

Pharmanex Vitox
Health Support Rating: ★ ★ ✒

Pure Encapsulations Men's Nutrients
Health Support Rating: ★ ★ ★ ★ ✒

Pure Encapsulations Women's Nutrients
Health Support Rating: ★ ★ ★ ★ ✒

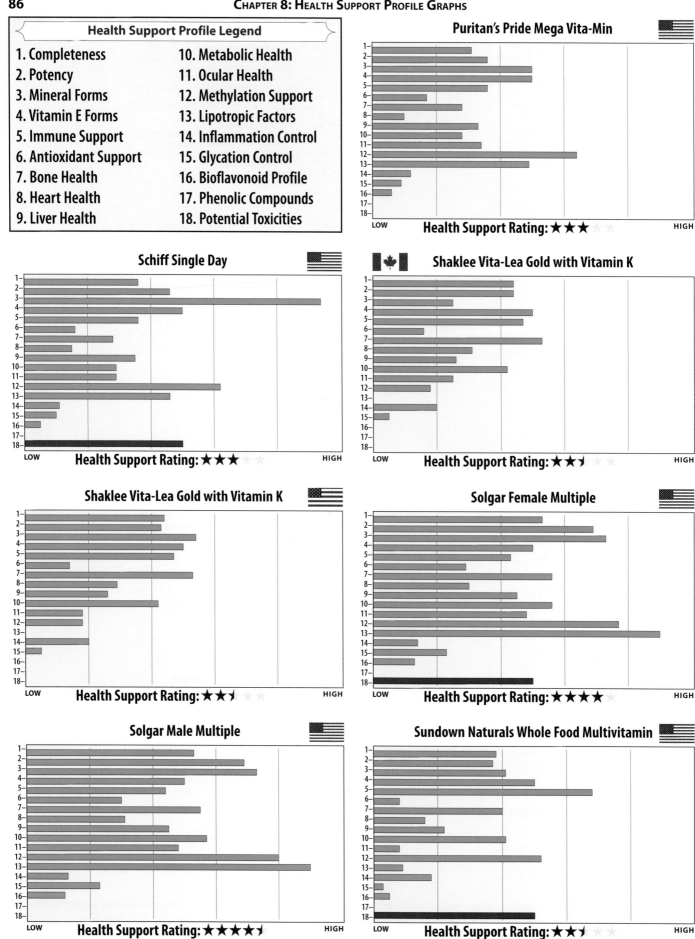

Health Support Profile Legend

1. Completeness
2. Potency
3. Mineral Forms
4. Vitamin E Forms
5. Immune Support
6. Antioxidant Support
7. Bone Health
8. Heart Health
9. Liver Health
10. Metabolic Health
11. Ocular Health
12. Methylation Support
13. Lipotropic Factors
14. Inflammation Control
15. Glycation Control
16. Bioflavonoid Profile
17. Phenolic Compounds
18. Potential Toxicities

Puritan's Pride Mega Vita-Min

Health Support Rating: ★ ★ ★ ☆ ☆

Schiff Single Day

Health Support Rating: ★ ★ ★ ☆ ☆

Shaklee Vita-Lea Gold with Vitamin K

Health Support Rating: ★ ★ ☆ ☆ ☆

Shaklee Vita-Lea Gold with Vitamin K

Health Support Rating: ★ ★ ☆ ☆ ☆

Solgar Female Multiple

Health Support Rating: ★ ★ ★ ★ ☆

Solgar Male Multiple

Health Support Rating: ★ ★ ★ ★ ☆

Sundown Naturals Whole Food Multivitamin

Health Support Rating: ★ ★ ★ ☆ ☆

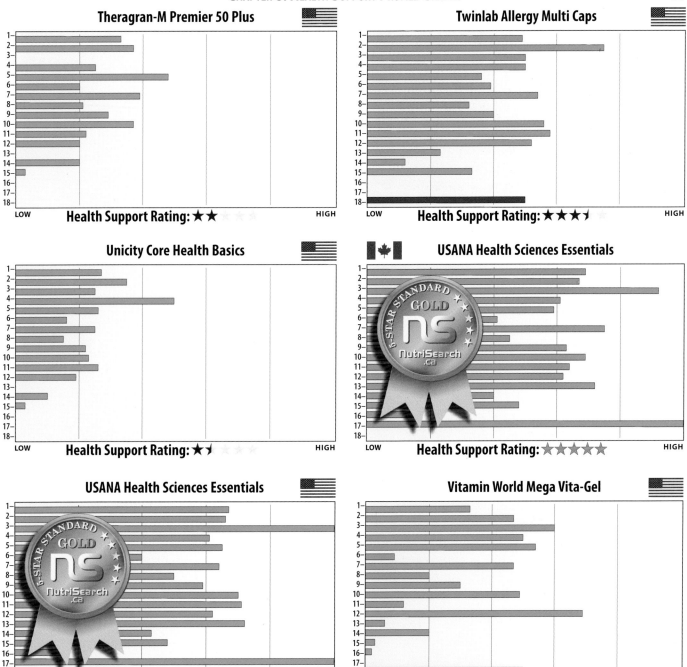

Theragran-M Premier 50 Plus

Health Support Rating: ★★

Twinlab Allergy Multi Caps

Health Support Rating: ★★★↙

Unicity Core Health Basics

Health Support Rating: ★↙

USANA Health Sciences Essentials

Health Support Rating: ★★★★★

USANA Health Sciences Essentials

Health Support Rating: ★★★★★

Vitamin World Mega Vita-Gel

Health Support Rating: ★★↙

CHAPTER NINE:

PRODUCT RATINGS

Ratings of each product examined by NutriSearch, from zero to five stars, displayed in alphabetical order. NutriSearch GOLD Medal of Achievement recipients are shown with a Gold, Five-Star Rating.

Where known, the country of manfacture is denoted by a Canadian or US flag in the country column. Some products may be sold in both countries and in other countries around the world; however, product formulations may vary in other jurisdictions due to local regulations or restrictions.

Manufacturer & Product Name	Country	Rating
1st Endurance Multi-V	USA	★★★
1st Step for Energy 71 Vitamins and Minerals	USA	★½
21st Century Mega Multi for Men	USA	★★★½
21st Century Mega Multi for Women	USA	★★★
21st Century One Daily Adults 50+	USA	★½
21st Century One Daily Cholesterol Health	USA	★
21st Century One Daily Maximum	USA	½
21st Century One Daily Men's 50+	USA	★½
21st Century One Daily Men's Health	USA	★
21st Century One Daily Women's	USA	½
21st Century One Daily Women's 50+	USA	★½
21st Century Sentry	USA	★
21st Century Sentry Cardio Support	USA	★
21st Century Sentry Perform	USA	★
21st Century Sentry Senior	USA	★
4Life Multiplex	USA	★★★½
Absolute Nutrition Uno Diario Hombres	USA	★
Absolute Nutrition Uno Diario Mujeres	USA	½
Action Labs Action-Tabs Made For Men	USA	★★½
Adëeva All-In-One	USA	★★★★½
Adrien Gagnon Multi Active Men	Canada	★★½
Adrien Gagnon Multi Active Men 50+	Canada	★★
Adrien Gagnon Multi Active Women	Canada	★★½
Adrien Gagnon Multi Active Women 50+	Canada	★★
Adrien Gagnon Multi Adults	Canada	★
Advanced Nutritional Innovations (ANI) CoralAdvantage	USA	★★
Advanced Nutritional Innovations (ANI) Joint Health	USA	★★★★
Advocare CorePlex Chewable	USA	★★½
Advocare CorePlex with Iron	USA	★★★★½
Advocare V100 Multivitamin	USA	★★½
Agel Min	USA	★★
Ageloss (see Nature's Plus)		
Albi Naturals Multi Vita-Mineral	Canada	★★★
Albi Naturals Super Rocky	Canada	★★★½
All One Active Seniors	USA	★★★★½
All One Fruit Antioxidant	USA	★★★★
All One Green Phyto Base	USA	★★★★
All One Original Formula	USA	★★★★
All One Rice Base	USA	★★★★½
All One Tablets for Travel	USA	★★★★½
Allergy Research Group Multi-Vi-Min	USA	★★
Allergy Research Group Multi-Vi-Min without Copper & Iron	USA	★★
Allergy Research Group Steady On Powder	USA	★★★★½
Alpha Betic Multivitamin Plus Extended Energy	USA	★★★★
AlternaVites Multivitamins & Minerals	USA	★★★½
American Health Nutri-Mega	USA	★★★
American Nutrition Active Man's Formula	USA	★★★★
American Nutrition Active Woman's Multi	USA	★★★½
American Nutrition Life Essentials	USA	★★★½
Anabolic Laboratories Aved-Eze Multi	USA	★★
Anabolic Laboratories Aved-Multi	USA	★★★½
Anabolic Laboratories Aved-Multi Iron Free	USA	★★★½
Anabolic Laboratories Multigel Caps	USA	★★★★½
Analytical Research Labs Endo-Mins	USA	★★½
Analytical Research Labs Megapan	USA	★★½
AOR Advanced Series Multi Basics Complete	Canada	★★★★½
AOR Advanced Series Multi Basics-3	Canada	★★★★½
AOR Classic Series Essential Mix	Canada	★★★★
Apex 50 Plus Multivitamin	USA	★★★½
Apex Performance Multivitamin	USA	★★★★½
Apex Women's Multivitamin	USA	★★
Applied Nutriceuticals Complete-Balance	USA	★★½
Ariix Vitamins & Minerals	USA	★★★★★½
AST Sports Science Multi Pro 32X	USA	★★★★½
Awareness Life Daily Complete	Canada	★★★½
Balance Nutraceuticals MultiBalance No Iron	USA	★★★★★½
Balance Nutraceuticals MultiBalance Plus Iron	USA	★★★★
Be True (see Truestar Health)		
Be Well Complete Multivitamin	USA	★★★★★½
Beachbody Nutritionals ActiVit	USA	★★★
Beachbody Shakeology (Chocolate)	USA	½
Beachbody Shakeology (Vanilla, Greenberry)	USA	★
Beyond Health Multi-Vitamin Formula	USA	★★★★½
Bio-Actif Phytobec	Canada	★★½
Bioclinic Naturals BioFoundation-G	Canada	★★★★★½
BioGenesis MultiGreens	USA	★★★★★½
BioGenesis Premiere Greens Multi	USA	★
BioGenesis Ultra Genesis	USA	★★★★
BioGenesis Ultra Genesis without Iron	USA	★★★★
BioGenesis Ultra Genesis without Iron & Copper	USA	★★★★
Bio-Life Naturals Super Bio-Balance	USA	★★★★½
Bio-Lumin Essense Daily Essense	USA	★★★½
Bio-Lumin Essense Living Essense	USA	★
Biomédic Advantage	Canada	★★
Biomédic Formule Forte	Canada	★
Biotics Research Bio Multi-Plus	USA	★★½
Biotics Research Bio Multi-Plus Iron and Copper Free	USA	★★
Biotics Research Bio Multi-Plus Iron Free	USA	★★
Biotics Research Bio-Trophic Plus	USA	★
Biotics Research Equi-Fem	USA	★★★
Biotics Research Equi-Fem Iron and Copper Free	USA	★★★½
Biotics Research ProMulti-Plus	USA	★★★★★½
BioX Ultimate Once A Day	Canada	★★★★
Blueberry Health Sciences Essentials Premium	USA	☆☆☆☆☆
Bluebonnet Age-less Choice for Men 50+	USA	★★★★½
Bluebonnet Age-less Choice for Women 50+	USA	★★★★½

Manufacturer & Product Name	Country	Rating
Bluebonnet Ladies' Choice Caplets	USA	★★★★½
Bluebonnet Maxi One Caplets	USA	★★★½
Bluebonnet Maxi Two Caplets	USA	★★★★
Bluebonnet Men's Choice Caplets	USA	★★★★½
Bluebonnet Multi One Vcaps	USA	★★½
Bluebonnet Multi-Vita Softgels	USA	★★★★
Bluebonnet Super Earth Multinutrient Formula	USA	★★★★
Bluebonnet Super Vita-CoQ10 Formula Caplets	USA	★★★★½
Bluebonnet Veggie Choice Caplets	USA	★★★★½
Body Rewards Daily Multi	USA	★★★
Body Wise Right Choice AM/PM	USA	★★★★★½
BodyBreak Energy & Vitality	Canada	★★
BodyBreak Silver 50+	Canada	★★
BodyBreak Total Health	Canada	★★
Botanic Choice Mega Multi Vitamin	USA	★★★
Botanic Choice Whole Foods Power Multi	USA	★★★½
Bronson Advanced Mature Gold	USA	★★★½
Bronson All Insurance Vitamin Powder	USA	★★★★
Bronson Chewable Vitamin & Mineral	USA	★★
Bronson Daily Multi + Joint Support	USA	★★½
Bronson Fortified Vitamin & Mineral Insurance Formula	USA	★★
Bronson GTC Formula	USA	★★
Bronson GTC Formula #2	USA	★
Bronson Mature Formula	USA	★★½
Bronson Mature Formula Without Iron	USA	★★
Bronson Mega Multi Softcaps	USA	★★
Bronson Men's Complete Formula	USA	★★★
Bronson Omega Complete for Men	USA	★★★★
Bronson Omega Complete For Women	USA	★★★★
Bronson Performance Edge for Men	USA	★★★
Bronson Performance Edge for Women	USA	★★★
Bronson The Bronson Formula	USA	★★
Bronson The Woman's Formula	USA	★★½
Bronson Therapeutic Formula	USA	★
Bronson Vegi Source	USA	★★★★½
Bronson Vitamin & Mineral Formula	USA	★★½
Bronson Vitamin & Mineral Insurance Formula	USA	★★★
BSC Multi-VMA	USA	★★★
Buried Treasure Active 55 Plus	USA	★★★★
Buried Treasure Daily Nutrition	USA	★★★
Buried Treasure VM-100 Complete	USA	★★★★½
Burns Drugs Multi-Max with Lutein	USA	★★
CanPrev Adult Multi	Canada	★★★★
CanPrev Immuno Multi	Canada	★★★★½
Carlson ACES Gold	USA	★★★½
Carlson Fish Oil Multi	USA	★★★½
Carlson Mini-Multi	USA	★★½
Carlson Super 1 Daily	USA	★★★
Carlson Super 2 Daily	USA	★★★★½
Centrum	Canada	½
Centrum Adults	USA	★
Centrum Advantage	Canada	★★
Centrum Flavor Burst Chew	USA	★
Centrum Flavor Burst Drink Mix	USA	★½
Centrum Flavour Burst Chews	Canada	★
Centrum for Men	Canada	★
Centrum for Women	Canada	★
Centrum Forte	Canada	★
Centrum Performance	Canada	★
Centrum Select 50+	Canada	★½
Centrum Select 50+ Chewables	Canada	★
Centrum Silver Adults 50+	USA	★
Centrum Silver Men	USA	★½
Centrum Silver Women	USA	★½
Centrum Women	USA	★
Century Systems Miracle 2000	USA	★★★★
Cooper Complete Basic One Iron Free	USA	★★★½
Cooper Complete Basic One With Iron	USA	★★★★½
Cooper Complete Elite Athlete	USA	★★★★
Cooper Complete Iron Free	USA	★★★★
Cooper Complete With Iron	USA	★★★★½
Country Life Beyond Food	USA	★★★★½
Country Life Chewable Adult Multi	USA	★★
Country Life Daily Multi-Sorb	USA	★★★½
Country Life Daily Total One	USA	★★★½
Country Life Essential Life	USA	★★★½
Country Life Liquid Multi	USA	★★★★
Country Life Max for Men	USA	★★★★
Country Life Max for Men Vegetarian Caps	USA	★★★★
Country Life Maxine Iron-Free	USA	★★★★
Country Life Maxi-Sorb Superior Multiple	USA	★★★★½
Country Life Multi-100	USA	★★★
Country Life Multi-Sorb Maxine	USA	★★★★½
Country Life Multi-Sorb Maxine Vegetarian Capsules	USA	★★★★½
Country Life Realfood Organics Men's Daily Nutrition	USA	★
Country Life Realfood Organics Ultimate Daily Nutrition	USA	★★½
Country Life Realfood Organics Women's Daily Nutrition	USA	★
Country Life Realfood Organics Your Daily Nutrition	USA	★
Country Life Seniority Multivitamin	USA	★★★½
Country Life Vegetarian Support	USA	★★★
Creating Wellness Purpose Vitalizing Men's Multi	USA	★
Creating Wellness Purpose Vitalizing Women's Multi	USA	★
CTD Labs Multi-elite	USA	★★★★

Manufacturer & Product Name	Country	Rating
CVS Pharmacy Daily Multiple	US	✦
CVS Pharmacy Daily Multiple for Men	US	★✦
CVS Pharmacy Daily Multiple for Women	US	★
CVS Pharmacy Daily Multiple Plus Minerals	US	✦
CVS Pharmacy Spectravite	US	★
CVS Pharmacy Spectravite Senior	US	★
Cyto-Charge Life Assurance	US	★★★
D'Adamo Personalized Nutrition Exakta	US	★
DaVinci Laboratories of Vermont Daily Best	US	★★★
DaVinci Laboratories of Vermont Daily Best Ultra	US	★★★✦
DaVinci Laboratories of Vermont Omni	US	★★
DaVinci Laboratories of Vermont Spectra	US	★★★★✦
DaVinci Laboratories of Vermont Spectra Infinite Nutrition	US	★★★★★
DaVinci Laboratories of Vermont Spectra Man	US	★★★★✦
DaVinci Laboratories of Vermont Spectra Multi Age	US	★★★★
DaVinci Laboratories of Vermont Spectra Senior	US	★★★★✦
DaVinci Laboratories of Vermont Spectra Without Copper & Iron	US	★★★★
DaVinci Laboratories of Vermont Spectra Woman	US	★★★★
DaVinci Laboratories of Vermont Ultimate Spectra	US	★★★★★
DC Formula 19	US	★✦
DC Formula 249	US	★✦
DC Formula 360	US	★
DC Formula 75	US	★★✦
DC Formula 784	US	★
DC Formula 814	US	★✦
DC Vita-Men	US	★★★
DC Vita-Women	US	★★✦
Dee Cee Laboratories (see DC)		
Designs for Health Complete Multi	US	★★★★✦
Designs for Health Complete Multi with Copper and Iron	US	★★★★★✦
Designs for Health Metabolic Synergy	US	★★★★★✦
Designs for Health Twice Daily Multi	US	★★★★
Designs for Health Vitavescence (Packets)	US	★★★★
Doctor David Williams Daily Basics Plus	US	★★★★✦
Doctor's Choice (see Enzymatic Therapy)		
Doctor's Nutrition Athletic Nutrients	US	★★★★✦
Doctor's Nutrition Mega Vites Man	US	★★★★
Doctor's Nutrition Mega Vites Senior	US	★★★✦
Doctor's Nutrition Mega Vites Without Copper & Iron	US	★★★★
Doctor's Nutrition Mega Vites Woman	US	★★★✦
Don Lemmon's Multi-Nutrient Support Formula	US	★★★★
DōTerra Microplex VMz	US	★★
DotFit ActiveMV	US	★★★
Douglas Laboratories Added Protection III Without Copper	US	★★★★
Douglas Laboratories Added Protection III Without Copper & Iron	US	★★★★✦
Douglas Laboratories Added Protection III Without Iron	US	★★★★✦
Douglas Laboratories Basic Preventive 1	US	★★★★✦
Douglas Laboratories Basic Preventive 2	US	★★★★✦
Douglas Laboratories Basic Preventive 3	US	★★★★✦
Douglas Laboratories Basic Preventive 4	US	★★★★★
Douglas Laboratories Basic Preventive 5	US	★★★★✦
Douglas Laboratories Essential Basics	US	★★★★
Douglas Laboratories Multivite	US	★
Douglas Laboratories Ultra Balance III	Canada	★★★★✦
Douglas Laboratories Ultra Balance III Capsules	Canada	★★★★
Douglas Laboratories Ultra Balance III with Copper & Iron	Canada	★★★★✦
Douglas Laboratories Ultra Balance III with Iron	Canada	★★★★✦
Douglas Laboratories Ultra Fem	US	★★★★
Douglas Laboratories Ultra Genic	US	★★★✦
Douglas Laboratories Ultra Preventive	US	★★★★★
Douglas Laboratories Ultra Preventive Beta	US	★★★★✦
Douglas Laboratories Ultra Preventive Beta with Copper	US	★★★★✦
Douglas Laboratories Ultra Preventive Beta with Copper & Iron	US	★★★★✦
Douglas Laboratories Ultra Preventive Forte-Chel	US	★★★★✦
Douglas Laboratories Ultra Preventive III	US	★★★★✦
Douglas Laboratories Ultra Preventive III Capsules	US	★★★✦
Douglas Laboratories Ultra Preventive III Capsules with Copper	US	★★★★
Douglas Laboratories Ultra Preventive III with Copper	US	★★★★✦
Douglas Laboratories Ultra Preventive III with Copper & Iron	US	★★★★✦
Douglas Laboratories Ultra Preventive III with Iron	US	★★★★✦
Douglas Laboratories Ultra Preventive III with Zinc Picolinate	US	★★★★✦
Douglas Laboratories Ultra Preventive IX with Vitamin K	US	★★★★★
Douglas Laboratories Ultra Preventive X	US	★★★★★
Douglas Laboratories Ultra Preventive X Vegetarian Capsules	Canada	★★★★✦
Douglas Laboratories Ultra Vite 75 II	US	★★★
Douglas Laboratories Vitaworx	US	★★★★
Dr. Ben Kim Natural Health Solutions Comprehensive Formula	Canada	★★
Dr. Cranton's PrimeNutrients	US	★★★★✦
Dr. Donsbach Agua Vitae Mens	US	★★★★✦
Dr. Donsbach Agua Vitae Unisex	US	★★★★✦
Dr. Donsbach Agua Vitae Women's Formula	US	★★★★✦

Manufacturer & Product Name	Country	Rating
Dr. Fuhrman Gentle Care Formula	USA	★★
Dr. Fuhrman Men's Daily Formula +D3	USA	★★
Dr. Fuhrman Women's Daily Formula + D3	USA	★★
Dr. Mercola Whole Food Multivitamin Plus Vital Minerals	USA	★★★★½
Dr. Rath's Vitacor Plus	USA	★★
Dr. Sinatra Multivitamin for Men	USA	★★★½
Dr. Sinatra Multivitamin for Women	USA	★★★½
Dr. Weil Multivitamin & Antioxidant	USA	★★★½
Dr. Whitaker Forward	USA	★★★★½
Drinkables Liquid Multi Vitamins	USA	★½
Drucker Labs IntraMax	USA	★★★½
Dymatize Nutrition Super Multi	USA	★★½
Eclectic Institute Optimum ii, iv, vi Without Iron	USA	★★★★
Eclectic Institute Vital Force	USA	★★★½
Eclectic Institute Vital Force Ultra-Caps	USA	★★★½
Eclectic Institute Vital Force without Iron	USA	★★★★
EcoNugenics Men's Longevity Essentials Plus	USA	★★★½
EcoNugenics Women's Longevity Rhythms	USA	★★★½
Edom Labs Active Man's Formula	USA	★★★★
Edom Labs Active Woman's Multi	USA	★★★½
Edom Labs Family-Vites	USA	½
Edom Labs Natural Organic Formula 75	USA	★★★
Edom Labs Natural Supervites	USA	★★
Edom Labs Timed Release Ultra-Vites	USA	★★★
Emergen-C Multi-Vitamin Plus	USA	★½
Endurance Products Company Endur-VM	USA	★
Endurance Products Company Endur-VM without Iron	USA	★½
Enerex Sona Multi Athletes & 55 Plus	Canada	★★★½
Enerex Sona Multi Original	Canada	★★★
Enerex Sona Pure	Canada	★★★
Enerex Supreme Once-A-Day	Canada	★★★
Enerex Supreme Twice-A-Day	Canada	★★★
Eniva Vibe Apple	Canada	★★
Eniva Vibe Fruit Sensation	Canada	★★
Enzymatic Therapy Doctor's Choice 45+ Women	USA	★★★★½
Enzymatic Therapy Doctor's Choice 50+ Men	USA	★★★★½
Enzymatic Therapy Doctor's Choice Men	USA	★★★★½
Enzymatic Therapy Doctor's Choice Women	USA	★★★★½
Enzyme Labs Multi-Life	USA	★★½
Equate Active Adults 50+	USA	★
Equate Adults Under 50	USA	★
Equate Century Advance	Canada	★½
Equate Century Complete	Canada	½
Equate Century Plus	Canada	★
Equate Century Preference	Canada	★
Equate Century Premium	Canada	★
Equate Century Silver	Canada	★½
Equate Complete Multivitamin	USA	½

Manufacturer & Product Name	Country	Rating
Equate Men's 50+	Canada	★½
Equate One Daily Men's Health	USA	★½
Equate One Daily Women's Health	USA	★
Equate Women 50+	USA	★½
Equate Women's 50+	Canada	½
Equate Women's Formula	Canada	½
Equate Women's Pro-Active	USA	★
Especially Yours (see Nature's Plus)		
Esteem Senior Total Man	USA	★★½
Esteem Senior Total Woman	USA	★★½
Esteem Total Man	USA	★★½
Esteem Total Woman	USA	★★
Exact Essentra Balance	Canada	½
Exact Essentra Elite	Canada	★
Exact Essentra Forte	Canada	★
Exact Essentra Performa	Canada	★
Exact Essentra Platinum	Canada	★
Exact Multi Max 1	Canada	★★½
Exact Vital 1	Canada	½
Exact Vital 1 Daily Men's 50+ Formula	Canada	★½
Exact Vital 1 Men's Formula	Canada	★½
Factor Nutrition Labs FOCUSfactor	USA	★★
First Organics Daily Multiple	USA	★½
Flora Multi Caps	USA	★★★
Food Research Vitamin & Mineral	USA	★½
Food Science of Vermont Daily Best	USA	★★★
Food Science of Vermont Men's Superior	USA	★★★★½
Food Science of Vermont Senior's Superior	USA	★★★★
Food Science of Vermont Superior Care	USA	★★★★½
Food Science of Vermont Superior Care Without Copper and Iron	USA	★★★★
Food Science of Vermont Total Care	USA	★★
Food Science of Vermont Ultimate Care	USA	★★★★★
Food Science of Vermont Women's Superior	USA	★★★★
Freeda Freedavite	USA	★
Freeda Geri-Freeda	USA	★★
Freeda Hi Kovite	USA	★
Freeda Monocaps	USA	★
Freeda Quintabs-M	USA	★½
Freeda Quintabs-M Iron Free	USA	★★
Freeda T-Vites	USA	★½
Freeda Ultra Freeda	USA	★★★
Freeda Ultra Freeda A Free	USA	★★★
Freeda Ultra Freeda Iron Free	USA	★★★½
Futurebiotics Hi Energy Multi for Men	USA	★★★½
Futurebiotics Multi Vitamin Energy Plus for Women	USA	★★
Futurebiotics Vegetarian Super Multi	USA	★★★
Futurebiotics Vitomega Men	USA	★★★½
Futurebiotics Vitomega Women	USA	★★★½

Manufacturer & Product Name	Country	Rating
Garden of Life Living Multi Optimal Formula	USA	★★
Garden of Life Living Multi Optimal Men's Formula	USA	★★½
Garden of Life Living Multi Optimal Women's Formula	USA	★★
Garden of Life Vitamin Code 50 & Wiser Men	USA	★★½
Garden of Life Vitamin Code 50 & Wiser Women	USA	★★½
Garden of Life Vitamin Code Family	USA	★★½
Garden of Life Vitamin Code Liquid Multivitamin Formula	USA	★★★
Garden of Life Vitamin Code Men	USA	★★
Garden of Life Vitamin Code Perfect Weight	USA	★★½
Garden of Life Vitamin Code Raw One for Women	USA	★½
Garden of Life Vitamin Code Raw One Men	USA	★½
Garden of Life Vitamin Code Women	USA	★★
Gary Null Super AM & Super PM Formulas	USA	★★★★½
Gary Null Supreme Health	USA	★★★★½
Genesis Super 100 Formula	USA	★★★½
Genesis Today GenEssentials Organic Total Nutrition	USA	★★
Genestra Almond Liquid Vite Min	Canada	★★★
Genestra Liquid Multi Vite Min	Canada	★★
Genestra Maxum Multi Vite	Canada	★★½
Genestra Multi Vite	Canada	★★
Genestra Super Orti Vite	Canada	★★
Genestra Vite Min Mix Vitamin Powder	Canada	★★★★
Geneva Levity+Plus	USA	★★★
Genuine Health Multi+ Complete	Canada	★★★
Genuine Health Multi+ Daily Energy	Canada	★★½
Genuine Health Multi+ Daily Glow	Canada	★★★
Genuine Health Multi+ Daily Joy	Canada	★★★½
Genuine Health Multi+ Daily Trim	Canada	★★★
Geritol Complete	USA	½
GNC be-WHOLE	USA	★★★½
GNC Mega Men	USA	★★★★
GNC Mega Men 50 Plus	USA	★★★
GNC Mega Men 50+ One Daily	USA	★★½
GNC Mega Men Energy & Metabolism	USA	★★★★
GNC Mega Men Liquid	USA	★★★★
GNC Mega Men Maximum Nutrition	USA	★★★½
GNC Mega Men One Daily	USA	★★½
GNC Mega Men Sport	USA	★★★
GNC Solotron Chewable	USA	★
GNC Ultra Mega Gold	USA	★★★½
GNC Ultra Mega Green Men's	USA	★★★½
GNC Ultra Mega Green Men's 50+	USA	★★★½
GNC Ultra Mega Green Men's Sport	USA	★★★½
GNC Ultra Mega Green Women's	USA	★★★
GNC Ultra Mega Green Women's 50 Plus	USA	★★★½
GNC Ultra Mega Green Women's Active	USA	★★★
GNC Women's Ultra Mega	USA	★★★

Manufacturer & Product Name	Country	Rating
GNC Women's Ultra Mega 50 Plus	USA	★★★
GNC Women's Ultra Mega 50 Plus One Daily	USA	★★
GNC Women's Ultra Mega Active	USA	★★★
GNC Women's Ultra Mega Bone Density Without Iron And Iodine	USA	★★★½
GNC Women's Ultra Mega Energy & Metabolism	USA	★★★½
GNC Women's Ultra Mega Maximum Nutrition	USA	★★★
GNC Women's Ultra Mega One Daily	USA	★★
GNC Women's Ultra Mega Without Iron and Iodine	USA	★★★
GNLD Formula IV	USA	★½
GNLD Vegetarian Multi	USA	★★
Great American Products Green Supreme Multi	USA	★★★½
Great American Products Liquid Master Multi	USA	★½
Great American Products Master Green Multi	USA	★★★★
Greens Today Men's Formula	USA	★★★
Greens Today Original Formula	USA	★★½
Greens Today Powerhouse Formula	USA	★★½
Greens Today Vegan Formula	USA	★★★
Health Direct Nature's Optimal Nutrition	USA	★★★
Health First Multi-First	USA	★★½
H-E-B Complete	USA	★
H-E-B One Daily for Men	USA	★½
H-E-B One Daily for Women	USA	★
H-E-B Ultimate Men's	USA	★
H-E-B Ultimate Women's	USA	★
Herbalife Multivitamin Complex	USA	★★
Highland Laboratories (see Mt. Angel Vitamin Company)		
Hillestad Pharmaceuticals Sterling	USA	★★★
Hillestad Summit Gold	USA	★★½
Hillestad Summit Gold Special Formula	USA	★★★
Hillestad Summit MAX	USA	★★★
Immunotec Research Vitamin and Mineral Supplement	USA	★★½
Immuvit Plus Q10	USA	½
Innate Response Formulas Food Multi II	USA	★½
Innate Response Formulas Food Multi III BioMax	USA	★★
Innate Response Formulas Food Multi IV	USA	★★
Innate Response Formulas Maximum Food	USA	★½
Innate Response Formulas Men Over 40	USA	★★½
Innate Response Formulas Men over 40 One Daily	USA	★½
Innate Response Formulas One Daily	USA	★½
Innate Response Formulas One Daily Cap	USA	★★½
Innate Response Formulas One Daily without Iron	USA	★½
Innate Response Formulas Women Over 40	USA	★★
Innate Response Formulas Women Over 40 One Daily	USA	★½
Innate Response Formulas Women's Multi	USA	★★
Innate Response Formulas Women's One Daily	USA	★
Inno-Vite Formula H.H.	Canada	★★½

Manufacturer & Product Name	Country	Rating
Integrative Therapeutics Clinical Nutrients 45-Plus Women	USA	★★★★½
Integrative Therapeutics Clinical Nutrients 50-Plus Men	USA	★★★★½
Integrative Therapeutics Clinical Nutrients for Men	USA	★★★★½
Integrative Therapeutics Clinical Nutrients for Women	USA	★★★★½
Integrative Therapeutics Maximum Blue	USA	★★★★
Integrative Therapeutics Mega MultiVitamin Powder Mix	USA	★★★½
Integrative Therapeutics Multiplex-1 with Iron	USA	★★★★
Integrative Therapeutics Multiplex-1 without Iron	USA	★★★★½
Integrative Therapeutics Multiplex-2 with Iron	USA	★★★★
Integrative Therapeutics Multiplex-2 without Iron	USA	★★★★
Integrative Therapeutics NutriVitamin Enzyme Complex	USA	★★★½
Integrative Therapeutics NutriVitamin Enzyme Complex without Iron	USA	★★★★
Integrative Therapeutics Spectrient	USA	★★★½
Integrative Therapeutics Spectrient without Iron	USA	★★★
Integrative Therapeutics Spectrum 2C with Iron	USA	★★★
Integrative Therapeutics Spectrum 2C without Iron	USA	★★★½
Integrative Therapeutics Total Formula 2	USA	★★½
Integrative Therapeutics Total Formula 3 Advanced No Iron	USA	★★½
Intensive Nutrition Mega-VM	USA	★★★★½
Intensive Nutrition Multi-VM	USA	★★★★
Irwin Naturals Angel Multi	USA	★★★½
Irwin Naturals Men's Living Green Liquid-Gel Multi	USA	★★★½
Irwin Naturals Only One Liquid-Gel Multi	USA	★★
Irwin Naturals Only One Liquid-Gel Multi without Iron	USA	★★★½
Irwin Naturals Women's Living Green Liquid-Gel Multi	USA	★★★½
Isagenix Essentials For Men	USA	★★★½
Isagenix Essentials For Women	USA	★★★½
Isotonix Multivitamin	USA	★★★½
It Works! It's Vital Core Nutrition	USA	★★★½
Jamieson Mega-Vim	Canada	★★★
Jamieson Power Vitamins for Men	Canada	★★★½
Jamieson Vita Slim	Canada	★★
Jamieson Vita-Vim for Women	Canada	★½
Jamieson Vita-Vim Healthy Heart	Canada	★½
Jamieson Vita-Vim Regular	Canada	★★
Jamieson Vita-Vim Super	Canada	★★★½
Jarrow Formulas Multi 1-to-3 (with Lutein)	USA	★★★★
Jarrow Formulas Women's Multi	USA	★★★★
JD Premium MVX Daily	USA	★★★★★
Jean-Marc Brunet (see Le Naturiste)		

Manufacturer & Product Name	Country	Rating
Jeunesse (see Nutrigen)		
KAL Enhanced 75	USA	★★★½
KAL Enhanced Energy	USA	★★★★
KAL Enhanced Energy Supreme Iron Free	USA	★★★★½
KAL High Potency Soft Multiple	USA	★★★
KAL High Potency Soft Multiple Iron Free	USA	★★★½
KAL Mega Vita-Min	USA	★★★
KAL Multi-Active Iron Free	USA	★★★★
KAL Multi-Four +	USA	★★★★
KAL Multi-Max 1	USA	★★★½
KAL Multi-Max 1 50+ Sustained Release	USA	★★★½
KAL Multi-Max 1 for Men	USA	★★★
KAL Multi-Max 1 for Women Sustained Release	USA	★★½
KAL Multi-Max 1 Iron Free	USA	★★★
Karuna Maxxum 1	USA	★★★★½
Karuna Maxxum 2	USA	★★★★½
Karuna Maxxum 3	USA	★★★★½
Karuna Maxxum 4	USA	★★★★½
Karuna Maxxum Basic	USA	★★★
Kirkland Signature Daily Multi	USA	★
Kirkland Signature Formula Forte for Men	Canada	★
Kirkland Signature Formula Forte for Women	Canada	★
Kirkland Signature Formula Forte Senior	Canada	★½
Kirkland Signature Mature Multi	USA	★½
Kirkland Signature Premium Performance Multi	USA	★½
Kirkman EveryDay	USA	★½
Kirkman Spectrum Complete II	USA	★★½
Le Naturiste ABC Plus Senior	Canada	★
Le Naturiste Vitaminol Men's Multivitamin	Canada	★½
Le Naturiste Vitaminol Multivitamin for Adults 50+	Canada	★½
Leader Mega Multivitamin for Men	USA	★★
Leader Mega Multivitamin for Women	USA	★★★½
Leader One Daily Men's Health	USA	★
Leader One Daily Plus Iron	USA	½
Leader One Daily Weight Control	USA	★½
Leader One Daily Women's	USA	½
Levity+Plus Multivitamin for Women	USA	★★★
Life Adult Multivitamins for People Over 50	Canada	½
Life Daily-One for Men 50+	Canada	★½
Life Daily-One for Women	Canada	½
Life Solutions Super MultiVitamins and Minerals	USA	★★★
Life Spectrum Advanced	Canada	★★
Life Spectrum Forte	Canada	★
Life Spectrum Gold for Adults Over 50	Canada	★½
Life Spectrum with Lutein	Canada	½
LifeExtension LifeExtension Mix	USA	★★★★★
LifeExtension LifeExtension Mix Extra Niacin Without Copper	USA	★★★★★
LifeExtension LifeExtension Mix With Extra Niacin	USA	★★★★★

Manufacturer & Product Name	Country	Rating
LifeExtension LifeExtension Mix Without Copper	US	★★★★★
LifeExtension One-Per-Day	US	★★★★½
LifeExtension Two-Per-Day	US	★★★★½
LifeGive Men's Formula	US	★½
LifeGive Women's Formula	US	★½
Life-Line Vitamin Multimineral	US	★★½
LifePlus Daily BioBasics	US	★★★
LifePlus TVM-Plus	US	★★★
LifeScript Daily Essentials	US	★½
LifeSource Men's Superior	US	★★★★
LifeSource Multi Vitamin & Minerals	US	★★★½
LifeSource Women's Superior	US	★★★½
Lifetime Fitness Men's Performance Daily AM/PM	US	★★★★½
Lifetime Fitness Women's Performance Daily AM/PM	US	★★★★½
LifeTime Soft Gel	US	★★★
Liquid Health Complete Multiple	US	★★
LiquiMax Complete Nutrition	US	★
London Drugs Multi Complete	Canada	½
London Drugs Multi Plus	Canada	★
London Drugs Multi Vitamin & Minerals	Canada	★
London Drugs One Tablet Daily Adults 50+	Canada	★½
Mannatech PhytoMatrix	US	★½
Mason Natural Daily Multiple Vitamins with Minerals	US	★
Mason Natural Super Multiple Iron Free	US	★★
Mason Natural VitaTRUM	US	½
Matol Mega Vitamins	US	★★½
Mauves (see Trophic)		
Max International Max N-Fuze	US	★★
Maxi Vision Whole Body Formula	US	★★★★½
Maximized Living Women's Multi	US	★★½
Maximum Human Performance Activite	US	★★★
Maxion Max Multi	US	★★
MBi Bio-Naturalvite	US	★★
MD Healthline Advanced Green Multi	US	½
MD's Choice Complete Formula	US	★★★½
MD's Choice Complete Formula for Mature Women	US	★★★★½
MD's Choice Complete Formula for Men	US	★★★★½
MD's Choice Complete Formula for Young Women	US	★★★★½
MD's Choice Complete Liquid Formula	US	★★★½
MegaFood Lifestyle	US	★★
MegaFood Lifestyle One Daily	US	½
MegaFood Men over 40	US	★★½
MegaFood Men Over 40 One Daily	US	★½
MegaFood Men's	US	★★
MegaFood Men's One Daily	US	★½
MegaFood One Daily	US	★½
MegaFood Optimum Foods	US	★½
MegaFood Women Over 40	US	★★

Manufacturer & Product Name	Country	Rating
MegaFood Women Over 40 One Daily	US	★½
MegaFood Women's	US	★★
MegaFood Women's One Daily	US	★
Melaleuca Vitality Men's	US	★★½
Melaleuca Vitality Women's	US	★★
Member's Mark Complete Multi	US	½
Metabolic Maintenance Basic Maintenance	US	★★
Metabolic Maintenance Basic Maintenance Plus Vitamin D	US	★★½
Metagenics Multigenics	US	★★★★
Metagenics Multigenics Chewable	US	★★
Metagenics Multigenics Intensive Care	US	★★★★½
Metagenics Multigenics Intensive Care without Iron	US	★★★★½
Metagenics Multigenics Powder	US	★★★½
Metagenics Multigenics without Iron	US	★★★★½
Metagenics PhytoMulti	US	★★★
Metagenics PhytoMulti with Iron	US	★★★
Michael's Naturopathic Programs For Men	US	★★★½
Michael's Naturopathic Programs For Women	US	★★★★
Miracle 2000 Total Body Nutrition	US	★★★½
More Than a Multiple Iron-Free / Vegetarian Formula	US	★★★★
More Than a Multiple Multivitamin for Men	US	★★★★
More than a Multiple Multivitamin for Women	US	★★★½
More Than a Multiple Multivitamin Formula	US	★★★★
Mountain Naturals of Vermont Daily Best	US	★★★
Mountain Naturals of Vermont Superior Care without Copper & Iron	US	★★★★½
Mountain Peak Nutritionals Ultra High	US	★★★★
MRM Beyond Basics	US	★★★½
Mt. Angel Vitamin Company Men's 50+	US	★★★★
Mt. Angel Vitamin Company One Good Multi	US	★★½
Mt. Angel Vitamin Company Simply 4 Energy	US	★★★★
Mt. Angel Vitamin Company Women's 50+	US	★★★★
Multibionta Probiotic Multivitamin	Canada	½
Multibionta Probiotic Multivitamin 50+	Canada	½
MultiSure (see Webber Naturals)		
Myadec Multivitamin Multimineral Supplement	US	★
N.F. Formulas (see Integrative Therapeutics)		
Nāka Nutri Multi	Canada	★★½
Nāka Nutri Multi for Men	Canada	★★★★
Nāka Nutri Multi for Women	Canada	★★★★
Natrol My Favorite Multiple	US	★★½
Natrol My Favorite Multiple Energizer	US	★★
Natrol My Favorite Multiple for Women	US	★★★
Natrol My Favorite Multiple Iron Free	US	★★★½
Natrol My Favorite Multiple Prime	US	★★
Natrol My Favorite Multiple Prime 50+	US	★★★½
Natrol My Favorite Multiple Take One	US	★★½
Natural Factors Hi Potency Multi	Canada	★★½

Manufacturer & Product Name	Country	Rating
Natural Factors Men's 50+ MultiStart	USA	★★★★
Natural Factors Men's MultiStart	USA	★★★★½
Natural Factors MultiFactors Women's	Canada	★★★★½
Natural Factors MultiFactors Women's 50+	Canada	★★★★½
Natural Factors Women's MultiStart	USA	★★★★
Natural Factors Women's Plus MultiStart	USA	★★★★½
Natural Vitality Organic Life Vitamins	USA	★★★
Naturally Preferred Life Multi Complete	USA	★
Naturally Preferred Men's Multi	USA	★½
Naturally Preferred One Daily Multi	USA	★½
Naturally Preferred One Daily Multi Iron Free	USA	★½
Naturally Preferred Vita-Max	USA	★★★
Naturally Preferred Women's Multi	USA	★
Nature Made Multi Complete Liquid Softgel	USA	★
Nature Made Multi Complete Tablet	USA	★½
Nature Made Multi for Her	USA	★
Nature Made Multi for Her 50+	USA	★½
Nature Made Multi for Him 50+	USA	★★
Nature's Answer Multi-Daily	USA	★½
Nature's Answer Platinum Liquid Multiple Vitamin & Mineral	USA	★★½
Nature's Best A to Z	USA	★
Nature's Best Multi-Max 50 Plus	USA	★★
Nature's Best Multi-Max Complete	USA	★★★
Nature's Blend Multi-Vitamin with Minerals	USA	½
Nature's Bounty ABC Plus Senior	Canada	★
Nature's Bounty Mega Vita-Min	Canada	★★½
Nature's Bounty Multi-Day Plus Minerals	USA	½
Nature's Bounty Multi-Day Women's	USA	★
Nature's Bounty Your Life Adult Gummies	USA	★½
Nature's Bounty Your Life Men's 45+	USA	★½
Nature's Bounty Your Life Women's 45+	USA	★
Nature's Harmony Adult Chewable Superior One-Per-Day	Canada	★★½
Nature's Harmony High Potency One-Per-Day	Canada	★★★
Nature's Harmony Superior One-Per-Day	Canada	★½
Nature's Life Antioxidant Soft Multi	USA	★★★★
Nature's Life E-Z Vite Multiple	USA	★½
Nature's Life Great Greens Multi	USA	★★★½
Nature's Life Green-Pro 96 Multi	USA	★★
Nature's Life One Daily	USA	★★½
Nature's Life Soft Gelatin Multiple	USA	★★★
Nature's Life Vegan Super Mega Vite	USA	★★★
Nature's Plus Ageloss Men's Multi	USA	★★★★
Nature's Plus Ageloss Women's Multi	USA	★★★½
Nature's Plus Especially Yours	USA	★★★
Nature's Plus Mega Force	USA	★★★★
Nature's Plus Source of Life	USA	★★★½
Nature's Plus Source of Life (no iron)	USA	★★★★
Nature's Plus Source of Life Adult's Chewable	USA	★★★
Nature's Plus Source of Life Gold	USA	★★★★½
Nature's Plus Source of Life Green and Red	USA	★★★★
Nature's Plus Source of Life Men	USA	★★★★
Nature's Plus Source of Life Men Liquid	USA	★★★½
Nature's Plus Source of Life Red	USA	★★★★
Nature's Plus Source of Life Women	USA	★★★½
Nature's Plus Source of Life Women Liquid	USA	★★★½
Nature's Plus Ultra Source of Life	USA	★★★½
Nature's Plus Ultra Source of Life No Iron	USA	★★★★
Nature's Secret Women's 73 Nutrient Soft-Gel Multi	USA	★★½
Nature's Sunshine Super Supplemental	USA	★★★
Nature's Way Alive! Energy 50+	USA	★★
Nature's Way Alive! Liquid Multi	USA	★★★½
Nature's Way Alive! Men's Energy	USA	★★
Nature's Way Alive! Men's Multi	USA	★★★★
Nature's Way Alive! Men's Ultra Potency	USA	★★★½
Nature's Way Alive! Multi-Vitamin	USA	★★★½
Nature's Way Alive! Multi-Vitamin (No Iron Added)	USA	★★★★½
Nature's Way Alive! Multi-Vitamin Ultra Potency	USA	★★★
Nature's Way Alive! Women's Energy	USA	★½
Nature's Way Alive! Women's Multi	USA	★★★★
New Chapter every MAN	USA	★★
New Chapter Every Man II	USA	★★½
New Chapter Every Man's One Daily	USA	★★
New Chapter Every Man's One Daily 40+	USA	★★
New Chapter Every Woman	USA	★★
New Chapter Every Woman II	USA	★★½
New Chapter Every Woman's One Daily	USA	★★
New Chapter Every Woman's One Daily 40+	USA	★★
New Chapter Only One	USA	★★
New Chapter Perfect Calm	USA	★★½
New Chapter Perfect Energy	USA	★★½
New Chapter Perfect Immune	USA	★★
New Chapter Tiny Tabs	USA	★★
New Roots Multi	Canada	★★★
New Roots Multi-Max	Canada	★★★★
New Roots Multi-MaxImmune	Canada	★★★½
Neways Maximol Solutions	USA	½
Nikken Mega Daily 4 for Men	USA	★★½
Nikken Mega Daily 4 for Women	USA	★★½
NorthStar Nutritionals RegeneCell	USA	★★★★★
NorthStar Nutritionals Ultimate Daily Support	USA	★★★★½
NOW Adam	USA	★★★★
NOW Adam Superior	USA	★★★★
NOW Daily Vits	USA	★
NOW Eve	USA	★★★★
NOW Liquid Multi Gels	USA	★★★
NOW Special One	USA	★★

Manufacturer & Product Name	Country	Rating
NOW Special Two	USA	★★★★
NOW Vit-Min 100	USA	★★★½
NOW Vit-Min 75+	USA	★★★½
Nu-Life The Ultimate One Men 50+	Canada	★★★½
Nu-Life The Ultimate One Women 50+	Canada	★★★½
Nutra Perfect Dentra Perfect	USA	★★
Nutra Perfect VitaPerfect	USA	★★★½
Nutra Therapeutics (see Adëeva)		
Nutraceutical Research Institute Mega 2	USA	★★★
Nutralife Ultra Daily	USA	★★½
NutraMetrix Isotonix with Iron	USA	★★
NutraOrigin Men & Women	USA	★★★
NutraOrigin Men's	USA	★★★
NutraOrigin Women's	USA	★★½
Nutribetics Multi-Vitamin	Canada	★★★
NutriCology Complete Immune	USA	★★★★½
NutriCology Multi-Vi-Min	USA	★★
NutriCology Multi-Vi-Min without Copper and Iron	USA	★★
NutriCology MVM-A	USA	★★★
NutriCology WomanPrime	USA	★★
Nutriex Basic	USA	★★★★
Nutriex Health	USA	★★★★½
NutriGen AM & PM Essentials	USA	★★
Nutrilite Daily	USA	★½
Nutrilite Daily Free Multivitamin Multimineral	USA	★½
Nutrina Vitamax Powder	USA	★★★
Nutrina Vitamax Tablets	USA	★★
Nutrition Dynamics Optimum Health Essentials	USA	★★★★½
Nutrition House Men's Multi Extra	Canada	★★★½
Nutrition House Multi-Vitamin Extra	Canada	★★½
Nutrition House Women's Multi Extra	Canada	★★★½
Nutrition Now MultiVites	USA	★½
NuTriVene Adult Daily	USA	★★★★½
NuTriVene Full Spectrum Formula	USA	★★★★
Nutri-West Core Level Health Reserve	USA	★
Nutri-West Multi Complex	USA	★½
Nutri-West MultiBalance For Men	USA	★★½
Nutri-West MultiBalance For Women	USA	★★½
O'Brien Pharmacy Optimal Daily Allowance	USA	★★★★½
Ola Loa Energy Daily Multi	USA	★★★½
Olympian Labs Vita-Vitamin	USA	★★★½
Omninutrition Omni IV	USA	★
One A Day Energy	USA	★
One A Day for Men	Canada	★½
One A Day for Men 50 Plus	Canada	★½
One A Day for Women	Canada	½
One A Day for Women 50 Plus	Canada	½
One A Day Menopause Formula	USA	★½
One A Day Men's 50+ Advantage	USA	★½
One A Day Men's Health Formula	USA	★½
One A Day Men's Pro Edge	USA	★½
One A Day VitaCraves	USA	★
One A Day WeightSmart	Canada	★½
One A Day Women's	USA	★
One A Day Women's 50+ Advantage	USA	★½
One A Day Women's Active Metabolism	USA	★
One A Day Women's Petites	USA	★
One A Day Women's plus Healthy Skin Support	USA	★
OneSource Men's	USA	★★★½
OneSource Women's	USA	★★★
Only Natural For Women Only	USA	★½
Only Natural Mega Multi Energizer	USA	★★★★
Optima Multivit & Mineralex	Canada	★★
Optimox Androvite	USA	★★★★
Optimox Gynovite Plus	USA	★★★
Optimox Optivite P.M.T.	USA	★★★★
Optimum Nutrition Opti-Men	USA	★★★½
Optimum Nutrition Opti-Women	USA	★★½
Option+ Multi	Canada	★
Option+ Multi Adult	Canada	★½
Option+ Multi Forte	Canada	★
Option+ Multi Forte Senior	Canada	★
Oregon Health Multi-Guard	USA	★★★★
Orenda International All in One Female	USA	★★★½
Orenda International All in One Male	USA	★★★½
Orenda International All in One Young & Active	USA	★★★★
Organika Multiple Vitamins with Minerals	Canada	★
Organika One Daily	Canada	★★
Ortho Molecular Products Alpha Base with Iron	USA	★★★★½
Ortho Molecular Products Alpha Base without Iron	USA	★★★★½
OxyLife Liquid Oxy-Gold	USA	★★★
Perque Perque 2 Life Guard	USA	★★★★
Personnelle Complete	Canada	½
Personnelle Forte	Canada	★
Personnelle Senior	Canada	★
Personnelle Superia	Canada	★
Pharmacists Selection Multivitamin Multimineral	Canada	½
Pharmacists Selection Multivitamin Multimineral Plus	Canada	★
Pharmanex Life Essentials	USA	★★
Pharmanex Vitox	USA	★★½
PharmAssure Complete Multivite	USA	★½
PharmAssure Men's Biomultiple	USA	★★★
PharmAssure Women's Biomultiple	USA	★★
Pharmax Adult Formula	Canada	★★★
Physician Formulas MultiVit Rx	USA	★★★★½
Physician's Preference Dr. Hotze's Energy Formula	USA	★★★★½
Phytobec	Canada	★½

Manufacturer & Product Name	Country	Rating
Pioneer 1 + 1 Vitamin Mineral	USA	★★★★
Pioneer 1 + Vitamin Mineral	USA	★★★½
Pioneer 1 + Vitamin Mineral Iron Free	USA	★★★★
Pioneer Chewable	USA	★★★★
Pioneer Chewable Iron Free	USA	★★★½
Pioneer Vitamin Mineral	USA	★★★★½
Platinum Performance Platinum Multi-Vitamin & Mineral Formula	USA	★★
Poliquin Complete Multi 2.0	USA	★★★★
Poliquin Complete Multi 2.0 Iron Free	USA	★★★★½
Poliquin Multi Intense	USA	★★★★½
Poliquin Multi Intense Iron Free	USA	★★★★½
Poliquin Über Nutrients	USA	★★★
Poliquin Über Nutrients Iron Free	USA	★★★
Prairie Naturals Multi-Force	Canada	★★★★
Prairie Naturals Multi-Force Iron Free	Canada	★★★★½
Prairie Naturals MultiForce ORAC	Canada	★★½
Pro Grade VGF 25+ for Men	USA	★★½
Pro Grade VGF 25+ for Women	USA	★★½
Pro Health Super Multiple II	USA	★★★★
Pro Image Pro Vitamin Complete	USA	★
Pro-Caps Laboratories Essential 1	USA	★★½
Progressive Active Men	Canada	★★★★
Progressive Active Women	Canada	★★★★
Progressive Adult Men	Canada	★★★½
Progressive Adult Women	Canada	★★★½
Progressive Men 50+	Canada	★★★★
Progressive Women's 50+	Canada	★★★★
ProThera MultiThera 1	USA	★★★★½
ProThera MultiThera 2	USA	★★★★½
ProThera VitaTab Chewable	USA	★★½
Pure Encapsulations Men's Nutrients	USA	★★★★½
Pure Encapsulations Multi t/d	USA	★★★½
Pure Encapsulations Nutrient 950	USA	★★★★
Pure Encapsulations PureFood Nutrients	USA	★½
Pure Encapsulations Women's Nutrients	USA	★★★★½
Pure Essence Labs LifeEssence Powder	USA	★★★★½
Pure Essence Labs LifeEssence Vegetarian Formula	USA	★★★★½
Pure Essence Labs LifeEssence Women's Formula	USA	★★★★½
Pure Essence Labs Longevity Men's Formula	USA	★★★★½
Pure Essence Labs Longevity Women's Formula	USA	★★★★½
Pure Essence Labs One 'n' Only	USA	★★★★½
Pure Essence Labs One 'n' Only Men's Formula	USA	★★★★
Pure Essence Labs One 'n' Only Women's Formula	USA	★★★
Pure Synergy Organic Multi Vita-Min	USA	★★½
Pure Synergy Organic Vita-Min-Herb for Men	USA	★★★★
Pure Synergy Organic Vita-Min-Herb for Women	USA	★★★★
Puritan's Pride ABC Plus	USA	½
Puritan's Pride Mega Vita-Min	USA	★★★
Puritan's Pride One Daily Men's	USA	★★½

Manufacturer & Product Name	Country	Rating
Puritan's Pride Vita-Min Complete Formula #1	USA	★
Puritan's Pride Women's One Daily	USA	★
Purity Products Perfect Multi	USA	★★★★½
Purity Products Perfect Multi Essentials	USA	★★★★
Purity Products Perfect Multi Focus Formula	USA	★★★★
Purity Products Perfect Multi Liquid	USA	★★★½
Purity Products Perfect Multi Super Greens	USA	★★★★½
Purity Products Perfect Multi Super Greens for Canada	Canada	★★★★½
Purpose (See Creating Wellness)		
QCI Nutritionals Daily Preventive #1	USA	★★★★½
Quest Adult Chewables	Canada	★★½
Quest Mature Men 50+ His Daily One	Canada	★★★½
Quest Mature Women 50+ Her Daily One	Canada	★★★½
Quest Maximum Once A Day	Canada	★★★½
Quest Men His Daily One	Canada	★★★½
Quest Premium Multi-Cap	Canada	★★½
Quest Premium Multi-Cap iron-free	Canada	★★
Quest Super Once A Day	Canada	★★★½
Quest Women Her Daily One	Canada	★★
Quest Women Her Daily One Chewable	Canada	★★½
Rainbow Light 50+ Mini-Tab	USA	★★★
Rainbow Light Active Senior	USA	★★★
Rainbow Light Advanced Nutritional System	USA	★★★★½
Rainbow Light Advanced Nutritional System Iron-Free	USA	★★★★½
Rainbow Light Certified Organics Men's Multivitamin	USA	★★
Rainbow Light Certified Organics Women's Multivitamin	USA	★★
Rainbow Light Complete Nutritional System	USA	★★★★½
Rainbow Light Complete Nutritional System Iron-Free	USA	★★★★
Rainbow Light Energizer One	USA	★★★
Rainbow Light Just Once	USA	★★
Rainbow Light Just Once Iron-Free	USA	★★
Rainbow Light Men's One	USA	★★★½
Rainbow Light Performance Energy for Men	USA	★★★
Rainbow Light RejuvenAge 40+	USA	★★★★½
Rainbow Light Women's Nutritional System	USA	★★★★
Rainbow Light Women's One	USA	★★★½
Ray & Terry's Total Care Daily Formula	USA	★★★★½
Ray & Terry's Two-a-Day	USA	★★★½
Real Advantage Nutrients Ultimate Daily Support	USA	★★★★½
Rejuvenation Science Maximum Vitality	USA	★★★★★
Reliv Classic	USA	★★½
Reliv Now	USA	★★
Réservé 50+ Senior Formula	Canada	★
Réservé Forte Formula	Canada	★
Réservé Regular Formula	Canada	½

Manufacturer & Product Name	Country	Rating
Reserveage Organics Vibrance	🇺🇸	★★★★
Restorage Professional for Men & Women	🇺🇸	★½
Revival Firm Foundation Multivitamin Multimineral 100	🇺🇸	★★
Rexall US (see Sundown Naturals)		
Rexall Adult Formula	🇨🇦	½
Rexall Adults 50+ Formula	🇨🇦	★½
Rexall Complete	🇨🇦	½
Rexall Complete for Adults 50+	🇨🇦	★
Rexall Complete Forte	🇨🇦	★
Rexall Complete Premium	🇨🇦	★
Rexall Multivitamin + Multimineral Forte	🇨🇦	★
Rexall Women's Formula	🇨🇦	½
R-Garden Daily Complete	🇺🇸	★★★★
Rite Aid Central-Vite	🇺🇸	½
Rite Aid Central-Vite Cardio	🇺🇸	★
Rite Aid Central-Vite Men's Mature	🇺🇸	★½
Rite Aid Central-Vite Performance	🇺🇸	★
Rite Aid Central-Vite Select	🇺🇸	★
Rite Aid Central-Vite Women's Mature	🇺🇸	★½
Rite Aid One Daily Energy Formula	🇺🇸	★
Rite Aid One Daily Men's Multi	🇺🇸	★
Rite Aid One Daily Women's	🇺🇸	½
Rite Aid One Daily Women's 50+	🇺🇸	★½
Rite Aid ResurgenC	🇺🇸	★
Rite Aid Whole Source Men	🇺🇸	★★
Rite Aid Whole Source Women	🇺🇸	★½
Rx Vitamins ReVitalize	🇺🇸	★★★★
Safeway Active Performance	🇺🇸	★
Safeway Century	🇺🇸	★
Safeway Century Ultimate Men's	🇺🇸	★
Safeway Century Ultimate Women's	🇺🇸	★
Safeway Complete for Adults 50+	🇺🇸	★
Safeway One Daily Men's 50+ Advanced	🇺🇸	★½
Safeway One Daily Men's Health Formula	🇺🇸	★
Safeway Ultimate Women's 50+	🇺🇸	★½
Safeway Women's 50+	🇺🇸	★½
SAN Multi Nutrient Formula Basic	🇺🇸	★★★★
SAN Multi Nutrient Formula Gold	🇺🇸	★★★★½
SAN Multi Nutrient Formula Original	🇺🇸	★★★★½
SAN Multi Nutrient Formula Plus	🇺🇸	★★★★½
Sangster's Choice Apex	🇨🇦	★
Sangster's Men's Choice	🇨🇦	★★★½
Sangster's Women's Choice	🇨🇦	★★★
Saturn Supplements VitaPlex	🇺🇸	★½
Schiff Single Day	🇺🇸	★★★
Schiff Vegetarian Multiple	🇺🇸	★½
Schwartz Laboratories VitaPlex	🇺🇸	★★★★
Schwarzbein Institute Ultra Preventive III (Capsules)	🇺🇸	★★★½

Manufacturer & Product Name	Country	Rating
Schwarzbein Principle Ultra Preventive III (Tablets)	🇺🇸	★★★★½
Selekta Multi's (w/o Copper & Iron)	🇨🇦	★★★
Sentinel Mega Multi	🇺🇸	★★★
Sentinel One Daily	🇺🇸	½
Sentinel One Daily with Iron	🇺🇸	½
Sentinel Sentivites Senior	🇺🇸	★
Sentinel Therra M	🇺🇸	★
Shaklee CitriBoost	🇺🇸	★½
Shaklee Vita-Lea Gold Vitamin K	🇺🇸	★★½
Shaklee Vita-Lea Gold with Vitamin K	🇨🇦	★★½
Shaklee Vita-Lea Gold without Vitamin K	🇨🇦	★★½
Shaklee Vita-Lea Gold without Vitamin K	🇺🇸	★★½
Shaklee Vita-Lea Iron Formula	🇨🇦	★★
Shaklee Vita-Lea Iron Formula	🇺🇸	★★
Shaklee Vita-Lea Without Iron Formula	🇨🇦	★★
Shaklee Vita-Lea without Iron Formula	🇺🇸	★★½
Sīsū Multi Vi Min	🇨🇦	★★
Sīsū Optimal Health Multi 1	🇨🇦	★★★
Sīsū Supreme Multivitamin	🇨🇦	★★★½
Sīsū Supreme Multivitamin 50+	🇨🇦	★★★★
Sīsū Supreme Multivitamin with Iron	🇨🇦	★★★
Solaray Iron Free Spectro	🇺🇸	★★★
Solaray Men's Golden	🇺🇸	★★★½
Solaray Multi-Vita Mega-Mineral	🇺🇸	★★★½
Solaray Once Daily High Energy	🇺🇸	★★½
Solaray Provide	🇺🇸	★★★½
Solaray Spectro	🇺🇸	★★½
Solaray Spectro 3	🇺🇸	★★★
Solaray Spectro 3 Iron Free	🇺🇸	★★★½
Solaray Spectro 50-Plus	🇺🇸	★★★½
Solaray Spectro Man	🇺🇸	★★½
Solaray Spectro Vegetarian	🇺🇸	★★½
Solaray Spectro Woman	🇺🇸	★★½
Solaray Three Daily Super Energy	🇺🇸	★★★★
Solaray Three Daily Super Energy Iron Free	🇺🇸	★★★★
Solaray Twice Daily Multi Energy	🇺🇸	★★★
Solaray Twice Daily Multi Energy Iron Free	🇺🇸	★★★½
Solaray VitaPrime For Men	🇺🇸	★★★½
Solaray VitaPrime For Women	🇺🇸	★★★½
Solaray Women's Golden	🇺🇸	★★★½
Solgar Earth Source Multi-Nutrient	🇺🇸	★★★½
Solgar Female Multiple	🇺🇸	★★★★
Solgar Formula VM-75	🇺🇸	★★★
Solgar Formula VM-75 Iron-Free	🇺🇸	★★★
Solgar Male Multiple	🇺🇸	★★★★½
SomaLife SomaVit Plus	🇨🇦	★★★
Source Naturals Advanced One (No Iron)	🇺🇸	★★★★
Source Naturals Advanced One (with Iron)	🇺🇸	★★★½
Source Naturals Élan Vitàl Multiple	🇺🇸	★★★★½

Manufacturer & Product Name	Country	Rating
Source Naturals Life Force Green Multiple	USA	★★★★½
Source Naturals Life Force Multiple	USA	★★★★½
Source Naturals Life Force Vegan	USA	★★★★★
Source Naturals Life Force Vegan No Iron	USA	★★★★★
Source Naturals Mega-One	USA	★★★
Source Naturals Mega-One No Iron	USA	★★★½
Source Naturals Men's Life Force Multiple	USA	★★★★★
Source Naturals Ultra Multiple	USA	★★★
Source Naturals Wellness Multiple	USA	★★★½
Source Naturals Women's Life Force	USA	★★★★★
Source Naturals Women's Life Force Multiple, No Iron	USA	★★★★★
Spring Valley Adult Gummy Multivitamin	USA	½
Spring Valley Ultra Multivitamin For Women	USA	★★★
STS Fit Man Multi	USA	★★★½
STS Fit Woman Multi	USA	★★★½
Sundown Naturals Adult Multivitamin Gummies	USA	★½
Sundown Naturals Complete Daily	USA	★
Sundown Naturals Complete Women's	USA	★½
Sundown Naturals Daily	USA	½
Sundown Naturals SunVite	USA	★
Sundown Naturals SunVite Active Adults 50+	USA	★
Sundown Naturals Whole Food Multivitamin	USA	★★★½
Super Nutrition Men's Blend	USA	★★★★½
Super Nutrition Perfect Family	USA	★★★★½
Super Nutrition Super Immune Multi Vitamin	USA	★★★★★
Super Nutrition Women's Blend	USA	★★★★½
Swanson Active One with Iron	USA	★★
Swanson Active One without Iron	USA	★★½
Swanson Active One without Iron Mini-Tabs	USA	★★★
Swanson All-Day Complete for Seniors	USA	★★★★
Swanson Century Formula with Iron	USA	★
Swanson Century Formula without Iron	USA	★½
Swanson Daily Multi-Vitamin & Mineral	USA	★★
Swanson Geromulti without Iron	USA	★½
Swanson High Potency Softgel Iron Free	USA	★★★★½
Swanson Jack LaLanne Vita-Lanne Liquid	USA	★★★
Swanson Longevital	USA	★★★★★
Swanson Men's Prime Multi	USA	★★
Swanson Vital Multi for Men	USA	★★★½
Swanson Vital Multi for Women	USA	★★★½
Swanson Whole Food Multi without Iron	USA	★★★★½
Swanson Women's Prime Multi	USA	★★
Swiss Adult Chewable Multi Vitamin & Mineral	Canada	★★
Swiss Adult Multi One Formula	Canada	★★
Swiss Iron Free Vege	Canada	★★★½
Swiss One	Canada	★
Swiss One 25	Canada	★½
Swiss One 50	Canada	★★★½
Swiss One 80	Canada	★★★

Manufacturer & Product Name	Country	Rating
Swiss Total One Antioxidant	Canada	★★★½
Swiss Total One Men	Canada	★★★½
Swiss Total One Men 50+	Canada	★★★½
Swiss Total One Sport	Canada	★★★½
Swiss Total One Women	Canada	★★
Swiss Total One Women 50+	Canada	★★★½
Tanta Formula Forte Senior	Canada	★
The Results Company (see Vitamost)		
The Synergy Company (see Pure Synergy)		
Theragran-M Advanced	USA	★
Theragran-M Advanced 50 Plus	USA	★
Theragran-M Premier	USA	★½
Theragran-M Premier 50 Plus	USA	★★
Theralogix 50+ Companion Women's Multivitamin	USA	★½
Theralogix Essentia Women's Multivitamin	USA	★★
Thompson Adult-Plex	USA	★★★½
Thompson All-In-One	USA	★½
Thompson Coach's Formula	USA	★★★½
Thompson Mega 80	USA	★★★½
Thompson Multi Formula For Women	USA	★
Thompson Multi Vitamins With Minerals	USA	★½
Thompson Nuplex	USA	★½
Thorne Research Al's Formula	USA	★★★★
Thorne Research Basic Nutrients V	USA	★★★★
Thorne Research Extra Nutrients	USA	★★★★
Thorne Research Meta-Fem	USA	★★★★½
Thorne Research Nutri-Fem	USA	★★★★
To Your Health Liquid Vitamins	USA	★★★★½
Trace Minerals Research Liquid Multi Vita-Mineral	USA	★★★
Trace Minerals Research Liquimins Maxi Multi	USA	★★
Trader Joe's Men's Once Daily	USA	★★★
Trader Joe's Multi Vitamin & Mineral Antioxidant	USA	★★
Trader Joe's Women's Once Daily	USA	★★★½
TriVita VitaDaily AM Formula & PM Formula	USA	★★★
TriVita Wellavoh for Men AM Formula & PM Formula	USA	★★★½
TriVita Wellavoh for Women AM Formula & PM Formula	USA	★★★
Trophic Complete One	Canada	★★★½
Trophic Men's 50+	Canada	★★★★★½
Trophic Men's Ultra Complete	Canada	★★★★★½
Trophic Vita Balance & Minero Balance	Canada	★★★½
Trophic Women's 50+	Canada	★★★★★½
Trophic Women's Ultra Complete	Canada	★★★★★½
Tropical Oasis Multiple Vitamin Mineral for Adults	USA	★
True Essentials Adult Chewable	USA	★½
True Essentials Everyday Essentials	USA	★★★½
True Essentials Men's Everyday	USA	★★★
True Essentials Women's Everyday	USA	★★★
True Essentials Women's Gold	USA	★★★

Manufacturer & Product Name	Country	Rating
Truehope EMPowerplus	Canada	★★★
Truestar Health TrueBASICS Solo	Canada	★★★★★
Twinlab Allergy Multi Caps	USA	★★★½
Twinlab Daily One Caps With Iron	USA	★★½
Twinlab Daily One Caps Without Iron	USA	★★½
Twinlab Daily Two Caps with Iron	USA	★★★
Twinlab Daily Two Caps without iron	USA	★★★½
Twinlab Dualtabs	USA	★★★½
Twinlab Mega 6	USA	★★★½
Twinlab Women's Ultra Daily	USA	★★★½
Ultimate Nutrition Daily Complete Formula	USA	★★★★
Ultimate Nutrition Super Complete Formula	USA	★★★★½
Unicity Core Health Basics	USA	★½
Univera MultiVitamin	USA	★★
Universal Formulas Quint-Essence	USA	★★★½
Up & Up Adults' Multivitamin/Multimineral	USA	★
Up & Up Men's Daily	USA	★½
Up & Up Multivitamin/Multimineral	USA	★
Up & Up Women's Daily	USA	★
Up &Up Multivitamin/Multimineral Adults 50+	USA	★
Usana Health Sciences Essentials	Canada	★★★★★
Usana Health Sciences Essentials	USA	★★★★★
Usana Health Sciences Essentials Kosher	USA	★★★★½
Växa Daily Essentials	USA	★½
VegLife MultiVeg Energy	USA	★★★
VegLife MultiVeg Energy Iron Free	USA	★★★½
VegLife SpectroVeg High Energy	USA	★★½
VegLife Vegan One	USA	★★½
VegLife Vegan One Iron Free	USA	★★½
Visalus Multi Mineral & Vitamin	USA	★★½
Vita Springs Anti-Aging Multi-Vitamins	USA	★½
Vita-Complete AA	Canada	★½
Vita-Complete Vita29	Canada	★
Vitacost Men's 50 Plus	USA	★★★½
Vitacost Synergy 3000	USA	★★★★½
Vitacost Synergy Basic	USA	★★★★½
Vitacost Synergy Complete	USA	★★★★
Vitacost Synergy Men's	USA	★★★★½
Vitacost Synergy NeroPower	USA	★★★★½
Vitacost Synergy Viva! No Added Iron	USA	★★★★½
Vitacost Synergy Viva! with Iron	USA	★★★★½
Vitacost Synergy Women's	USA	★★★★½
Vitacost Synergy Women's with Iron	USA	★★★★½
Vitacost The Woman	USA	★★★★
Vitacost Women's 50 Plus	USA	★★★
VitaFusion Men's	USA	★½
VitaFusion MultiVites	USA	★½
VitaFusion MultiVites Sour	USA	★½
VitaFusion Women's	USA	★½
Vital Nutrients Minimal and Essential	USA	★★★★

Manufacturer & Product Name	Country	Rating
Vital Nutrients Multi-Nutrients 2	USA	★★★★
Vital Nutrients Multi-Nutrients 3	USA	★★★★
Vital Nutrients Multi-Nutrients 4	USA	★★★★
Vital Nutrients Multi-Nutrients 5	USA	★★★★
Vital Nutrients Multi-Nutrients Veg	USA	★★★★
Vital Nutrients Multi-Nutrients with Iron and Iodine	USA	★★★½
Vital Nutrients Vital Clear	USA	★★★★
VitaLabs Mega-2	USA	★★½
Vitalert Energy Multi	USA	★★
Vitality Men's Multi	USA	★★
Vitality Multivite	USA	★★½
Vitality Women's Multi	USA	★★
Vitalux Healthy Eyes	Canada	★★
Vitalux Timed Release Multivitamin/Multimineral	Canada	★★
Vitamark Primalux	USA	★★★
VitaMedica Multi-Vitamin & Mineral	USA	★★★★
Vitamin Code (see Garden of Life)		
Vitamin Power Advanced Multi-Vites & Mins	USA	★
Vitamin Power Complete Men's Multiple	USA	★★½
Vitamin Power Mega Multiple 85	USA	★★
Vitamin Power Power Source 100	USA	★★★
Vitamin Power Super Vite	USA	★★
Vitamin Power Ultra Multi 90 Plus	USA	★★★
Vitamin Research Products Extend Core	USA	★★★★½
Vitamin Research Products Extend Liquid	USA	★★★★
Vitamin Research Products Extend One	USA	★★★½
Vitamin Research Products Extend Plus	USA	★★★★½
Vitamin Research Products Extend Ultra	USA	★★★★½
Vitamin Research Products Optimum Protection	USA	★★★★
Vitamin Research Products Optimum Silver	USA	★★★★½
Vitamin Research Products Women's Essentials	USA	★★★★
Vitamin World Mega Vita-Gel	USA	★★½
Vitamin World Mega Vita-Min	USA	★★½
Vitamin World Mega Vita-Min Adult Chewable	USA	★½
Vitaminol (see Le Naturiste)		
Vitamins Direct Time Fighters for Men	USA	★★★½
Vitamost Prime	USA	★★★★½
Vitanica Mid-Life Symmetry	USA	★★★½
Vitanica Women's Symmetry	USA	★★★½
Vitapril	USA	★★
Vitazan Professional Multi	Canada	★★★
VIVA DailyGuard	USA	★★★
VIVA for Life	USA	★★
Viva Vitamins Complete Multi Extra Strength	USA	★★½
Viva Vitamins Complete Multi Extra Strength Iron and Copper Free	USA	★★★
Viva Vitamins Complete Multi Regular Strength	USA	★★
Viva Vitamins Complete Multi Regular Strength Iron and Copper Free	USA	★★

Manufacturer & Product Name	Country	Rating
Viva Vitamins Complete Multi Ultra Strength	USA	★★★
Viva Vitamins V.M.T. Extra Strength	USA	★★★★
Viva Vitamins V.M.T. Regular Strength	USA	★★★
Viva Vitamins VegiSource	USA	★★★½
Vivitas Woman One for Her	Canada	★★
Vivitas Woman One for Her 50+	Canada	★★½
Walgreens A thru Z Active Performance	USA	★
Walgreens A thru Z Select Ultimate Men's	USA	★½
Walgreens A thru Z Select Ultimate Women's	USA	★½
Walgreens A thru Z Ultimate Women's	USA	★
Walgreens Advanced Formula A thru Z	USA	★
Walgreens Advanced Formula A thru Z Select Adults 50+	USA	★½
Walgreens One Daily Energy	USA	★
Walgreens One Daily for Men	USA	★
Walgreens One Daily for Men 50+ Advanced	USA	★½
Walgreens One Daily for Woman	USA	★
Walgreens One Daily for Women 50+ Advanced	USA	★½
Walgreens One Daily Healthy Weight	USA	½
Wampole Adult Multivitamin Chewable	Canada	½
Watkins Daily Vitamin	USA	★★
Webber Naturals Multi Vitamin	Canada	★
Webber Naturals MultiSure For Men	Canada	★★★½
Webber Naturals MultiSure For Men 50+	Canada	★★★★
Webber Naturals MultiSure for Women	Canada	★★★
Webber Naturals MultiSure For Women 50+	Canada	★★★½
Webber Naturals MultiSure Healthy Aging	Canada	★★★
Wellgenix Balanced Essentials	USA	★★
Wellness International Network Phyto-Vite	USA	★★½
Wellness Resources Daily Energy Multiple Vitamin	USA	★★★★
WellnessPro Multivitamin Complex for Men	USA	★★
WellnessPro Multivitamin Complex for Women	USA	★★
Westcoast Naturals Multi-One	Canada	★★½
World Organic Liqui-Vite & Liqui-Mins	USA	★★½
Xymogen ActivNutrients	USA	★★★½
Xymogen ActivNutrients without Iron	USA	★★★½
Yoli Vitamin & Mineral	USA	★★★★
YOR Health YOR Essential Vitamin	USA	★★★★
Young Again All Your Vitamins & All Your Minerals	USA	★★
Young Living Master Formula Hers	USA	★★★½
Young Living Master Formula His	USA	★★★★
Youngevity Beyond Tangy Tangerine	USA	★★★★
Youngevity Majestic Earth Tropical Plus	USA	★★
Youngevity Ultimate Classic	USA	★★★★½
Youngevity Ultimate Tangy Tangerine	USA	★★★★½
Zeal For Life Wellness Formula	USA	★½
Ziquin Mind and Body Tonic	USA	★★

BIBLIOGRAPHY

Chapter 1 Reference List

(1) Marler JB, Wallin JR. Human Health, the Nutritional Quality of Harvested Food and Sustainable Farming Systems. *Nutrition Security Institute* [serial online] 2006; Accessed November 4, 2009.

(2) Thomas D. The mineral depletion of foods available to us as a nation (1940-2002)--a review of the 6th Edition of McCance and Widdowson. Nutr Health 2007;19:21-55.

(3) Farm Land Mineral Depletion. *Medical Missionary Press* [serial online] 2009; Accessed November 4, 2009.

(4) Horrigan L, Lawrence RS, Walker P. How sustainable agriculture can address the environmental and human health harms of industrial agriculture. *Environ Health Perspect* 2002;110:445-456.

(5) Lilburne LR, Hewitt AE, Sparling GP, Selvarajah N. Soil quality in New Zealand: policy and the science response. *J Environ Qual* 2002;31:1768-1773.

(6) McMichael AJ. Global environmental change and human health: new challenges to scientist and policy-maker. *J Public Health Policy* 1994;15:407-419.

(7) Boardman J, Shepheard ML, Walker E, Foster ID. Soil erosion and risk-assessment for on- and off-farm impacts: a test case using the Midhurst area, West Sussex, UK. *J Environ Manage* 2009;90:2578-2588.

(8) Griffin TS, Honeycutt CW. Effectiveness and efficacy of conservation options after potato harvest. *J Environ Qual* 2009;38:1627-1635.

(9) Gunderson PD. Biofuels and North American agriculture--implications for the health and safety of North American producers. *J Agromedicine* 2008;13:219-224.

(10) Liu YY, Ukita M, Imai T, Higuchi T. Recycling mineral nutrients to farmland via compost application. *Water Sci Technol* 2006;53:111-118.

(11) Robert M. [Degradation of soil quality: health and environmental risks]. Bull Acad Natl Med 1997;181:21-40.

(12) Davis DR, Epp MD, Riordan HD. Changes in USDA food composition data for 43 garden crops, 1950 to 1999. *J Am Coll Nutr* 2004;23:669-682.

(13) Vegetables without Vitamins. Life Extension Foundation [March]. 2001.

(14) Thomas D. A study on the mineral depletion of the foods available to us as a nation over the period 1940 to 1991. *Nutr Health* 2003;17:85-115.

(15) Picard A. Today's fruits and vegetables lack yesterday's nutrition. *Globe and Mail* [serial online] 2002; Accessed November 4, 9 A.D.

(16) Fan MS, Zhao FJ, Fairweather-Tait SJ, Poulton PR, Dunham SJ, McGrath SP. Evidence of decreasing mineral density in wheat grain over the last 160 years. *J Trace Elem Med Biol* 2008;22:315-324.

(17) Karr M. Mineral Depletion in Soils. longevitylibrary com [serial online] 2009; Accessed November 4, 2009.

(18) Drucker R. Depleted Soil and Compromised Food Sources: What You Can Do about It. *Nutrition Wellness* [serial online] 2006; Accessed May 11, 2009.

(19) Soil Mineral Depletion: Can a Healthy diet be sufficient in today's world? *Physical Nutrition* [serial online] 2009; Available from: Botanica Medica. Accessed May 11, 2009.

(20) Stockdale T. A speculative discussion of some problems arising from the use of ammonium nitrate fertiliser on acid soil. *Nutr Health* 1992;8:207-222.

(21) Soil Depletion. TJ Clark com [serial online] 2006; Accessed November 4, 2009.

(22) Ackerman LB. Overview of human exposure to dieldrin residues in the environment and current trends of residue levels in tissue. *Pestic Monit J* 1980;14:64-69.

(23) Albers JM, Kreis IA, Liem AK, van ZP. Factors that influence the level of contamination of human milk with poly-chlorinated organic compounds. *Arch Environ Contam Toxicol* 1996;30:285-291.

(24) Baillie-Hamilton PF. Chemical toxins: a hypothesis to explain the global obesity epidemic. *J Altern Complement Med* 2002;8:185-192.

(25) Bharadwaj L, Dhami K, Schneberger D, Stevens M, Renaud C, Ali A. Altered gene expression in human hepatoma HepG2 cells exposed to low-level 2,4-dichlorophenoxyacetic acid and potassium nitrate. *Toxicol In Vitro* 2005;19:603-619.

(26) Biscardi D, De FR, Feretti D et al. [Genotoxic effects of pesticide-treated vegetable extracts using the Allium cepa chromosome aberration and micronucleus tests]. *Ann Ig* 2003;15:1077-1084.

(27) Carpy SA, Kobel W, Doe J. Health risk of low-dose pesticides mixtures: a review of the 1985-1998 literature on combination toxicology and health risk assessment. *J Toxicol Environ Health B Crit Rev* 2000;3:1-25.

(28) Dougherty CP, Henricks HS, Reinert JC, Panyacosit L, Axelrad DA, Woodruff TJ. Dietary exposures to food contaminants across the United States. *Environ Res* 2000;84:170-185.

(29) Grote K, Andrade AJ, Grande SW et al. Effects of peripubertal exposure to triphenyltin on female sexual development of the rat. *Toxicology* 2006;222:17-24.

(30) Gupta PK. Pesticide exposure--Indian scene. *Toxicology* 2004;198:83-90.

(31) Jiang QT, Lee TK, Chen K et al. Human health risk assessment of organochlorines associated with fish consumption in a coastal city in China. *Environ Pollut* 2005;136:155-165.

(32) Katz JM, Winter CK. Comparison of pesticide exposure from consumption of domestic and imported fruits and vegetables. *Food Chem Toxicol* 2009;47:335-338.

(33) Kawahara J, Yoshinaga J, Yanagisawa Y. Dietary exposure to organophosphorus pesticides for young children in Tokyo and neighboring area. *Sci Total Environ* 2007;378:263-268.

(34) Luo Y, Zhang M. Multimedia transport and risk assessment of organophosphate pesticides and a case study in the northern San Joaquin Valley of California. *Chemosphere* 2009;75:969-978.

(35) Moser VC, Simmons JE, Gennings C. Neurotoxicological interactions of a five-pesticide mixture in preweanling rats. *Toxicol Sci* 2006;92:235-245.

(36) Nakata H, Kawazoe M, Arizono K et al. Organochlorine pesticides and polychlorinated biphenyl residues in foodstuffs and human tissues from china: status of contamination, historical trend, and human dietary exposure. *Arch Environ Contam Toxicol* 2002;43:473-480.

(37) Peng J, Peng L, Stevenson FF, Doctrow SR, Andersen JK. Iron and paraquat as synergistic environmental risk factors in sporadic Parkinson's disease accelerate age-related neurodegeneration. *J Neurosci* 2007;27:6914-6922.

(38) Reed L, Buchner V, Tchounwou PB. Environmental toxicology and health effects associated with hexachlorobenzene exposure. *Rev Environ Health* 2007;22:213-243.

(39) Rivas A, Cerrillo I, Granada A, Mariscal-Arcas M, Olea-Serrano F. Pesticide exposure of two age groups of women and its relationship with their diet. *Sci Total Environ* 2007;382:14-21.

(40) Tryphonas H. The impact of PCBs and dioxins on children's health: immunological considerations. *Can J Public Health* 1998;89 Suppl 1:S49-7.

(41) Tsydenova OV, Sudaryanto A, Kajiwara N, Kunisue T, Batoev VB, Tanabe S. Organohalogen compounds in human breast milk from Republic of Buryatia, Russia. *Environ Pollut* 2007;146:225-232.

(42) Viquez OM, Valentine HL, Friedman DB, Olson SJ, Valentine WM. Peripheral nerve protein expression and carbonyl content in N,N-diethlydithiocarbamate myelinopathy. *Chem Res Toxicol* 2007;20:370-379.

(43) Wade MG, Parent S, Finnson KW et al. Thyroid toxicity due to subchronic exposure to a complex mixture of 16 organochlorines, lead, and cadmium. *Toxicol Sci* 2002;67:207-218.

(44) Waliszewski SM, Pardio VT, Waliszewski KN et al. Organochlorine pesticide residues in cow's milk and butter in Mexico. *Sci Total Environ* 1997;208:127-132.

(45) Weiss J, Papke O, Bergman A. A worldwide survey of polychlorinated dibenzo-p-dioxins, dibenzofurans, and related contaminants in butter. *Ambio* 2005;34:589-597.

(46) Bloom MS, Vena JE, Swanson MK, Moysich KB, Olson JR. Profiles of ortho-polychlorinated biphenyl congeners, dichlorodiphenyldichloroethylene, hexachlorobenzene, and Mirex among male Lake Ontario sportfish consumers: the New York State Angler cohort study. *Environ Res* 2005;97:178-194.

(47) Carpy SA, Kobel W, Doe J. Health risk of low-dose pesticides mixtures: a review of the 1985-1998 literature on combination toxicology and health risk assessment. *J Toxicol Environ Health B Crit Rev* 2000;3:1-25.

(48) Swirsky GL, Stern BR, Slone TH, Brown JP, Manley NB, Ames BN. Pesticide residues in food: investigation of disparities in cancer risk estimates. *Cancer Lett* 1997;117:195-207.

(49) Gammon DW, Aldous CN, Carr WC, Jr., Sanborn JR, Pfeifer KF. A risk assessment of atrazine use in California: human health and ecological aspects. *Pest Manag Sci* 2005;61:331-355.

(50) Abhilash PC, Singh N. Pesticide use and application: an Indian scenario. *J Hazard Mater* 2009;165:1-12.

(51) Gupta PK. Pesticide exposure--Indian scene. *Toxicology* 2004;198:83-90.

(52) Moser VC, Simmons JE, Gennings C. Neurotoxicological interactions of a five-pesticide mixture in preweanling rats. *Toxicol Sci* 2006;92:235-245.

(53) Boyd CA, Weiler MH, Porter WP. Behavioral and neurochemical changes associated with chronic exposure to low-level concentration of pesticide mixtures. *J Toxicol Environ Health* 1990;30:209-221.

(54) Porter WP, Green SM, Debbink NL, Carlson I. Groundwater pesticides: interactive effects of low concentrations of carbamates aldicarb and methomyl and the triazine metribuzin on thyroxine and somatotropin levels in white rats. *J Toxicol Environ Health* 1993;40:15-34.

(55) Porter WP, Jaeger JW, Carlson IH. Endocrine, immune, and behavioral effects of aldicarb (carbamate), atrazine (triazine) and nitrate (fertilizer) mixtures at groundwater concentrations. *Toxicol Ind Health* 1999;15:133-150.

(56) Thiruchelvam M, Richfield EK, Baggs RB, Tank AW, Cory-Slechta DA. The nigrostriatal dopaminergic system as a preferential target of repeated exposures to combined paraquat and maneb: implications for Parkinson's disease. *J Neurosci* 2000;20:9207-9214.

(57) Charlier C, Albert A, Herman P et al. Breast cancer and serum organochlorine residues. *Occup Environ Med* 2003;60:348-351.

(58) Brucker-Davis F, Wagner-Mahler K, Delattre I et al. Cryptorchidism at birth in Nice area (France) is associated with higher prenatal exposure to PCBs and DDE, as assessed by colostrum concentrations. *Hum Reprod* 2008;23:1708-1718.

(59) Noren K, Meironyte D. Certain organochlorine and organobromine contaminants in Swedish human milk in perspective of past 20-30 years. *Chemosphere* 2000;40:1111-1123.

(60) Wigle DT, Arbuckle TE, Walker M, Wade MG, Liu S, Krewski D. Environmental hazards: evidence for effects on child health. *J Toxicol Environ Health B Crit Rev* 2007;10:3-39.

(61) Stefanidou M, Maravelias C, Spiliopoulou C. Human exposure to endocrine disruptors and breast milk. *Endocr Metab Immune Disord Drug Targets* 2009;9:269-276.

(62) Curl CL, Fenske RA, Elgethun K. Organophosphorus pesticide exposure of urban and suburban preschool children with organic and conventional diets. *Environ Health Perspect* 2003;111:377-382.

(63) Lester GE, Manthey JA, Buslig BS. Organic vs conventionally grown Rio Red whole grapefruit and juice: comparison of production inputs, market quality, consumer acceptance, and human health-bioactive compounds. *J Agric Food Chem* 2007;55:4474-4480.

(64) Worthington V. Nutritional quality of organic versus conventional fruits, vegetables, and grains. *J Altern Complement Med* 2001;7:161-173.

(65) Mitchell A. A two-year comparison of several quality and nutritional characteristics in tomatoes and peppers. University of California (Davis Campus) website [serial online] 2009; Accessed June 11, 2009.

(66) Carbonaro M, Mattera M, Nicoli S, Bergamo P, Cappelloni M. Modulation of antioxidant compounds in organic vs conventional fruit (peach, Prunus persica L., and pear, Pyrus communis L.). *J Agric Food Chem* 2002;50:5458-5462.

(67) Asami DK, Hong YJ, Barrett DM, Mitchell AE. Comparison of the total phenolic and ascorbic acid content of freeze-dried and air-dried marionberry, strawberry, and corn grown using conventional, organic, and sustainable agricultural practices. *J Agric Food Chem* 2003;51:1237-1241.

(68) Brandt K, Molgaard JP. Organic agriculture: does it enhance or reduce the nutritional value of plants foods? *Journal of Science and Food Agriculture* 2001;81:924-931.

Chapter 2 Reference List

(1) Fletcher RH, Fairfield KM. Vitamins for chronic disease prevention in adults: clinical applications. JAMA 2002;287:3127-3129.

(2) Fairfield KM, Fletcher RH. Vitamins for chronic disease prevention in adults: scientific review. JAMA 2002;287:3116-3126.

(3) Faloon W. Vindication for Linus Pauling. Life Extension [June]. 2011. Hollywood, FL, Life Extension Foundation.

(4) Enstrom JE, Kanim LE, Klein MA. Vitamin C intake and mortality among a sample of the United States population. Epidemiology 1992;3:194-202.

(5) Losonczy KG, Harris TB, Havlik RJ. Vitamin E and vitamin C supplement use and risk of all-cause and coronary heart disease mortality in older persons: the Established Populations for Epidemiologic Studies of the Elderly. Am J Clin Nutr 1996;64:190-196.

(6) Nyyssonen K, Parviainen MT, Salonen R, Tuomilehto J, Salonen JT. Vitamin C deficiency and risk of myocardial infarction: prospective population study of men from eastern Finland. BMJ 1997;314:634-638.

(7) Giovannucci E, Stampfer MJ, Colditz GA et al. Multivitamin use, folate, and colon cancer in women in the Nurses' Health Study. Ann Intern Med 1998;129:517-524.

(8) Mansoor MA, Kristensen O, Hervig T et al. Plasma total homocysteine response to oral doses of folic acid and pyridoxine hydrochloride (vitamin B6) in healthy individuals. Oral doses of vitamin B6 reduce concentrations of serum folate. Scand J Clin Lab Invest 1999;59:139-146.

(9) Aksenov V, Long J, Lokuge S, Foster JA, Liu J, Rollo CD. Dietary amelioration of locomotor, neurotransmitter and mitochondrial aging. Exp Biol Med (Maywood) 2010;235:66-76.

(10) Lemon JA, Boreham DR, Rollo CD. A complex dietary supplement extends longevity of mice. J Gerontol A Biol Sci Med Sci 2005;60:275-279.

(11) Macchia A, Monte S, Pellegrini F et al. Omega-3 fatty acid supplementation reduces one-year risk of atrial fibrillation in patients hospitalized with myocardial infarction. Eur J Clin Pharmacol 2008;64:627-634.

(12) Gopinath B, Buyken AE, Flood VM, Empson M, Rochtchina E, Mitchell P. Consumption of polyunsaturated fatty acids, fish, and nuts and risk of inflammatory disease mortality. Am J Clin Nutr 2011;93:1073-1079.

(13) Leon H, Shibata MC, Sivakumaran S, Dorgan M, Chatterley T, Tsuyuki RT. Effect of fish oil on arrhythmias and mortality: systematic review. BMJ 2008;337:a2931.

(14) Marik PE, Varon J. Omega-3 dietary supplements and the risk of cardiovascular events: a systematic review. Clin Cardiol 2009;32:365-372.

(15) Zhao YT, Chen Q, Sun YX et al. Prevention of sudden cardiac death with omega-3 fatty acids in patients with coronary heart disease: a meta-analysis of randomized controlled trials. Ann Med 2009;41:301-310.

(16) Einvik G, Klemsdal TO, Sandvik L, Hjerkinn EM. A randomized clinical trial on n-3 polyunsaturated fatty acids supplementation and all-cause mortality in elderly men at high cardiovascular risk. Eur J Cardiovasc Prev Rehabil 2010;17:588-592.

(17) Garland C, Shekelle RB, Barrett-Connor E, Criqui MH, Rossof AH, Paul O. Dietary vitamin D and calcium and risk of colorectal cancer: a 19-year prospective study in men. Lancet 1985;1:307-309.

(18) Gorham ED, Garland CF, Garland FC et al. Vitamin D and prevention of colorectal cancer. J Steroid Biochem Mol Biol 2005;97:179-194.

(19) Garland CF, Garland FC, Gorham ED et al. The role of vitamin D in cancer prevention. Am J Public Health 2006;96:252-261.

(20) Ingraham BA, Bragdon B, Nohe A. Molecular basis of the potential of vitamin D to prevent cancer. Curr Med Res Opin 2008;24:139-149.

(21) Grant WB, Mohr SB. Ecological studies of ultraviolet B, vitamin D and cancer since 2000. Ann Epidemiol 2009;19:446-454.

(22) Miller ER, III, Pastor-Barriuso R, Dalal D, Riemersma RA, Appel LJ, Guallar E. Meta-analysis: high-dosage vitamin E supplementation may increase all-cause mortality. Ann Intern Med 2005;142:37-46.

(23) Wood T. The Case for Nutritional Supplements. article submitted for publication 2006.

Chapter 3 Reference List

(1) Vitamin D. Wikipedia [serial online] 2011; Accessed June 14, 2011.

(2) Holick MF. Evolution and function of vitamin D. Recent Results Cancer Res 2003;164:3-28.

(3) Davis W. Vitamin D's Crucial Role in Cardiovascular Protection. *Life Extension Magazine* [September]. 2007.

(4) Holick M. The Vitamin D Solution. New York: Hudson Street Press, 2010.

(5) Holick M. Fish, Phytoplankton, Dinosaurs, Lizards and You. The Vitamin D Solution. New York: Hudson Street Press; 2010;25-55.

(6) Hildebrand AR, Penfield GT, Kring DA et al. Chicxulub Crater; a possible Cretaceous/Tertiary boundary impact crater on the Yucatan Peninsula, Mexico. Geology 1991;19(9):867-871.

(7) Harrub B. Neanderthals - Missing Link or Diseased? apologeticsarticles ws/articles/364 [serial online] 2011; Accessed June 18, 2011.

(8) Clemens TL, Adams JS, Henderson SL, Holick MF. Increased skin pigment reduces the capacity of skin to synthesise vitamin D3. Lancet 1982;1:74-76.

(9) Holick M. What is Vitamin D? The Vitamin D Solution. New York: Hudson Street Press; 2010;3-24.

(10) Light Therapy. Wikipedia [serial online] 2011; Accessed June 18, 2011.

(11) Ellinger F. Medical Radiation Biology. Springfiled, Ill: Charles C.Thomas, 1957.

(12) Dunn PM. Francis Glisson (1597-1677) and the "discovery" of rickets. Arch Dis Child Fetal Neonatal Ed 1998;78:F154-F155.

(13) Holick M. What is Vitamin D? The Vitamin D Solution. New York: Hudson Street Press; 2010;3-24.

(14) Berwick M, Armstrong BK, Ben-Porat L et al. Sun exposure and mortality from melanoma. J Natl Cancer Inst 2005;97:195-199.

(15) Holick M. Dethroning the Cover-Up. The Vitamin D Solution. New York: Hudson Street Press; 2010;242-248.

(16) Jensen SS, Madsen MW, Lukas J, Binderup L, Bartek J. Inhibitory effects of 1alpha,25-dihydroxyvitamin D(3) on the G(1)-S phase-controlling machinery. Mol Endocrinol 2001;15:1370-1380.

(17) Lowe L, Hansen CM, Senaratne S, Colston KW. Mechanisms implicated in the growth regulatory effects of vitamin D compounds in breast cancer cells. Recent Results Cancer Res 2003;164:99-110.

(18) Swami S, Raghavachari N, Muller UR, Bao YP, Feldman D. Vitamin D growth inhibition of breast cancer cells: gene expression patterns assessed by cDNA microarray. Breast Cancer Res Treat 2003;80:49-62.

(19) Colston KW, Hansen CM. Mechanisms implicated in the growth regulatory effects of vitamin D in breast cancer. Endocr Relat Cancer 2002;9:45-59.

(20) Weitsman GE, Koren R, Zuck E, Rotem C, Liberman UA, Ravid A. Vitamin D sensitizes breast cancer cells to the action of H2O2: mitochondria as a convergence point in the death pathway. Free Radic Biol Med 2005;39:266-278.

(21) Welsh J. Vitamin D and breast cancer: insights from animal models. Am J Clin Nutr 2004;80:1721S-1724S.

(22) Grant WB. Epidemiology of disease risks in relation to vitamin D insufficiency. Prog Biophys Mol Biol 2006;92:65-79.

(23) Grant WB. A multicountry ecologic study of risk and risk reduction factors for prostate cancer mortality. Eur Urol 2004;45:271-279.

(24) Grant WB. An estimate of premature cancer mortality in the U.S. due to inadequate doses of solar ultraviolet-B radiation. Cancer 2002;94:1867-1875.

(25) Johnson TD. Guarding Against the Dangers of Vitamin D Deficiency. Life Extension Magazine [May]. 2007.

(26) Holick M. Adventures in Globe-trotting. The Vitamin D Solution. New York: Hudson Street Press; 2010;74-98.

(27) Garland C, Shekelle RB, Barrett-Connor E, Criqui MH, Rossof AH, Paul O. Dietary vitamin D and calcium and risk of colorectal cancer: a 19-year prospective study in men. Lancet 1985;1:307-309.

(28) Gorham ED, Garland CF, Garland FC et al. Vitamin D and prevention of colorectal cancer. J Steroid Biochem Mol Biol 2005;97:179-194.

(29) Garland CF, Garland FC, Gorham ED et al. The role of vitamin D in cancer prevention. Am J Public Health 2006;96:252-261.

(30) Grant WB. An ecological study of cancer incidence and mortality rates in France with respect to latitude, an index for vitamin D production. Dermatoendocrinol 2010;2:62-67.

(31) Oh EY, Ansell C, Nawaz H, Yang CH, Wood PA, Hrushesky WJ. Global breast cancer seasonality. Breast Cancer Res Treat 2010;123:233-243.

(32) Bakhru A, Mallinger JB, Buckanovich RJ, Griggs JJ. Casting light on 25-hydroxyvitamin D deficiency in ovarian cancer: a study from the NHANES. Gynecol Oncol 2010;119:314-318.

(33) Karami S, Boffetta P, Stewart P et al. Occupational sunlight exposure and risk of renal cell carcinoma. Cancer 2010;116:2001-2010.

(34) Mohr SB, Gorham ED, Garland CF, Grant WB, Garland FC. Low ultraviolet B and increased risk of brain cancer: an ecological study of 175 countries. Neuroepidemiology 2010;35:281-290.

(35) Mohr SB, Garland CF, Gorham ED, Grant WB, Garland FC. Ultraviolet B irradiance and vitamin D status are inversely associated with incidence rates of pancreatic cancer worldwide. Pancreas 2010;39:669-674.

(36) Neale RE, Youlden DR, Krnjacki L, Kimlin MG, van der Pols JC. Latitude variation in pancreatic cancer mortality in Australia. Pancreas 2009;38:387-390.

(37) Mohr SB, Garland CF, Gorham ED, Grant WB, Garland FC. Ultraviolet B and incidence rates of leukemia worldwide. Am J Prev Med 2011;41:68-74.

(38) Musselman JR, Spector LG. Childhood cancer incidence in relation to sunlight exposure. Br J Cancer 2011;104:214-220.

(39) Ingraham BA, Bragdon B, Nohe A. Molecular basis of the potential of vitamin D to prevent cancer. Curr Med Res Opin 2008;24:139-149.

(40) Grant WB, Mohr SB. Ecological studies of ultraviolet B, vitamin D and cancer since 2000. Ann Epidemiol 2009;19:446-454.

(41) Pierrot-Deseilligny C, Souberbielle JC. Widespread vitamin D insufficiency: A new challenge for primary prevention, with particular reference to multiple sclerosis. Presse Med 2011;40:349-356.

(42) Lappe JM, Travers-Gustafson D, Davies KM, Recker RR, Heaney RP. Vitamin D and calcium supplementation reduces cancer risk: results of a randomized trial. Am J Clin Nutr 2007;85:1586-1591.

(43) Grimes DS, Hindle E, Dyer T. Sunlight, cholesterol and coronary heart disease. QJM 1996;89:579-589.

(44) Scragg R, Jackson R, Holdaway IM, Lim T, Beaglehole R. Myocardial infarction is inversely associated with plasma 25-hydroxyvitamin D3 levels: a community-based study. Int J Epidemiol 1990;19:559-563.

(45) Spencer FA, Goldberg RJ, Becker RC, Gore JM. Seasonal distribution of acute myocardial infarction in the second National Registry of Myocardial Infarction. J Am Coll Cardiol 1998;31:1226-1233.

(46) Ku CS, Yang CY, Lee WJ, Chiang HT, Liu CP, Lin SL. Absence of a seasonal variation in myocardial infarction onset in a region without temperature extremes. Cardiology 1998;89:277-282.

(47) Lind L, Hanni A, Lithell H, Hvarfner A, Sorensen OH, Ljunghall S. Vitamin D is related to blood pressure and other cardiovascular risk factors in middle-aged men. Am J Hypertens 1995;8:894-901.

(48) Martins D, Wolf M, Pan D et al. Prevalence of cardiovascular risk factors and the serum levels of 25-hydroxyvitamin D in the United States: data from the Third National Health and Nutrition Examination Survey. Arch Intern Med 2007;167:1159-1165.

(49) Pfeifer M, Begerow B, Minne HW, Nachtigall D, Hansen C. Effects of a short-term vitamin D(3) and calcium supplementation on blood pressure and parathyroid hormone levels in elderly women. J Clin Endocrinol Metab 2001;86:1633-1637.

(50) Timms PM, Mannan N, Hitman GA et al. Circulating MMP9, vitamin D and variation in the TIMP-1 response with VDR genotype: mechanisms for inflammatory damage in chronic disorders? QJM 2002;95:787-796.

(51) Achinger SG, Ayus JC. The role of vitamin D in left ventricular hypertrophy and cardiac function. Kidney Int Suppl 2005;S37-S42.

(52) London GM, Guerin AP, Verbeke FH et al. Mineral metabolism and arterial functions in end-stage renal disease: potential role of 25-hydroxyvitamin D deficiency. J Am Soc Nephrol 2007;18:613-620.

(53) Zittermann A, Schleithoff SS, Tenderich G, Berthold HK, Korfer R, Stehle P. Low vitamin D status: a contributing factor in the pathogenesis of congestive heart failure? J Am Coll Cardiol 2003;41:105-112.

(54) Giovannucci E, Liu Y, Hollis BW, Rimm EB. 25-hydroxyvitamin D and risk of myocardial infarction in men: a prospective study. Arch Intern Med 2008;168:1174-1180.

(55) Lindqvist PG, Epstein E, Olsson H. Does an active sun exposure habit lower the risk of venous thrombotic events? A D-lightful hypothesis. J Thromb Haemost 2009;7:605-610.

(56) Schleithoff SS, Zittermann A, Tenderich G, Berthold HK, Stehle P, Koerfer R. Vitamin D supplementation improves cytokine profiles in patients with congestive heart failure: a double-blind, randomized, placebo-controlled trial. Am J Clin Nutr 2006;83:754-759.

(57) Kiefer D. Why is flu risk so much higher in the winter? Life Extension Magazine [February], 22-28. 2007. Life Extension Media.

(58) Lochner JD, Schneider DJ. [The relationship between tuberculosis, vitamin D, potassium and AIDS. A message for South Africa?]. S Afr Med J 1994;84:79-82.

(59) Bellamy R, Ruwende C, Corrah T et al. Tuberculosis and chronic hepatitis B virus infection in Africans and variation in the vitamin D receptor gene. J Infect Dis 1999;179:721-724.

(60) Schauber J, Dorschner RA, Coda AB et al. Injury enhances TLR2 function and antimicrobial peptide expression through a vitamin D-dependent mechanism. J Clin Invest 2007;117:803-811.

(61) Holick M. Finding Immunity. The Vitamin D Solution. New York: Hudson Street Press; 2010;99-115.

(62) Strohle A, Wolters M, Hahn A. Micronutrients at the interface between inflammation and infection--ascorbic acid and calciferol. Part 2: calciferol and the significance of nutrient supplements. Inflamm Allergy Drug Targets 2011;10:64-74.

(63) Hoeck AD, Pall ML. Will vitamin D supplementation ameliorate diseases characterized by chronic inflammation and fatigue? Med Hypotheses 2011;76:208-213.

(64) Sundar IK, Hwang JW, Wu S, Sun J, Rahman I. Deletion of vitamin D receptor leads to premature emphysema/COPD by increased matrix metalloproteinases and lymphoid aggregates formation. Biochem Biophys Res Commun 2011;406:127-133.

(65) Bahar-Shany K, Ravid A, Koren R. Upregulation of MMP-9 production by TNFalpha in keratinocytes and its attenuation by vitamin D. J Cell Physiol 2010;222:729-737.

(66) Vieth R. Vitamin D supplementation, 25-hydroxyvitamin D concentrations, and safety. Am J Clin Nutr 1999;69:842-856.

(67) Holick M. What is Vitamin D? The Vitamin D Solution. New York: Hudson Street Press; 2010;3-24.

(68) Holick M. Supplement Safely. The Vitamin D Solution. New York: Hudson Street Press; 2010;212-228.

(69) MacWilliam LD. Degenerative Disease. Comparative Guide to Nutritional Supplements. 4th ed. Vernon, BC: Northern Dimensions Publishing; 2007;6-8.

Chapter 4 Reference List

(1)   Miller DW. Iodine For Health. www lewrockwell com 2006; Available at: URL: www.lewrockwell.com/miller/miller20.html AccessedJune 26, 2012.

(2)   Crockford SJ. Evolutionary roots of iodine and thyroid hormones in cell-cell signaling. Integr Comp Biol 2009 August;49(2):155-66.

(3)   Hunt S. Halogenated tyrosine derivatives in invertebrate scleroproteins: isolation and identification. In: Wold F, Moldave K, editors. Methods in Enzymology. Volume 107 Postrsanslational Modifications Part B ed. New York: Academic Press; 1984. p. 413-38.

(4)   Patrick L. Iodine: deficiency and therapeutic considerations. Altern Med Rev 2008 June;13(2):116-27.

(5)   Zimmerman MB. Research on Iodine Deficiency and Goiter in the 19th and 20th Centuries. The Journal of Nutrition 2008;2060-2063. Available at: URL: http://jn.nutrition.org/content/138/11/2060.short AccessedAugust 7, 2012.

(6)   Kelly FC. Iodine in Medicine and Pharmacy Since it Discovery 1811-1961. Proc Royal Soc Med 1961;54:831-6.

(7)   Abraham GE. The History of Iodine in Medicine Part I: From Discovery to Essentiality. The Original Internist 2006;(Spring):34-40.

(8)   Salter WT. The Endocrine Function of Iodine. Harvard University Press; 1940.

(9)   Redisch W, Perloff WH. The Medical Treatment of Hyperthyroidism. Endocrinology 1940 January 2;26(2):221-8.

(10) Marine D, Kimball OP. Prevention of Simple Goiter in Man - 4th Paper. Arch Intern Med 1920;25(6):661-72.

(11) Davis W. Halt on Salt Sparks Iodine Controversy. Life Extension Magazine [October]. 2012.

(12) Braverman LE. Adequate Iodine Intake - the good far outweighs the bad. Eur J Endocrinol 1998;139:14-5.

(13) Patrick L. Iodine: deficiency and therapeutic considerations. Altern Med Rev 2008 June;13(2):116-27.

(14) Higdon J. Iodine. Linus Pauling Institute . 2010. 6-4-2012.

(15) Wolff J. Iodide goiter and the pharmacologic effects of excess iodide. Am J Med 1969 July;47(1):101-24.

(16) Ghent WR, Eskin BA, Low DA, Hill LP. Iodine replacement in fibrocystic disease of the breast. Can J Surg 1993 October;36(5):453-60.

(17) Backer H, Hollowell J. Use of iodine for water disinfection: iodine toxicity and maximum recommended dose. Environ Health Perspect 2000 August;108(8):679-84.

(18) Dunn JT. Seven deadly sins in confronting endemic iodine deficiency, and how to avoid them. J Clin Endocrinol Metab 1996 April;81(4):1332-5.

(19) World Health Organization. Iodine Deficiency Disorders: Fact Sheet No. 121. 1996. Geneva, Switzerland, World Health Organization.

(20) Triggiani V, Tafaro E, Giagulli VA et al. Role of iodine, selenium and other micronutrients in thyroid function and disorders. Endocr Metab Immune Disord Drug Targets 2009 September;9(3):277-94.

(21) Zimmermann M. Assessing Iodine Status and Monitoring Progress of Iodized Salt Programs. J Nutr 2004;134(7):1673-7.

(22) Fruhwald FM, Ramschak-Schwarzer S, Pichler B et al. Subclinical thyroid disorders in patients with dilated cardiomyopathy. Cardiology 1997 March;88(2):156-9.

(23) Grzesiuk W, Kondracka A, Slon M, Wojda M, Nauman J. Salt iodination as a effective method of iodine supplementation. Med Sci Monit 2002 April;8(4):CR288-CR291.

(24) Simpson FO, Thaler BI, Paulin JM, Phelan EL, Cooper GJ. Iodide excretion in a salt-restriction trial. N Z Med J 1984 December 26;97(770):890-3.

(25) Hoption Cann SA. Hypothesis: dietary iodine intake in the etiology of cardiovascular disease. J Am Coll Nutr 2006 February;25(1):1-11.

(26) Buchinger W, Lorenz-Wawschinek O, Semlitsch G et al. Thyrotropin and thyroglobulin as an index of optimal iodine intake: correlation with iodine excretion of 39,913 euthyroid patients. Thyroid 1997 August;7(4):593-7.

(27) Thomson CD. Selenium and iodine intakes and status in New Zealand and Australia. Br J Nutr 2004 May;91(5):661-72.

(28) Gunton JE, Hams G, Fiegert M, McElduff A. Iodine deficiency in ambulatory participants at a Sydney teaching hospital: is Australia truly iodine replete? Med J Aust 1999 November 1;171(9):467-70.

(29) Valeix P, Zarebska M, Preziosi P, Galan P, Pelletier B, Hercberg S. Iodine deficiency in France. Lancet 1999 May 22;353(9166):1766-7.

(30) Patrick L. Iodine: deficiency and therapeutic considerations. Altern Med Rev 2008 June;13(2):116-27.

(31) Caldwell KL, Jones R, Hollowell JG. Urinary iodine concentration: United States National Health And Nutrition Examination Survey 2001-2002. Thyroid 2005 July;15(7):692-9.

(32) Haddow JE, Palomaki GE, Allan WC et al. Maternal thyroid deficiency during pregnancy and subsequent neuropsychological development of the child. N Engl J Med 1999 August 19;341(8):549-55.

(33) Pearce EN. Effects of iodine deficiency in pregnancy. J Trace Elem Med Biol 2012 May 5.

(34) Pizzorno J. How Much Iodine Should We Prescribe? Int Med 2012 June;11(3):8-13.

(35) Abraham GE. Validation of the orthoiodosupplementation program: a rebuttal of Dr. Gaby's editorial on iodine. The Original Internist 2005;12(4):184-94.

(36) Miller DW. Extrathyroidal Benefits of Iodine. J Am Phys Surg 2006;11(4):106-10.

(37) Suzuki H, Higuchi T, Sawa K, Ohtaki S, Horiuchi Y. "Endemic coast goitre" in Hokkaido, Japan. Acta Endocrinol (Copenh) 1965 October;50(2):161-76.

(38) Nagataki S. The average of dietary iodine intake due to the ingestion of seaweeds is 1.2 mg/day in Japan. Thyroid 2008 June;18(6):667-8.

(39) Nagataki S, Shizume K, Nakao K. Thyroid function in chronic excess iodide ingestion: comparison of thyroidal absolute iodine uptake and degradation of thyroxine in euthyroid Japanese subjects. J Clin Endocrinol Metab 1967 May;27(5):638-47.

(40) Piccone N. The Silent Epidemic of Iodine Deficiency. Life Extension Magazine October. 2011.

(41) Ziegler RG, Hoover RN, Pike MC et al. Migration patterns and breast cancer risk in Asian-American women. J Natl Cancer Inst 1993 November 17;85(22):1819-27.

(42) Ghent WR, Eskin BA, Low DA, Hill LP. Iodine replacement in fibrocystic disease of the breast. Can J Surg 1993 October;36(5):453-60.

(43) Theodoropoulou A, Vagenakis AG, Makri M, Markou KB. Thyroid hormone synthesis and secretion in humans after 80 milligrams of iodine for 15 days and subsequent withdrawal. J Clin Endocrinol Metab 2007 January;92(1):212-4.

(44) Clark CD, Bassett B, Burge MR. Effects of kelp supplementation on thyroid function in euthyroid subjects. Endocr Pract 2003 September;9(5):363-9.

(45) Winkler R, Griebenow S, Wonisch W. Effect of iodide on total antioxidant status of human serum. Cell Biochem Funct 2000 June;18(2):143-6.

(46) Venturi S. Is there a role for iodine in breast diseases? Breast 2001 October;10(5):379-82.

(47) Poncin S, Gerard AC, Boucquey M et al. Oxidative stress in the thyroid gland: from harmlessness to hazard depending on the iodine content. Endocrinology 2008 January;149(1):424-33.

(48) Maier J, van SH, van OC, Paschke R, Weiss RE, Krohn K. Iodine deficiency activates antioxidant genes and causes DNA damage in the thyroid gland of rats and mice. Biochim Biophys Acta 2007 June;1773(6):990-9.

(49) Paschke R. Molecular pathogenesis of nodular goiter. Langenbecks Arch Surg 2011 December;396(8):1127-36.

(50) Dohan O, De l, V, Paroder V et al. The sodium/iodide Symporter (NIS): characterization, regulation, and medical significance. Endocr Rev 2003 February;24(1):48-77.

(51) Pizzorno L. Iodine: the Next Vitamin D? Part II. Longevity Medicine Review 2010 May;Available at: URL: http://www.lmreview.com/articles/view/iodine-the-next-vitamin-d-part-I/ AccessedNovember 7, 2012.

(52) DeLong GR, Leslie PW, Wang SH et al. Effect on infant mortality of iodination of irrigation water in a severely iodine-deficient area of China. Lancet 1997 September 13;350(9080):771-3.

(53) Klein RZ, Sargent JD, Larsen PR, Waisbren SE, Haddow JE, Mitchell ML. Relation of severity of maternal hypothyroidism to cognitive development of offspring. J Med Screen 2001;8(1):18-20.

(54) Vermiglio F, Lo P, V, Moleti M et al. Attention deficit and hyperactivity disorders in the offspring of mothers exposed to mild-moderate iodine deficiency: a possible novel iodine deficiency disorder in developed countries. J Clin Endocrinol Metab 2004 December;89(12):6054-60.

(55) Abnet CC, Fan JH, Kamangar F et al. Self-reported goiter is associated with a significantly increased risk of gastric noncardia adenocarcinoma in a large population-based Chinese cohort. Int J Cancer 2006 September 15;119(6):1508-10.

(56) Burgess JR, Dwyer T, McArdle K, Tucker P, Shugg D. The changing incidence and spectrum of thyroid carcinoma in Tasmania (1978-1998) during a transition from iodine sufficiency to iodine deficiency. J Clin Endocrinol Metab 2000 April;85(4):1513-7.

(57) Franceschi S, Preston-Martin S, Dal ML et al. A pooled analysis of case-control studies of thyroid cancer. IV. Benign thyroid diseases. Cancer Causes Control 1999 December;10(6):583-95.

(58) Mellemgaard A, From G, Jorgensen T, Johansen C, Olsen JH, Perrild H. Cancer risk in individuals with benign thyroid disorders. Thyroid 1998 September;8(9):751-4.

(59) Schaller RT, Jr., Stevenson JK. Development of carcinoma of the thyroid in iodine-deficient mice. Cancer 1966 August;19(8):1063-80.

(60) Shakhtarin VV, Tsyb AF, Stepanenko VF, Orlov MY, Kopecky KJ, Davis S. Iodine deficiency, radiation dose, and the risk of thyroid cancer among children and adolescents in the Bryansk region of Russia following the Chernobyl power station accident. Int J Epidemiol 2003 August;32(4):584-91.

(61) Biondi B, Klein I. Hypothyroidism as a risk factor for cardiovascular disease. Endocrine 2004 June;24(1):1-13.

(62) Dillmann WH. Cellular action of thyroid hormone on the heart. Thyroid 2002 June;12(6):447-52.

(63) Flechas JD. Orthoiodosupplementation in a Prmary Care Practice. The Orginal Internist 2005;(Summer):89-96.

(64) Sekiya M, Funahashi H, Tsukamura K et al. Intracellular signaling in the induction of apoptosis in a human breast cancer cell line by water extract of Mekabu. Int J Clin Oncol 2005 April;10(2):122-6.

(65) Shrivastava A, Tiwari M, Sinha RA et al. Molecular iodine induces caspase-independent apoptosis in human breast carcinoma cells involving the mitochondria-mediated pathway. J Biol Chem 2006 July 14;281(28):19762-71.

(66) Zhang L, Sharma S, Zhu LX et al. Nonradioactive iodide effectively induces apoptosis in genetically modified lung cancer cells. Cancer Res 2003 August 15;63(16):5065-72.

(67) Aceves C, Anguiano B, Delgado G. Is iodine a gatekeeper of the integrity of the mammary gland? J Mammary Gland Biol Neoplasia 2005 April;10(2):189-96.

(68) Garcia-Solis P, Alfaro Y, Anguiano B et al. Inhibition of N-methyl-N-nitrosourea-induced mammary carcino-genesis by molecular iodine (I2) but not by iodide (I-) treatment Evidence that I2 prevents cancer promotion. Mol Cell Endocrinol 2005 May 31;236(1-2):49-57.

(69) Wiseman RA. Breast cancer hypothesis: a single cause for the majority of cases. J Epidemiol Community Health 2000 November;54(11):851-8.

(70) Eskin BA, Bartuska DG, Dunn MR, Jacob G, Dratman MB. Mammary gland dysplasia in iodine deficiency. Studies in rats. JAMA 1967 May 22;200(8):691-5.

(71) Eskin BA. Iodine and mammary cancer. Adv Exp Med Biol 1977;91:293-304.

(72) Ghent WR, Eskin BA, Low DA, Hill LP. Iodine replacement in fibrocystic disease of the breast. Can J Surg 1993 October;36(5):453-60.

(73) Smyth PP. Thyroid disease and breast cancer. J Endocrinol Invest 1993 May;16(5):396-401.

(74) Golkowski F, Szybinski Z, Rachtan J et al. Iodine prophylaxis--the protective factor against stomach cancer in iodine deficient areas. Eur J Nutr 2007 August;46(5):251-6.

(75) Clur A. Di-iodothyronine as part of the oestradiol and catechol oestrogen receptor--the role of iodine, thyroid hormones and melatonin in the aetiology of breast cancer. Med Hypotheses 1988 December;27(4):303-11.

(76) Aranda N, Sosa S, Delgado G, Aceves C, Anguiano B. Uptake and antitumoral effects of iodine and 6-iodolactone in differentiated and undifferentiated human prostate cancer cell lines. Prostate 2013 January;73(1):31-41.

(77) Stadel BV. Dietary iodine and risk of breast, endometrial, and ovarian cancer. Lancet 1976 April 24;1(7965):890-1.

(78) Thomas BS, Bulbrook RD, Goodman MJ et al. Thyroid function and the incidence of breast cancer in Hawaiian, British and Japanese women. Int J Cancer 1986 September 15;38(3):325-9.

(79) Stoddard FR, Brooks AD, Eskin BA, Johannes GJ. Iodine alters gene expression in the MCF7 breast cancer cell line: evidence for an anti-estrogen effect of iodine. Int J Med Sci 2008;5(4):189-96.

(80) Eichler I, Winkler R. [Effect and effectiveness of iodine brine baths in a spa]. Wien Klin Wochenschr 1994;106(9):265-71.

(81) HITZENBERGER G. [Comparative studies on the effects of the Bad Hall iodine cure in hypertensives]. Arch Phys Ther (Leipz) 1961 January;13:91-4.

(82) Klieber M, Czerwenka-Howorka K, Homan R, Pirker R. [Ergospirometric studies of circulation in healthy humans. Effect of iodine brine baths on work-induced changes in blood pressure, respiratory gas exchange and metabolic parameters]. Med Welt 1982 August 20;33(33):1123-6.

(83) Lu HC. Chinese Foods for Longevity. New York: Sterling; 1990.

(84) Mikhno LE, Novikov SA. [The use of local iodobromine baths in the early sanatorium rehabilitation of myocardial infarct patients with arterial hypertension]. Lik Sprava 1992 January;(1):89-91.

(85) Pitchford P. Healing with Whole Foods: Oriental Traditions and Modern Nutrition. Berkeley, CA: North Atlantic Books; 1993.

(86) Vinogradova MN, Mandrykina TA, Lavrov GK, Shchegoleva EA. [The effect of molecular-iodine baths on the central hemodynamics of patients with hypertension and ischemic heart disease]. Vopr Kurortol Fizioter Lech Fiz Kult 1990 July;(4):15-8.

(87) Bastido WA. Pharmacology, Therapeutics and Prescription Writing for Students and Practitioners. 5th ed. Philadelphia: WB Saunders; 1947.

(88) McGuigan HA. Applied Pharmacology. St Louis, CV Mosby; 1940.

(89) Sollmann TH. A Manual of Pharmacology and Its Applications to Therapeutics and Toxicology. 7th ed. Philadelphia: 1948.

(90) Fazio S, Palmieri EA, Lombardi G, Biondi B. Effects of thyroid hormone on the cardiovascular system. Recent Prog Horm Res 2004;59:31-50.

(91) Molnar I, Magyari M, Stief L. [Iodine deficiency in cardiovascular diseases]. Orv Hetil 1998 August 30;139(35):2071-3.

(92) Cacace MG, Landau EM, Ramsden JJ. The Hofmeister series: salt and solvent effects on interfacial phenomena. Q Rev Biophys 1997 August;30(3):241-77.

(93) Hatefi Y, Hanstein WG. Solubilization of particulate proteins and nonelectrolytes by chaotropic agents. Proc Natl Acad Sci U S A 1969 April;62(4):1129-36.

(94) Hoption Cann SA, van Netten JP, van NC. Iodized salt and hypertension. Arch Intern Med 2002 January 14;162(1):104-5.

(95) Canturk Z, Cetinarslan B, Tarkun I, Canturk NZ, Ozden M. Lipid profile and lipoprotein (a) as a risk factor for cardiovascular disease in women with subclinical hypothyroidism. Endocr Res 2003 August;29(3):307-16.

(96) Kahaly GJ. Cardiovascular and atherogenic aspects of subclinical hypothyroidism. Thyroid 2000 August;10(8):665-79.

(97) Park YJ, Lee YJ, Choi SI, Chun EJ, Jang HC, Chang HJ. Impact of subclinical hypothyroidism on the coronary artery disease in apparently healthy subjects. Eur J Endocrinol 2011 July;165(1):115-21.

(98) Haentjens P, Van MA, Poppe K, Velkeniers B. Subclinical thyroid dysfunction and mortality: an estimate of relative and absolute excess all-cause mortality based on time-to-event data from cohort studies. Eur J Endocrinol 2008 September;159(3):329-41.

(99) Auer J, Berent R, Weber T, Lassnig E, Eber B. Thyroid function is associated with presence and severity of coronary atherosclerosis. Clin Cardiol 2003 December;26(12):569-73.

(100) Bruckert E, Giral P, Chadarevian R, Turpin G. Low free-thyroxine levels are a risk factor for subclinical atherosclerosis in euthyroid hyperlipidemic patients. J Cardiovasc Risk 1999 October;6(5):327-31.

(101) Dagre AG, Lekakis JP, Protogerou AD et al. Abnormal endothelial function in female patients with hypothyroidism and borderline thyroid function. Int J Cardiol 2007 January 18;114(3):332-8.

(102) Yun KH, Jeong MH, Oh SK et al. Relationship of thyroid stimulating hormone with coronary atherosclerosis in angina patients. Int J Cardiol 2007 October 31;122(1):56-60.

(103) Cappola AR, Ladenson PW. Hypothyroidism and atherosclerosis. J Clin Endocrinol Metab 2003 June;88(6):2438-44.

(104) den Hollander JG, Wulkan RW, Mantel MJ, Berghout A. Correlation between severity of thyroid dysfunction and renal function. Clin Endocrinol (Oxf) 2005 April;62(4):423-7.

(105) Klein I, Danzi S. Thyroid disease and the heart. Circulation 2007 October 9;116(15):1725-35.

(106) Muller B, Tsakiris DA, Roth CB, Guglielmetti M, Staub JJ, Marbet GA. Haemostatic profile in hypothyroidism as potential risk factor for vascular or thrombotic disease. Eur J Clin Invest 2001 February;31(2):131-7.

(107) Tomanek RJ, Busch TL. Coordinated capillary and myocardial growth in response to thyroxine treatment. Anat Rec 1998 May;251(1):44-9.

(108) Iqbal A, Jorde R, Figenschau Y. Serum lipid levels in relation to serum thyroid-stimulating hormone and the effect of thyroxine treatment on serum lipid levels in subjects with subclinical hypothyroidism: the Tromso Study. J Intern Med 2006 July;260(1):53-61.

(109) Rizos CV, Elisaf MS, Liberopoulos EN. Effects of thyroid dysfunction on lipid profile. Open Cardiovasc Med J 2011;5:76-84.

(110) Asvold BO, Bjoro T, Nilsen TI, Vatten LJ. Association between blood pressure and serum thyroid-stimulating hormone concentration within the reference range: a population-based study. J Clin Endocrinol Metab 2007 March;92(3):841-5.

(111) Asvold BO, Bjoro T, Nilsen TI, Gunnell D, Vatten LJ. Thyrotropin levels and risk of fatal coronary heart disease: the HUNT study. Arch Intern Med 2008 April 28;168(8):855-60.

(112) Hartoft-Nielsen ML, Rasmussen AK, Bock T, Feldt-Rasmussen U, Kaas A, Buschard K. Iodine and tri-iodo-thyronine reduce the incidence of type 1 diabetes mellitus in the autoimmune prone BB rats. Autoimmunity 2009 February;42(2):131-8.

(113) Okten A, Akcay S, Cakir M, Girisken I, Kosucu P, Deger O. Iodine status, thyroid function, thyroid volume and thyroid autoimmunity in patients with type 1 diabetes mellitus in an iodine-replete area. Diabetes Metab 2006 September;32(4):323-9.

(114) Vondra K, Vrbikova J, Dvorakova K. Thyroid gland diseases in adult patients with diabetes mellitus. Minerva Endocrinol 2005 December;30(4):217-36.

(115) Szybinski Z. [Iodine deficiency in pregnancy--a continuing public health problem]. Endokrynol Pol 2005 January;56(1):65-71.

(116) DI Gilio AR, Greco P, Vimercati A et al. [Incidence of thyroid diseases in pregnant women with type I diabetes mellitus]. Acta Biomed Ateneo Parmense 2000;71 Suppl 1:387-91.

(117) Brownstein D. Clinical Experience with Inorganic, Non-radioactive Iodine/Iodide. The Original Internist 2005;(Fall):105-8.

(118) American Cancer Society. Benign Breast Conditions. cancer org 2001;Available at: URL: cancer.org.

(119) Smyth PP. Role of iodine in antioxidant defence in thyroid and breast disease. Biofactors 2003;19(3-4):121-30.

(120) Bretthauer EW, Mullen AL, Moghissi AA. Milk transfer comparisons of different chemical forms of radioiodine. Health Phys 1972 March;22(3):257-60.

(121) Vishniakova VV, Murav'eva NI. [On the treatment of dyshormonal hyperplasia of mammary glands]. Vestn Akad Med Nauk SSSR 1966;21(9):19-22.

(122) Low DE, Ghent WR, Hill LD. Diatomic iodine treatment for fibrocystic breast disease: special report of efficacy and safety results. donaldmiller com 1995;submission to the FDA:1-38.

(123) Kessler JH. The effect of supraphysiologic levels of iodine on patients with cyclic mastalgia. Breast J 2004 July;10(4):328-36.

(124) Eskin BA, Grotkowski CE, Connolly CP, Ghent WR. Different tissue responses for iodine and iodide in rat thyroid and mammary glands. Biol Trace Elem Res 1995 July;49(1):9-19.

(125) Baker DH. Iodine toxicity and its amelioration. Exp Biol Med (Maywood) 2004 June;229(6):473-8.

(126) Backer H, Hollowell J. Use of iodine for water disinfection: iodine toxicity and maximum recommended dose. Environ Health Perspect 2000 August;108(8):679-84.

(127) Abraham GE, Flechas JD, Hakala JC. Optimal levels of iodine for greatest menatl and physical health. The Original Internist 2002;(September):5-18.

(128) Braverman LE. Iodine and the thyroid: 33 years of study. Thyroid 1994;4(3):351-6.

(129) Koutras DA. Control of efficiency and results, and adverse effects of excess iodine administration on thyroid function. Ann Endocrinol (Paris) 1996;57(6):463-9.

(130) Boyages SC, Bloot AM, Maberly GF et al. Thyroid autoimmunity in endemic goitre caused by excessive iodine intake. Clin Endocrinol (Oxf) 1989 October;31(4):453-65.

(131) Corvilain B, Van SJ, Dumont JE, Bourdoux P, Ermans AM. Autonomy in endemic goiter. Thyroid 1998 January;8(1):107-13.

(132) Tajiri J, Higashi K, Morita M, Umeda T, Sato T. Studies of hypothyroidism in patients with high iodine intake. J Clin Endocrinol Metab 1986 August;63(2):412-7.

(133) Wolff J. Iodide goiter and the pharmacologic effects of excess iodide. Am J Med 1969 July;47(1):101-24.

(134) Thomson CD, Campbell JM, Miller J, Skeaff SA. Minimal impact of excess iodate intake on thyroid hormones and selenium status in older New Zealanders. Eur J Endocrinol 2011 November;165(5):745-52.

(135) Fradkin JE, Wolff J. Iodide-induced thyrotoxicosis. Medicine (Baltimore) 1983 January;62(1):1-20.

Chapter 6 Reference List

(1) Balch PA. Minerals. Prescription for Nutritional Healing. 2 ed. New York, NY: Avery; 2002;53-76.

(2) Albion Laboratories. A Healthy Start. Alblion Research Notes Newsletter 1997;6:1-5.

(3) Knudsen E et al. Zinc, copper and magnesium absorption from a fiber-rich diet. J Trace Elem Med Biol 1996;2:68-76.

(4) Schardt FZ. Effects of doses of certain cereal foods and zinc on different blood parameters in performing althletes. Ernahrungswuiss 1994;3:207-216.

(5) Greger JL, Krashoc CL. Effects of a variety of calcium sources on mineral metabolism in anemic rats. Drug Nutr Interact 1988;5:387-394.

(6) Murray MT. Magnesium. Encyclopedia of Nutritional Supplements. Rocklin, CA: Prima Health; 1996;159-175.

(7) Reavley N. Vitamins, minerals and diet: the basics. New Encyclopedia of Vitamins, Minerals and Herbs. New York, NY: M. Evans and Company; 1998;4-30.

(8) Kushi LH, Folsom AR, Prineas RJ, Mink PJ, Wu Y, Bostick RM. Dietary antioxidant vitamins and death from coronary heart disease in postmenopausal women. N Engl J Med 1996;334:1156-1162.

(9) Yochum LA, Folsom AR, Kushi LH. Intake of antioxidant vitamins and risk of death from stroke in postmenopausal women. Am J Clin Nutr 2000;72:476-483.

(10) Stampfer MJ, Hennekens CH, Manson JE, Colditz GA, Rosner B, Willett WC. Vitamin E consumption and the risk of coronary disease in women. N Engl J Med 1993;328:1444-1449.

(11) Keaney JF, Jr., Simon DI, Freedman JE. Vitamin E and vascular homeostasis: implications for atherosclerosis. FASEB J 1999;13:965-975.

(12) Greenwell I. Newly Discovered Benefits of Gamma Tocopherol. Life Extension Magazine [Collector's edition], 61-64. 2003. Ft. Lauderdale, FL, LE Publications Inc.

(13) Olmedilla B, Granado F, Southon S et al. Serum concentrations of carotenoids and vitamins A, E, and C in control subjects from five European countries. Br J Nutr 2001;85:227-238.

(14) Friedrich MJ. To "E" or not to "E," vitamin E's role in health and disease is the question. JAMA 2004;292:671-673.

(15) Traber MG. The Biological Activity of Vitamin E. 1998. Linus Pauling Institute, Oregon State University.

(16) National Academies Press. Dietary Reference Intakes for Vitamin C, Vitamin E, Selenium, and Carotenoids. 2000. Washington, DC, Food and Nutrition Board, Institute of Medicine.

(17) Dietary supplementation with n-3 polyunsaturated fatty acids and vitamin E after myocardial infarction: results of the GISSI-Prevenzione trial. Gruppo Italiano per lo Studio della Sopravvivenza nell'Infarto miocardico. Lancet 1999;354:447-455.

(18) Yusuf S, Dagenais G, Pogue J, Bosch J, Sleight P. Vitamin E supplementation and cardiovascular events in high-risk patients. The Heart Outcomes Prevention Evaluation Study Investigators. N Engl J Med 2000;342:154-160.

(19) Kushi LH, Folsom AR, Prineas RJ, Mink PJ, Wu Y, Bostick RM. Dietary antioxidant vitamins and death from coronary heart disease in postmenopausal women. N Engl J Med 1996;334:1156-1162.

(20) Jha P, Flather M, Lonn E, Farkouh M, Yusuf S. The antioxidant vitamins and cardiovascular disease. A critical review of epidemiologic and clinical trial data. Ann Intern Med 1995;123:860-872.

(21) The effect of vitamin E and beta carotene on the incidence of lung cancer and other cancers in male smokers. The Alpha-Tocopherol, Beta Carotene Cancer Prevention Study Group. N Engl J Med 1994;330:1029-1035.

(22) Campbell SE, Stone WL, Whaley SG, Qui M, Krishnan K. Gamma (gamma) tocopherol upregulates peroxisome proliferator activated receptor (PPAR) gamma (gamma) expression in SW 480 human colon cancer cell lines. BMC Cancer 2003;3:25.

(23) Huang HY, Appel LJ. Supplementation of diets with alpha-tocopherol reduces serum concentrations of gamma- and delta-tocopherol in humans. J Nutr 2003;133:3137-3140.

(24) Saldeen T, Li D, Mehta JL. Differential effects of alpha- and gamma-tocopherol on low-density lipoprotein oxidation, superoxide activity, platelet aggregation and arterial thrombogenesis. J Am Coll Cardiol 1999;34:1208-1215.

(25) Tomasch R, Wagner KH, Elmadfa I. Antioxidative power of plant oils in humans: the influence of alpha- and gamma-tocopherol. Ann Nutr Metab 2001;45:110-115.

(26) Li D, Saldeen T, Romeo F, Mehta JL. Relative Effects of alpha- and gamma-Tocopherol on Low-Density Lipoprotein Oxidation and Superoxide Dismutase and Nitric Oxide Synthase Activity and Protein Expression in Rats. J Cardiovasc Pharmacol Ther 1999;4:219-226.

(27) Jiang Q, Elson-Schwab I, Courtemanche C, Ames BN. gamma-tocopherol and its major metabolite, in contrast to alpha-tocopherol, inhibit cyclooxygenase activity in macrophages and epithelial cells. Proc Natl Acad Sci U S A 2000;97:11494-11499.

(28) Stone WL, Krishnan K, Campbell SE, Qui M, Whaley SG, Yang H. Tocopherols and the treatment of colon cancer. Ann N Y Acad Sci 2004;1031:223-233.

(29) Azzi A, Gysin R, Kempna P et al. The role of alpha-tocopherol in preventing disease: from epidemiology to molecular events. Mol Aspects Med 2003;24:325-336.

(30) Williamson KS, Gabbita SP, Mou S et al. The nitration product 5-nitro-gamma-tocopherol is increased in the Alzheimer brain. Nitric Oxide 2002;6:221-227.

(31) Kupper FC, Carpenter LJ, McFiggans GB et al. Iodide accumulation provides kelp with an inorganic antioxidant impacting atmospheric chemistry. Proc Natl Acad Sci U S A 2008;105:6954-6958.

(32) Patrick L. Iodine: deficiency and therapeutic considerations. Altern Med Rev 2008;13:116-127.

(33) Venturi S, Venturi M. Iodine in evolution of salivary glands and in oral health. Nutr Health 2009;20:119-134.

(34) Murray MT and Pizzorno J. Immune Support. Encyclopedia of Natural Medicine. Prima Health, Rocklin CA; 1998;145-160.

(35) Crary EJ, McCarty MF. Potential clinical applications for high-dose nutritional antioxidants. Med Hypotheses 1984;13:77-98.

(36) Saldeen T, Li D, Mehta JL. Differential effects of alpha- and gamma-tocopherol on low-density lipoprotein oxidation, superoxide activity, platelet aggregation and arterial thrombogenesis. J Am Coll Cardiol 1999;34:1208-1215.

(37) Handelman GJ. Carotenoids as scavengers of active oxygen species. In: Cadenas E, Parker L, eds. Handbook of Antioxidants. New York, NY: Marcel Dekker Inc.; 1996;259-314.

(38) Balch PA, Balch JF. Antioxidants. Prescription for Nutritional Healing. New York, NY: Avery; 2000;53-62.

(39) Cocchi M, Venturi S. Iodine, antioxidant function and omega-6 and omega-3 fatty acids: a new hypothesis of biochemical ciooperation? Prog Nutr 2000;2:15-19.

(40) Katamine S, Hoshino N, Totsuka K, Suzuki M. Effects of the long-term (17-19 months) feeding of high-iodine eggs on lipid metabolism and thyroid function in rats. J Nutr Sci Vitaminol (Tokyo) 1985;31:339-353.

(41) Tseng YL, Latham KR. Iodothyronines: oxidative deiodination by hemoglobin and inhibition of lipid peroxidation. Lipids 1984;19:96-102.

(42) Venturi S. Is there a role for iodine in breast diseases? Breast 2001;10:379-382.

(43) Murray MT, Pizzorno J. Osteoporosis. Encyclopedia of Natural Medicine. 2nd ed. Rocklin, CA: Prima Publishing; 1998;706-721.

(44) Reavley N. Osteoporosis. New Encyclopedia of Vitamins, Minerals and Herbs. New York, NY: M. Evans and Company; 1998;653-660.

(45) Murray MT. Zinc. Encyclopedia of Nutritional Supplements. Rocklin, CA: Prima Health; 1996;181-189.

(46) Mancini M, Parfitt VJ, Rubba P. Antioxidants in the Mediterranean diet. Can J Cardiol 1995;11 Suppl G:105G-109G.

(47) Steinberg D. Antioxidants in the prevention of human atherosclerosis. Summary of the proceedings of a National Heart, Lung, and Blood Institute Workshop: September 5-6, 1991, Bethesda, Maryland. Circulation 1992;85:2337-2344.

(48) Gottlieb SS, Baruch L, Kukin ML, Bernstein JL, Fisher ML, Packer M. Prognostic importance of the serum magnesium concentration in patients with congestive heart failure. J Am Coll Cardiol 1990;16:827-831.

(49) Bellizzi MC, Franklin MF, Duthie GG, James WP. Vitamin E and coronary heart disease: the European paradox. Eur J Clin Nutr 1994;48:822-831.

(50) Rimm EB, Stampfer MJ, Ascherio A, Giovannucci E, Colditz GA, Willett WC. Vitamin E consumption and the risk of coronary heart disease in men. N Engl J Med 1993;328:1450-1456.

(51) Eichler I, Winkler R. [Effect and effectiveness of iodine brine baths in a spa]. Wien Klin Wochenschr 1994;106:265-271.

(52) Hitzenberger G. [Comparative studies on the effects of the Bad Hall iodine cure in hypertensives]. Arch Phys Ther (Leipz) 1961;13:91-94.

(53) Klieber M, Czerwenka-Howorka K, Homan R, Pirker R. [Ergospirometric studies of circulation in healthy humans. Effect of iodine brine baths on work-induced changes in blood pressure, respiratory gas exchange and metabolic parameters]. Med Welt 1982;33:1123-1126.

(54) Lu HC. Chinese Foods for Longevity. New York: Sterling, 1990.

(55) Mikhno LE, Novikov SA. [The use of local iodobromine baths in the early sanatorium rehabilitation of myocardial infarct patients with arterial hypertension]. Lik Sprava 1992;89-91.

(56) Pitchford P. Healing with Whole Foods: Oriental Traditions and Modern Nutrition. Berkeley, CA: North Atlantic Books, 1993.

(57) Vinogradova MN, Mandrykina TA, Lavrov GK, Shchegoleva EA. [The effect of molecular-iodine baths on the central hemodynamics of patients with hypertension and ischemic heart disease]. Vopr Kurortol Fizioter Lech Fiz Kult 1990;15-18.

(58) Bastido WA. Pharmacology, Therapeutics and Prescription Writing for Students and Practitioners. 5th ed. Philadelphia: WB Saunders, 1947.

(59) McGuigan HA. Applied Pharmacology. St Louis, CV Mosby, 1940.

(60) Sollmann TH. A Manual of Pharmacology and its Applications to Therapeutics and Toxicology. 7th ed. Philadelphia: 1948.

(61) Cacace MG, Landau EM, Ramsden JJ. The Hofmeister series: salt and solvent effects on interfacial phenomena. Q Rev Biophys 1997;30:241-277.

(62) Hatefi Y, Hanstein WG. Solubilization of particulate proteins and nonelectrolytes by chaotropic agents. Proc Natl Acad Sci U S A 1969;62:1129-1136.

(63) Hoption Cann SA, van Netten JP, van NC. Iodized salt and hypertension. Arch Intern Med 2002;162:104-105.

(64) Hoption Cann SA. Hypothesis: dietary iodine intake in the etiology of cardiovascular disease. J Am Coll Nutr 2006;25:1-11.

(65) Cappuccio FP, Elliott P, Allender PS, Pryer J, Follman DA, Cutler JA. Epidemiologic association between dietary calcium intake and blood pressure: a meta-analysis of published data. Am J Epidemiol 1995;142:935-945.

(66) Murray MT. Calcium. Encyclopedia of Nutritional Supplements. Rocklin, CA: Prima Health; 1996;149-158.

(67) Karppanen H, Karppanen P, Mervaala E. Why and how to implement sodium, potassium, calcium, and magnesium changes in food items and diets? J Hum Hypertens 2005;19 Suppl 3:S10-S19.

(68) Zemel MB. Calcium modulation of hypertension and obesity: mechanisms and implications. J Am Coll Nutr 2001;20:428S-435S.

(69) Altura BM. Ischemic heart disease and magnesium. Magnesium 1988;7:57-67.

(70) Altura BM. Basic biochemistry and physiology of magnesium: a brief review. Magnes Trace Elem 1991;10:167-171.

(71) McLean RM. Magnesium and its therapeutic uses: a review. Am J Med 1994;96:63-76.

(72) Purvis JR, Movahed A. Magnesium disorders and cardiovascular diseases. Clin Cardiol 1992;15:556-568.

(73) Galland LD, Baker SM, McLellan RK. Magnesium deficiency in the pathogenesis of mitral valve prolapse. Magnesium 1986;5:165-174.

(74) Simoes FJ, Pereira T, Carvalho J et al. Therapeutic effect of a magnesium salt in patients suffering from mitral valvular prolapse and latent tetany. Magnesium 1985;4:283-290.

(75) Brodsky MA, Orlov MV, Capparelli EV et al. Magnesium therapy in new-onset atrial fibrillation. Am J Cardiol 1994;73:1227-1229.

(76) Langsjoen PH, Vadhanavikit S, Folkers K. Response of patients in classes III and IV of cardiomyopathy to therapy in a blind and crossover trial with coenzyme Q10. Proc Natl Acad Sci U S A 1985;82:4240-4244.

(77) Digiesi V, Cantini F, Oradei A et al. Coenzyme Q10 in essential hypertension. Mol Aspects Med 1994;15 Suppl:s257-s263.

(78) Langsjoen P, Langsjoen P, Willis R, Folkers K. Treatment of essential hypertension with coenzyme Q10. Mol Aspects Med 1994;15 Suppl:S265-S272.

(79) Langsjoen PH, Langsjoen PH, Folkers K. Isolated diastolic dysfunction of the myocardium and its response to CoQ10 treatment. Clin Investig 1993;71:S140-S144.

(80) Duke RC, Ojcius DM, Young JD. Cell suicide in health and disease. Sci Am 1996;275:80-87.

(81) Slater AF, Stefan C, Nobel I, van den Dobbelsteen DJ, Orrenius S. Signalling mechanisms and oxidative stress in apoptosis. Toxicol Lett 1995;82-83:149-153.

(82) Kidd PM. Glutathione: Systemic Protectant aginst Oxidative and Free Radical Damage. www thorne com/ altmedrev [serial online] 2002; Accessed March 3, 2002.

(83) Forman HJ, Boveris A. Superoxide radical and hydrogen peroxide in mitochondria. In: Pryor WA, ed. New York, NY: Academy Press; 1982;65-90.

(84) Kidd PM. Natural Antioxidants' First Line of Defense. Living with the AIDS Virus: A Strategy for Long-term Survival. Albany, CA: PMK Biomedical-Nutritional Consulting; 1991;115-142.

(85) Cross CE, Halliwell B, Borish ET et al. Oxygen radicals and human disease. Ann Intern Med 1987;107:526-545.

(86) Meister A. Glutathione-ascorbic acid antioxidant system in animals. J Biol Chem 1994;269:9397-9400.

(87) Anderson ME. Glutathione and glutathione delivery compounds. Adv Pharmacol 1997;38:65-78.

(88) Meister A. Mitochondrial changes associated with glutathione deficiency. Biochim Biophys Acta 1995;1271:35-42.

(89) Hunjan MK, Evered DF. Absorption of glutathione from the gastro-intestinal tract. Biochim Biophys Acta 1985;815:184-188.

(90) Witschi A, Reddy S, Stofer B, Lauterburg BH. The systemic availability of oral glutathione. Eur J Clin Pharmacol 1992;43:667-669.

(91) Miller DW. Extrathyroidal Benefits of Iodine. J Am Phys Surg 2006;11:106-109.

(92) Campbell PJ, Carlson MG. Impact of obesity on insulin action in NIDDM. Diabetes 1993;42:405-410.

(93) Hughes TA, Gwynne JT, Switzer BR, Herbst C, White G. Effects of caloric restriction and weight loss on glycemic control, insulin release and resistance, and atherosclerotic risk in obese patients with type II diabetes mellitus. Am J Med 1984;77:7-17.

(94) Murray MT. Vitamin A and Carotenoids. Encyclopedia of Nutritional Supplements. Rocklin, CA: Prima Health; 1996;19-38.

(95) Pitchon E, Sahli O, Borruat FX. Night blindness, yellow vision, and yellow skin: symptoms and signs of malabsorption. Klin Monatsbl Augenheilkd 2006;223:443-446.

(96) Chichili GR, Nohr D, Schaffer M, von LJ, Biesalski HK. beta-Carotene conversion into vitamin A in human retinal pigment epithelial cells. Invest Ophthalmol Vis Sci 2005;46:3562-3569.

(97) Hammond BR, Jr., Wooten BR, Snodderly DM. Density of the human crystalline lens is related to the macular pigment carotenoids, lutein and zeaxanthin. Optom Vis Sci 1997;74:499-504.

(98) Knekt P, Heliovaara M, Rissanen A, Aromaa A, Aaran RK. Serum antioxidant vitamins and risk of cataract. BMJ 1992;305:1392-1394.

(99) Jacques PF, Chylack LT, Jr., McGandy RB, Hartz SC. Antioxidant status in persons with and without senile cataract. Arch Ophthalmol 1988;106:337-340.

(100) Robertson JM, Donner AP, Trevithick JR. Vitamin E intake and risk of cataracts in humans. Ann N Y Acad Sci 1989;570:372-382.

(101) Burton GW, Ingold KU. beta-Carotene: an unusual type of lipid antioxidant. Science 1984;224:569-573.

(102) Palozza P, Krinsky NI. beta-Carotene and alpha-tocopherol are synergistic antioxidants. Arch Biochem Biophys 1992;297:184-187.

(103) Glueck CJ, Shaw P, Lang JE, Tracy T, Sieve-Smith L, Wang Y. Evidence that homocysteine is an independent risk factor for atherosclerosis in hyperlipidemic patients. Am J Cardiol 1995;75:132-136.

(104) Landgren F, Israelsson B, Lindgren A, Hultberg B, Andersson A, Brattstrom L. Plasma homocysteine in acute myocardial infarction: homocysteine-lowering effect of folic acid. J Intern Med 1995;237:381-388.

(105) Bates CJ, Fuller NJ. The effect of riboflavin deficiency on methylenetetrahydrofolate reductase (NADPH) (EC 1.5.1.20) and folate metabolism in the rat. Br J Nutr 1986;55:455-464.

(106) Ames BN, Elson-Schwab I, Silver EA. High-dose vitamin therapy stimulates variant enzymes with decreased coenzyme binding affinity (increased K(m)): relevance to genetic disease and polymorphisms. Am J Clin Nutr 2002;75:616-658.

(107) Wilcken DE, Dudman NP, Tyrrell PA. Homocystinuria due to cystathionine beta-synthase deficiency--the effects of betaine treatment in pyridoxine-responsive patients. Metabolism 1985;34:1115-1121.

(108) Dudman NP, Guo XW, Gordon RB, Dawson PA, Wilcken DE. Human homocysteine catabolism: three major pathways and their relevance to development of arterial occlusive disease. J Nutr 1996;126:1295S-1300S.

(109) Flora SJ, Singh S, Tandon SK. Prevention of lead intoxication by vitamin-B complex. Z Gesamte Hyg 1984;30:409-411.

(110) Shakman RA. Nutritional influences on the toxicity of environmental pollutants: a review. Arch Environ Health 1974;28:105-113.

(111) Schmidt MA. Smart Fats: How Dietary Fats and Oils affect Mental, Physical, and Emotional Intelligence. Berkely, CA: Frog Ltd., 1997.

(112) Kelley VE, Ferretti A, Izui S, Strom TB. A fish oil diet rich in eicosapentaenoic acid reduces cyclooxygenase metabolites, and suppresses lupus in MRL-lpr mice. J Immunol 1985;134:1914-1919.

(113) Watanabe S, Katagiri K, Onozaki K et al. Dietary docosahexaenoic acid but not eicosapentaenoic acid suppresses lipopolysaccharide-induced interleukin-1 beta mRNA induction in mouse spleen leukocytes. Prostaglandins Leukot Essent Fatty Acids 2000;62:147-152.

(114) Murray MT. Essential Fatty Acid Supplementation. Encyclopedia of Nutritional Supplements. Rocklin, CA: Prima Health; 1996;249-278.

(115) Christen S, Jiang Q, Shigenaga MK, Ames BN. Analysis of plasma tocopherols alpha, gamma, and 5-nitro-gamma in rats with inflammation by HPLC coulometric detection. J Lipid Res 2002;43:1978-1985.

(116) Christen S, Woodall AA, Shigenaga MK, Southwell-Keely PT, Duncan MW, Ames BN. gamma-tocopherol traps mutagenic electrophiles such as NO(X) and complements alpha-tocopherol: physiological implications. Proc Natl Acad Sci U S A 1997;94:3217-3222.

(117) Jiang Q, Ames BN. Gamma-tocopherol, but not alpha-tocopherol, decreases proinflammatory eicosanoids and inflammation damage in rats. FASEB J 2003;17:816-822.

(118) Moini H, Packer L, Saris NE. Antioxidant and prooxidant activities of alpha-lipoic acid and dihydrolipoic acid. Toxicol Appl Pharmacol 2002;182:84-90.

(119) Greenwell I. The Role of Inflammation in Chronic Disease. Life Extension Magazine Feb. 2001. Life Extension Media.

(120) Majewicz J, Rimbach G, Proteggente AR, Lodge JK, Kraemer K, Minihane AM. Dietary vitamin C down-regulates inflammatory gene expression in apoE4 smokers. Biochem Biophys Res Commun 2005;338:951-955.

(121) Tahir M, Foley B, Pate G et al. Impact of vitamin E and C supplementation on serum adhesion molecules in chronic degenerative aortic stenosis: a randomized controlled trial. Am Heart J 2005;150:302-306.

(122) Korantzopoulos P, Kolettis TM, Kountouris E et al. Oral vitamin C administration reduces early recurrence rates after electrical cardioversion of persistent atrial fibrillation and attenuates associated inflammation. Int J Cardiol 2005;102:321-326.

(123) Carcamo JM, Pedraza A, Borquez-Ojeda O, Golde DW. Vitamin C suppresses TNF alpha-induced NF kappa B activation by inhibiting I kappa B alpha phosphorylation. Biochemistry 2002;41:12995-13002.

(124) Pleiner J, Mittermayer F, Schaller G, Macallister RJ, Wolzt M. High doses of vitamin C reverse Escherichia coli endotoxin-induced hyporeactivity to acetylcholine in the human forearm. Circulation 2002;106:1460-1464.

(125) Rossig L, Hoffmann J, Hugel B et al. Vitamin C inhibits endothelial cell apoptosis in congestive heart failure. Circulation 2001;104:2182-2187.

(126) Aggarwal BB, Shishodia S. Suppression of Nuclear Factor-kB Activation Pathway by Spice-Derived Phytochemicals: Reasoning for Seasoning. Ann N Y Acad Sci 2004;1030:-434.

(127) Chen CC, Chow MP, Huang WC, Lin YC, Chang YJ. Flavonoids inhibit tumor necrosis factor-alpha-induced up-regulation of intercellular adhesion molecule-1 (ICAM-1) in respiratory epithelial cells through activator protein-1 and nuclear factor-kappaB: structure-activity relationships. Mol Pharmacol 2004;66:683-693.

(128) Lim H, Son KH, Chang HW, Kang SS, Kim HP. Inhibition of chronic skin inflammation by topical anti-inflammatory flavonoid preparation, Ato Formula. Arch Pharm Res 2006;29:503-507.

(129) Lotito SB, Frei B. Dietary flavonoids attenuate TNFalpha -induced adhesion molecule expression in human aortic endothelial cells: Structure-function relationships and activity after first-pass metabolism. J Biol Chem 2006.

(130) O'Leary KA, de Pascual-Tereasa S, Needs PW, Bao YP, O'Brien NM, Williamson G. Effect of flavonoids and vitamin E on cyclooxygenase-2 (COX-2) transcription. Mutat Res 2004;551:245-254.

(131) Gutierrez-Venegas G, Kawasaki-Cardenas P, rroyo-Cruz SR, Maldonado-Frias S. Luteolin inhibits lipopolysaccharide actions on human gingival fibroblasts. Eur J Pharmacol 2006;541:95-105.

(132) Birrell MA, McCluskie K, Wong S, Donnelly LE, Barnes PJ, Belvisi MG. Resveratrol, an extract of red wine, inhibits lipopolysaccharide induced airway neutrophilia and inflammatory mediators through an NF-kappaB-independent mechanism. FASEB J 2005;19:840-841.

(133) Manna SK, Mukhopadhyay A, Aggarwal BB. Resveratrol suppresses TNF-induced activation of nuclear transcription factors NF-kappa B, activator protein-1, and apoptosis: potential role of reactive oxygen intermediates and lipid peroxidation. J Immunol 2000;164:6509-6519.

(134) Mandel S, Youdim MB. Catechin polyphenols: neurodegeneration and neuroprotection in neurodegenerative diseases. Free Radic Biol Med 2004;37:304-317.

(135) Weinreb O, Mandel S, Amit T, Youdim MB. Neurological mechanisms of green tea polyphenols in Alzheimer's and Parkinson's diseases. J Nutr Biochem 2004;15:506-516.

(136) Bengmark S. Curcumin, an atoxic antioxidant and natural NFkappaB, cyclooxygenase-2, lipooxygenase, and inducible nitric oxide synthase inhibitor: a shield against acute and chronic diseases. JPEN J Parenter Enteral Nutr 2006;30:45-51.

(137) Bitler CM, Viale TM, Damaj B, Crea R. Hydrolyzed olive vegetation water in mice has anti-inflammatory activity. J Nutr 2005;135:1475-1479.

(138) El Seweidy MM, El-Swefy SE, Abdallah FR, Hashem RM. Dietary fatty acid unsaturation levels, lipoprotein oxidation and circulating chemokine in experimentally induced atherosclerotic rats. J Pharm Pharmacol 2005;57:1467-1474.

(139) Perez-Jimenez F, varez de CG, Badimon L et al. International conference on the healthy effect of virgin olive oil. Eur J Clin Invest 2005;35:421-424.

(140) Camuesco D, Galvez J, Nieto A et al. Dietary olive oil supplemented with fish oil, rich in EPA and DHA (n-3) polyunsaturated fatty acids, attenuates colonic inflammation in rats with DSS-induced colitis. J Nutr 2005;135:687-694.

(141) Baynes JW. The Maillard hypothesis on aging: time to focus on DNA. Ann N Y Acad Sci 2002;959:360-367.

(142) le-Donne I, Giustarini D, Colombo R, Rossi R, Milzani A. Protein carbonylation in human diseases. Trends Mol Med 2003;9:169-176.

(143) Berlett BS, Stadtman ER. Protein oxidation in aging, disease, and oxidative stress. J Biol Chem 1997;272:20313-20316.

(144) Baynes JW. The role of AGEs in aging: causation or correlation. Exp Gerontol 2001;36:1527-1537.

(145) Stadtman ER, Levine RL. Protein oxidation. Ann N Y Acad Sci 2000;899:191-208.

(146) DeGroot J. The AGE of the matrix: chemistry, consequence and cure. Curr Opin Pharmacol 2004;4:301-305.

(147) Harding JJ. Viewing molecular mechanisms of ageing through a lens. Ageing Res Rev 2002;1:465-479.

(148) Onorato JM, Jenkins AJ, Thorpe SR, Baynes JW. Pyridoxamine, an inhibitor of advanced glycation reactions, also inhibits advanced lipoxidation reactions. Mechanism of action of pyridoxamine. J Biol Chem 2000;275:21177-21184.

(149) Vlassara H. Advanced glycation in health and disease: role of the modern environment. Ann N Y Acad Sci 2005;1043:452-460.

(150) Jordan KG. Carnosine - Nature's pluripotent life extension agent. Life Extension Magazine [January]. 2001. Ft. Lauderdale, FL, Life Extension Media.

(151) Gallant S, Semyonova M, Yuneva M. Carnosine as a potential anti-senescence drug. Biochemistry (Mosc) 2000;65:866-868.

(152) Guiotto A, Calderan A, Ruzza P, Borin G. Carnosine and carnosine-related antioxidants: a review. Curr Med Chem 2005;12:2293-2315.

(153) Hipkiss AR. Carnosine, a protective, anti-ageing peptide? Int J Biochem Cell Biol 1998;30:863-868.

(154) Rosick ER. How Carnosine Protects Against Age-Related Disease. Life Extension Magazine [January]. 2006. Ft. Lauderdale, FL, Life Extension Media.

(155) Brownson C, Hipkiss AR. Carnosine reacts with a glycated protein. Free Radic Biol Med 2000;28:1564-1570.

(156) Miller PL, Reinagel M. Preventing Glycation: Age-Proofing Your Organs. Life Extension Revolution. New York, NY: Bantam Dell; 2005;220-231.

(157) Hipkiss AR, Michaelis J, Syrris P. Non-enzymatic glycosylation of the dipeptide L-carnosine, a potential anti-protein-cross-linking agent. FEBS Lett 1995;371:81-85.

(158) Balch PA, Balch JF. Diabetes. Prescription for Nutritional Healing. 3rd ed. New York, NY: Avery; 2000;321-326.

(159) Murray MT, Pizzorno J. Diabetes Mellitus. Encyclopedia of Natural Medicine. 2nd ed. Rocklin, CA: Prima Publishing; 1998;401-430.

(160) Rutter K, Sell DR, Fraser N et al. Green tea extract suppresses the age-related increase in collagen crosslinking and fluorescent products in C57BL/6 mice. Int J Vitam Nutr Res 2003;73:453-460.

(161) Qian P, Cheng S, Guo J, Niu Y. [Effects of vitamin E and vitamin C on nonenzymatic glycation and peroxidation in experimental diabetic rats]. Wei Sheng Yan Jiu 2000;29:226-228.

(162) Boeing H, Weisgerber UM, Jeckel A, Rose HJ, Kroke A. Association between glycated hemoglobin and diet and other lifestyle factors in a nondiabetic population: cross-sectional evaluation of data from the Potsdam cohort of the European Prospective Investigation into Cancer and Nutrition Study. Am J Clin Nutr 2000;71:1115-1122.

(163) Suzuki YJ, Tsuchiya M, Packer L. Lipoate prevents glucose-induced protein modifications. Free Radic Res Commun 1992;17:211-217.

(164) Munch G, Kuhla B, Luth HJ, Arendt T, Robinson SR. Anti-AGEing defences against Alzheimer's disease. Biochem Soc Trans 2003;31:1397-1399.

(165) Visioli F, Galli C. Natural antioxidants and prevention of coronary heart disease: the potential role of olive oil and its minor constituents. Nutr Metab Cardiovasc Dis 1995;5:306-314.

(166) Visioli F, Bellomo G, Montedoro G, Galli C. Low density lipoprotein oxidation is inhibited in vitro by olive oil constituents. Atherosclerosis 1995;117:25-32.

(167) Block G. The data support a role for antioxidants in reducing cancer risk. Nutr Rev 1992;50:207-213.

(168) Hertog MGL, et al. Content of potentially anticarcinogenic flavonoids of 28 vegetables and 9 fruits commonly consumed in the Netherlands. J Agric Food Chem 1992;40:2379-2383.

(169) Havsteen B. Flavonoids, a class of natural products of high pharmacological potency. Biochem Pharmacol 1983;32:1141-1148.

(170) Muosi I, Pragai BM. Inhibition of virus multiplication and alteration of cyclic AMP level in cell cultures by flavonoids. Experimentia 1985;41:930-931.

(171) Bagchi D, Bagchi M, Stohs SJ et al. Free radicals and grape seed proanthocyanidin extract: importance in human health and disease prevention. Toxicology 2000;148:187-197.

(172) Masquelier J. Procyanidolic Oligomers. J Parfums Cosm Arom 1990;95:89-97.

(173) Schwitters B, Masquelier J. OPC in Practice: Bioflavonoids and their Application. Alpha Omega 1993.

(174) Hertog MG, Feskens EJ, Hollman PC, Katan MB, Kromhout D. Dietary antioxidant flavonoids and risk of coronary heart disease: the Zutphen Elderly Study. Lancet 1993;342:1007-1011.

(175) Hertog MG, Kromhout D, Aravanis C et al. Flavonoid intake and long-term risk of coronary heart disease and cancer in the seven countries study. Arch Intern Med 1995;155:381-386.

(176) Cavallini L, Bindoli A, Siliprandi N. Comparative evaluation of antiperoxidative action of silymarin and other flavonoids. Pharmacol Res Commun 1978;10:133-136.

(177) Duarte J, Perez VF, Utrilla P, Jimenez J, Tamargo J, Zarzuelo A. Vasodilatory effects of flavonoids in rat aortic smooth muscle. Structure-activity relationships. Gen Pharmacol 1993;24:857-862.

(178) Hanasaki Y, Ogawa S, Fukui S. The correlation between active oxygens scavenging and antioxidative effects of flavonoids. Free Radic Biol Med 1994;16:845-850.

(179) Hope WC, Welton AF, Fiedler-Nagy C, Batula-Bernardo C, Coffey JW. In vitro inhibition of the biosynthesis of slow reacting substance of anaphylaxis (SRS-A) and lipoxygenase activity by quercetin. Biochem Pharmacol 1983;32:367-371.

(180) Ratty AK, Das NP. Effects of flavonoids on nonenzymatic lipid peroxidation: structure-activity relationship. Biochem Med Metab Biol 1988;39:69-79.

(181) Hasegawa R, Chujo T, Sai-Kato K, Umemura T, Tanimura A, Kurokawa Y. Preventive effects of green tea against liver oxidative DNA damage and hepatotoxicity in rats treated with 2-nitropropane. Food Chem Toxicol 1995;33:961-970.

(182) Visioli F, Vinceri FF, Galli C. 'Waste waters' from olive oil production are rich in natural antioxidants. Experientia 1995;51:32-34.

(183) Reavley N. Vitamin A and Carotenes. New Encyclopedia of Vitamins, Minerals and Herbs. New York, NY: M. Evans and Company; 1998;33-57.

(184) Cooper K. Nutrimedicine from A to Z: Vitamin A and its Relatives. Advanced Nutritional Therapies. Nashville, TN: Thomas Nelson Publishers; 1996;65-72.

(185) Murray MT. Vitamin A and Carotenes. Encyclopedia of Nutritional Supplements. Rocklin, CA: Prima Health; 1996;19-38.

(186) Rothman KJ, Moore LL, Singer MR, Nguyen US, Mannino S, Milunsky A. Teratogenicity of high vitamin A intake. N Engl J Med 1995;333:1369-1373.

(187) Cooper K. Nutrimedicine from A to Z: Iron. Advanced Nutritional Therapies. Nashville, TN: Thomas Nelson Publishers; 1996;263-267.

(188) Kiechl S, Willeit J, Egger G, Poewe W, Oberhollenzer F. Body iron stores and the risk of carotid atherosclerosis: prospective results from the Bruneck study. Circulation 1997;96:3300-3307.

(189) Tuomainen TP, Punnonen K, Nyyssonen K, Salonen JT. Association between body iron stores and the risk of acute myocardial infarction in men. Circulation 1998;97:1461-1466.

(190) Gordeuk VR, Bacon BR, Brittenham GM. Iron overload: causes and consequences. Annu Rev Nutr 1987;7:485-508.

(191) Reavley N. Iron. New Encyclopedia of Vitamins, Minerals and Herbs. New York, NY: M. Evans and Company; 1998;249-262.

(192) Stevens RG, Graubard BI, Micozzi MS, Neriishi K, Blumberg BS. Moderate elevation of body iron level and increased risk of cancer occurrence and death. Int J Cancer 1994;56:364-369.

(193) Canavese C, Bergamo D, Ciccone G et al. Low-dose continuous iron therapy leads to a positive iron balance and decreased serum transferrin levels in chronic haemodialysis patients. Nephrol Dial Transplant 2004;19:1564-1570.

Lyle MacWilliam, MSc, FP
President, *NutriSearch* Corporation

Author, educator and biochemist, Lyle MacWilliam is president and CEO of NutriSearch Corporation, a Canadian research company serving the needs of the natural health products industry in the global marketplace.

A scientific consultant and public advocate for the supplement industry, Mr. MacWilliam's research and communication skills have been solicited by several agencies. Mr. MacWilliam served at the behest of Canada's former Minister of Health as a member of an expert advisory team charged with developing an innovative framework to ensure Canadians access to safe, effective and high quality natural health products. He has also served as a management consultant with Health Canada, Environment Canada, Human Resources Development Canada, and the British Columbia Science Council, and he has been engaged as a scientific consultant for nutritional manufacturers in the United States, Canada and Mexico.

Mr. MacWilliam has served as a contributory writer for Life Extension Foundation, a US-based non-profit agency dedicated to the scientific exploration of optimal health and longevity. His creative works, including the popular *NutriSearch Comparative Guide to Nutritional Supplements,*™ are available in English, Spanish, French and Chinese. They are used by leading nutritional manufacturers, healthcare professionals and informed consumers, alike, as reliable evidence-based tools with which to sort through the maze of nutritional supplements in the market today. Mr. MacWilliam is a member of the Society of Industry leaders, an international organization dedicated to bringing together authorities from all fields in a global network connecting industry veterans and academia professionals with institutional investors.

A former Canadian Member of Parliament and Member of the Legislative Assembly for British Columbia, Mr. MacWilliam is also an accomplished martial artist with a passionate commitment to personal fitness and health. His written works hit hard at today's lifestyle and dietary patterns and their role

in the development of degenerative disease. His scientifically rigorous, no-nonsense delivery, served with a touch of humour, has earned him praise internationally as a sought-after speaker on the importance of optimal nutrition and lifestyle in preventive health.